HUNTERS
OF THE NORTHERN
FOREST

HUNTERS
OF THE NORTHERN
FOREST

Designs for Survival among the
Alaskan Kutchin

Richard K. Nelson

The University of Chicago Press   Chicago and London

Richard K. Nelson, assistant professor of anthropology at the Memorial University of Newfoundland, is the author of *Hunters of the Northern Ice*. He has spent three and a half years conducting studies of means for wilderness living in remote parts of the North, including the Aleutian Islands, Kodiak Island, the Arctic Slope, and various parts of the Interior.

1973

The University of Chicago Press, Chicago 60637
The University of Chicago Press, Ltd., London
© 1973 by The University of Chicago
All rights reserved. Published 1973
Printed in the United States of America
International Standard Book Number: 0-226-57177-7
Library of Congress Catalog Card Number: 72-97941

This book is respectfully dedicated
to the people of Chalkyitsik, Alaska,
and to my parents

Contents

Illustrations

Acknowledgments

This study is based on a year's field research among the Kutchin and Koyukon Indians of interior subarctic Alaska, done from August 1969 until July 1970 and from April to June of 1971. The investigation was supported by National Institutes of Health predoctoral research fellowships (numbers 1 F01 MH 44916-01 and 5 F01 MH44916-02) and a field research training grant (number MH 12211-01) from the Behavioral Sciences Training Branch of the National Institute of Mental Health. Additional support was provided by a Patent Fund grant from the University of California at Santa Barbara.

My deepest appreciation is to the people of Chalkyitsik, Huslia, and Hughes, Alaska, the villages where field research was carried out. I owe a special debt to the people of Chalkyitsik, where I lived for nine months. Although every person in Chalkyitsik gave his assistance and friendship in some way, there are some I would especially like to thank. Mr. Sam Herbert, Jr., my trapping partner and companion on many hunts, was a good friend and a patient teacher. Another frequent hunting and trapping companion, Mr. Harry Carroll, provided many hours of instruction and entertainment and served as a model of the expert native outdoorsman. Mr. Jim Ward, Sr., gave excellent instruction in the trapper's art.

I also want to thank two old-timers, favorite visitors to our cabin, Mr. Henry William and Mr. Moses Peter. Their stories of the old

days and their lessons in the ways of animals and men were as
pleasant as they were instructive. Others who were very kind and
helpful were Mr. Ben Thomas, Mrs. Lily Herbert, Mrs. Leah
Druck, Mrs. Bessie Edwin, Mr. Paul Thomas, Mr. Carl Moses,
Mr. and Mrs. Abraham Henry, Mr. Simon Francis, Mr. Charlie
Thomas, Mr. William Fredson, Mr. Richard Marten, and Mr. Phil-
lip Peter. In Huslia, Mr. Fred Bifelt, Mr. Edwin Simon, and Mr.
Sam Tony were especially helpful. Out of respect to individuals
who may wish to remain anonymous, all names mentioned in the
text are pseudonyms.

This book is based in large measure on my Ph.D. dissertation,
which was submitted to the Department of Anthropology, University of California at Santa Barbara. I owe special thanks to several
members of that department. Dr. Albert C. Spaulding, chairman
of my dissertation committee, persevered through several readings
of a very long manuscript, and yet never failed to give detailed
suggestions which reflected his concern for quality and conciseness.
I am also grateful to Dr. Thomas G. Harding, Dr. Elman R. Ser-
vice, and Dr. David W. Brokensha. Each has contributed importantly to the final outcome of this study.

Mr. Jack A. Barnes, of the Department of Anthropology, University of Iowa, gave helpful comments during and after the fieldwork.
Dr. James W. VanStone, Department of Anthropology, Field
Museum of Natural History, offered comparative observations and
critical suggestions during the course of fieldwork. Other persons
who have given their kind assistance include Dr. Frederick A.
Milan, Dr. Frederick Hadleigh West, Dr. Catherine McClellan,
and Mr. and Mrs. Ray Nicholson.

The crucial problems of management, business, and finance were
ably handled by Mrs. Betty Langefeld of the Department of
Anthropology, University of California at Santa Barbara. I am also
very grateful to Mrs. Phyllis L. Reese for her assistance with the
submission of research proposals.

Mr. and Mrs. G. Ray Bane of Hughes, Alaska, stimulated my
initial interest in Athapaskans and spread to me their contagious
love for the north country. They have also provided many insights
and observations which I have incorporated throughout this
research. For all of these things, and for enduring friendship, I
am most deeply grateful.

My parents, Mr. and Mrs. Robert K. Nelson, gave fully of their encouragement and kind assistance. They typed, proofread, and helped to edit the entire manuscript. But this was only the most tangible of their contributions, for they have given of themselves in countless ways that are far more important.

This study would probably never have been done without Carol Burch. An anthropology student herself, she made a great contribution to this research by passing along information from her conversations and activities and by offering intelligent suggestions and criticisms in every facet of the study. But she did far more than this in helping to make the total experience a fruitful one, and a word of thanks to her is hardly enough.

I THE STUDY

1   Introduction

The Topic

The boreal forest, or taiga, is a broad expanse of timberland stretching across most of Canada and Alaska, bounded by the Arctic tundra on the north and the temperate forest on the south. It is dominated by vast stands of spruce and birch, interspersed with swampy muskeg, meandering rivers, and literally millions of lakes. For many it is the Great North Woods, a true wilderness that promises solitude, abundant supplies of fish and game, and perhaps a return in mind to ways of living now lost in the distant past.

The western part of the taiga zone, including interior Alaska and the northwest Canadian provinces, is inhabited by a far-flung and diverse family of Indian tribes who speak languages of a stock called Athapaskan. These tribes include the Dogrib, Slave, Yellowknife, Chipewyan, Ingalik, Koyukon, and Kutchin, to name only a few. Despite the intrinsic fascination of their environment and lifeways, few people other than northwoodsmen and anthropologists are even aware that these groups exist. Little is known of their origins, but archaeologists have unearthed fragments of Athapaskan cultures in Alaska and Canada which are at least a thousand years old. It is likely that remains not yet discovered will extend their history to a much earlier time.

The northern Athapaskans (they are called this to distinguish

3

them from southerly Athapaskan tribes such as the Apache and
Navajo) were traditionally hunters, gatherers, and fishermen. After
contact with the fur traders, they added trapping to these pursuits.
Although their technology and culture have changed, some groups
perpetuate their traditional life-on-the-land, stalking moose and
bear, fishing the abundant runs of salmon and whitefish, and trapping valuable furbearers that inhabit the forest.

This book focuses upon modes of environmental exploitation
among one of these remaining land-oriented tribes. It is a study
of the knowledge and techniques associated with hunting, fishing,
trapping, and general survival among the Athapaskan-speaking
Kutchin of interior subarctic Alaska. Northern peoples such as the
Kutchin have long attracted the attention of anthropologists and
explorers because of their ability to live in extreme and marginal
environments. But in spite of this interest, the adaptive skills of
Athapaskan Indians have never been subjected to intensive, specific
study. Nor has there been a systematic investigation of their modern
and traditional knowledge of the surrounding boreal forest and
riverine environments.

The general inadequacy of ethnographic information along these
lines has resulted primarily from the concern of anthropologists with
other aspects of culture, such as social organization or material
technology. Consequently, we know comparatively little about the
behavioral aspects of these unique systems of human adaptation.
This is particularly unfortunate today, when there is an emerging
recognition that hunting has been a key factor in influencing the
course of man's biological and social evolution. This comes at a
time when few peoples remain in the world who still rely heavily
upon a hunting-based subsistence.

Ethnographic studies of hunting and survival techniques provide
the basis for understanding many aspects of human evolution. They
also furnish the groundwork on which archaeological interpretations
can be built, both in regard to the behavioral components of past
technologies and in regard to the wider realm of ecological relationships between prehistoric societies and their environments. Beyond
this, peoples such as the Kutchin possess knowledge of their surroundings which can be useful to disciplines outside anthropology,
in fields such as zoology, botany, ecology, and geography. And
finally, there is much in the study of subsistence and survival among

"primitive" hunters that is of interest to anyone who spends time in the outdoors, who might wish to apply useful techniques in his own activities or recreation, or who wants to explore how people outside the urbanized world relate to their surroundings. This study is divided into four major parts. Part 1 begins with an outline of the topic and the method of research. Following this is a discussion of the general setting, which identifies the Kutchin, describes their environment, and summarizes their annual cycle. The chapters composing part 2 deal with hunting and fishing techniques, knowledge of important game species, uses of vegetation, and methods of travel and navigation. Part 3 is concerned with trapping. It includes chapters discussing the importance of trapping in Kutchin lifeways, techniques of winter travel and survival, and the methods of trapping, snaring, and hunting fur animals. The final section, part 4, deals with several problems of a comparative or theoretical nature. These include historical and ecological factors influencing settlement patterns, culture change and its effects upon environmental adaptation, and a comparison of adaptive success among the Kutchin and the North Alaskan Eskimos.

Before moving on to discuss the Kutchin and their environment, it will be useful to consider the method by which the information for this study was collected.

The Method of Study

This investigation originated from an interest in human and animal ecology, hunting adaptations, and northern peoples; and its specific design and implementation were based on two previous field experiences. The first, a study of exploitation of the sea ice environment, conducted among the North Alaskan Eskimos in 1964–66, was conceived as a means of obtaining survival information for the use of pilots downed on the Arctic ice. The present study was intended as a companion investigation and was almost identical in every respect. The second experience underlying this study was a stay among the Koyukon Athapaskans in Huslia, Alaska, during the summer of 1968, which convinced me that a study of Indian hunting and trapping would be both interesting and enjoyable.

During the following year I began planning a return to do field-work among the Athapaskans. Initial preparation and background reading were carried out in the spring and summer of 1969. Most of the fieldwork was done in the village of Chalkyitsik, Alaska, from August 1969 to June 1970. I then stayed for about a month in Huslia and Hughes, Alaska, acquiring comparative perspective on Athapaskans. After departing from the field, I spent a month at the University of Wisconsin reading the literature on Athapaskans before returning to the University of California at Santa Barbara to do further library research and compile the results. The following spring (1971) I spent six weeks among the Hughes Indians and the North Alaskan Eskimos, obtaining additional comparative data. Approximately twelve months were spent in the field, one and one-half months in library research, one month compiling field and literature notes, and seven months writing the final results.

The first problem in ethnographic fieldwork is selecting a study site. I wished to do this research in Alaska because of my previous experience there, but I had to choose a specific village. Athapaskan settlements vary tremendously; so before making a choice it was important that I undertake a careful inquiry by writing and talking to persons familiar with interior Alaska. From information gathered this way, the village of Chalkyitsik appeared most suitable and was finally selected. Since the major portion of this research was done in Chalkyitsik, its advantages and disadvantages as a study site are worth recounting briefly.

From the standpoint of this research, the most important single quality of Chalkyitsik is its dependence upon a land-based economy. I use the term "dependence" loosely, since, like all Alaskan natives, the Chalkyitsik Kutchin make considerable use of resources from "Outside" and take whatever wage labor they can obtain. Nonetheless, compared with other interior settlements, Chalkyitsik is perhaps the most concerned with exploiting local resources, though, as is true everywhere in Alaska, this concern is fading rapidly.

I was interested in finding a village which occupied a typical river flats environment, depended on moose, fish, and bear for meat, and trapped a wide variety of fur species. Chalkyitsik, situated on the edge of the great Yukon Flats, is ideally suited to all these requirements. Further, since moose are not common here, men are forced to use every available technique to hunt them, a great advantage for an ethnographer interested in a diversity of methods. Chalkyitsik is also an active and productive trapping settlement. The surrounding country is extremely rich in fur animals, and the Indians consider themselves trappers above all else.

Another advantage of Chalkyitsik is its small size (about ninety-five persons) and its isolation. Although smallness limits the number and variety of instructors (or "informants"), it also makes for better cooperation, more interest in one's activities, less animosity toward white men, and a more pleasant and quiet atmosphere. The Chalkyitsik people are generally pleased to have an Outsider join them in their activities, which is a considerable aid to research focusing on participation in hunting and travel. Unfortunately, there were no exceptionally knowledgeable and communicative old-timers, though two or three old men were very helpful. In a larger settlement, the chances of finding an outstanding old-timer would be considerably greater.

Although Chalkyitsik offers some extremely important advantages for an ethnographic study of this type, it has several disadvantages which ought to be mentioned as well. First, and most important, the people are not particularly sociable and tend to be uncommunicative. They also do not spend a great amount of time discussing hunting and related topics. Although they will talk about these subjects, sometimes at great length, considerable effort is often required to sustain such conversation.

Another difficulty is attempting to do research where English is comprehended only to a limited degree. Nearly all the Chalkyitsik people speak English, but only a few are truly fluent, and a year in the field was not sufficient time for me to learn Kutchin. This often made it rather difficult to communicate facts and ideas that were important to the study. Fortunately, the research was based primarily upon observation and participation, thus minimizing the language problem.

Ethnographic fieldwork among the Kutchin also requires a cautious skepticism about the accuracy of verbal information. The people often perpetrate mistruths or exaggerate far out of proportion to reality. Their intent is generally not malicious; it is a form of self-entertainment, or it stems from a desire to say what the listener might like to hear, particularly when the listener is an Outsider.

The Kutchin also tend to state individual opinions as facts. It is therefore important to ask the same questions time and again to separate fact, opinion, and fabrication.

Finally, the Kutchin are not traditionally oriented and have little interest in the past. Except for language, exploitative knowledge and techniques, and elements of personality, little of the aboriginal culture remains today. This limits the ethnographer's ability to study aspects of memory culture, but it is not a great disadvantage to a study of contemporary environmental exploitation.

Before going to Alaska, I wrote to the Chalkyitsik village council informing them of my desire to come there and describing the nature of my interests. I later met with the council president in Fort Yukon, received his permission to do the study, and arranged to rent a house in the village. We flew to Chalkyitsik on the regular mail plane, and there was remarkably little curiosity regarding our arrival. The people were friendly, and helpful when needed, but accepted our presence as a matter of course. An effort was made to explain the study to all persons who contributed to it, but this met with limited success. The purpose of our stay was so unusual (no anthropologist had ever worked among the Chalkyitsik Kutchin) that it was largely incomprehensible from beginning to end.

As soon as I had gotten settled and became somewhat acquainted with the people it was possible to begin participating in the activities around the village. The Chalkyitsik Indians are not at all bashful and get along well with newcomers. As we became increasingly familiar with one another, interaction grew fairly relaxed and comfortable. The actual beginning of data collection came quickly.

This research deals with a very specialized subject, one which cannot be handled adequately by methods commonly used in ethnographic fieldwork. The primary technique of data collection used in this study is based on observation, but not the traditional form of "participant observation," which involves living in a community and participating in it only to the extent of being there to watch what is going on. This kind of observation might more accurately be termed "passive participation."

The present study utilizes the technique of "active participation," in which the ethnographer attempts to replicate the behavior involved in the activities he is documenting and to learn to perform each technique at least at a minimal level of proficiency. In other words, he participates to the fullest possible extent; and by learning each skill he is able to do a far more complete job of documentation, for he learns not only by observing others but by observing himself as well.

In order to carry out any technique of hunting or related activity, it is necessary to follow through a sequence of interconnecting procedures, each dependent on the one before and prerequisite to the one following. Often these procedures can be seen easily by a detached observer, but sometimes not. Those which are "invisible" or likely to be overlooked are usually as essential to successful performance of the technique as those which are highly visible, but they are difficult or impossible to document without going through the process of internalization.

The Kutchin, like many hunting and gathering peoples, train their own providers by the active participation technique. Young men are not given verbal instruction; they watch, try for themselves, then are corrected for their mistakes. It is a form of on-the-job training, and if it is the best way for young hunters to learn their skills, then it is also the best way for an ethnographer to learn the same skills.

My own training followed much the same process. I was almost never given explicit instruction beyond being told how to carry out a specific operation: "Stand here and watch for moose to come out," or "Cut across the muscle here." Procedures were never outlined before they were undertaken, such as what would go on in a coming moose drive. Efforts to elicit verbal accounts of techniques over a cup of tea in the village always fell short of the data brought back from actual hunting or trapping excursions.

For example, it is possible to learn a great deal about setting traps by listening to descriptions of the techniques given by expert trappers; but somehow the accounts never tell as much as being right there to watch trap sets put together. And even after watching the same process time and again, you are almost certain to make a mistake when a man hands you a trap and says, "Set it over there." How long were the twigs he used here? Does the trap belong this far inside the cubby? How high did he place the bait? Did he push the spring against his knee when he set the trap? You put the set together, your instructor comes over, looks, and starts moving things around. One or two tries later you have it right.

Now you are ready to write a description of a trap set. One never realizes how little he knows until someone says, "Now you try it."

Much of what is involved in mastering techniques becomes internalized until it is almost intuitive. The driver of an automobile or the rider of a bicycle does not think consciously about everything he does to keep his vehicle moving smoothly. Should he attempt to give verbal instruction on his techniques, he will undoubtedly neglect to mention much that is essential. And no matter how long and involved the verbal instruction may be, even though it is coupled with actual observation, no one drives an automobile or rides a bicycle without error on his first try. A partial understanding comes through verbal accounts, a fuller understanding comes through observation, and the most "complete" understanding comes through actual participation.

It should be made clear, however, that this method is a specialized one and therefore useful only when certain kinds of information are desired. It is ideal for a study like this one, involving technical procedures; and it is useful for studying other forms of subsistence techniques, music or dance, art, or technology. But the student of kinship or social structure might find that it has little to offer.

There are some disadvantages to the use of active participation, even for a study like this. The high degree of personal involvement in the data makes it hard to maintain detached objectivity. It becomes difficult, both for the reader and for the ethnographer himself, to separate the observations and interpretations of the anthropologist from those of the people he is studying. When he learns by watching and by practicing what he has seen, the ethnographer may be documenting the culture as he sees it and perhaps as he believes the native sees it. For this reason it is best to couple observations with explanations and descriptions elicited from the people themselves. This is not to say that either the native's or the anthropologist's account is "correct," but at least both points of view are presented.

There is one other drawback to the use of active participation. During this fieldwork, I took part in regular hunting and trapping activities almost daily. In addition, every effort was made to be self-sufficient in village life. Thus I cut, hauled, and split my firewood, hauled water from the river, set my own nets for fish and snare lines for hares, and maintained my own dog team. Although it was highly instructive to follow the native patterns closely, all these tasks plus the added burdens of research often became an overwhelming work load.

Information obtained through participation in hunting and trapping was, of course, combined with verbal accounts. These included data on methods no longer in use or not actually observed, information concerning the physical and biological environment, and accounts of individual experiences. Formal or paid interviews were not necessary, since there was ample opportunity to engage in conversation; and the paid informant relationship was not considered desirable in this situation since it would interfere with efforts to elicit information through casual conversation and might cause jealousy and hostility in the community. Persons who were especially helpful were remunerated in less direct ways.

Verbal information was collected in the course of conversations, which I usually steered toward subjects of particular interest. The people were of course aware of my interests and knew quite well that I recorded what I learned. I never took notes in their presence, except for brief outline notations made while on the trapline, and when I made these notations I often told my companions what I was writing down.

My experience with Eskimos and Athapaskans has shown that they often tire rather quickly of extended questioning. Several individuals have remarked that "white men ask too many questions," and that they try to avoid people who repeatedly barrage them with queries. I feel that directed informal conversations are thus particularly useful. A comment inserted at the correct moment, or an occasional question, usually elicits the kind of information desired. As the ethnographer learns more about the people and their interests, he becomes increasingly skilled at participating in conversations and directing them without resorting to questions.

I generally wrote notes late at night, just before retiring, when the day's information could be put down all at once. During the day I would often make brief sketch notes, and if I had a long and very productive conversation, I would sit down immediately to record in detail what I had learned. Field notes were made in bound notebooks, and at the end of the study I had about 450 pages of notes.

I made an effort to carry a camera on every hunting and trapping excursion, to provide supplementary photographic documentation, but the North is hardly an ideal situation for photography with its extreme cold and often gloomy lighting. Many important activities take place in twilight or semidarkness, when a camera is merely an encumbrance; and using a camera in temperatures below zero is often difficult. While traveling, I generally carried a camera by a strap around my neck beneath my parka, which kept it from freezing or being jarred. I was able to photograph most of the important activities of the Kutchin, but in many cases the pictures were of low quality owing to the difficult conditions.

Near the beginning of this discussion I mentioned the research conducted during a six-week period at Huslia and Hughes. My previous acquaintance with those people considerably enhanced the ease of obtaining information there, and I acquired a great deal of information from G. Ray Bane, a schoolteacher with graduate training in anthropology. Mr. Bane has spent nine years among the Alaskan Indians and Eskimos and is thoroughly familiar with their hunting, travel, and survival techniques. There was little opportunity to participate in hunting activity in the Huslia area, and so I depended upon verbal information. Several older men in Huslia were extraordinarily good instructors with a good command of English, and this, coupled with a general interest in things of the past, made my brief stay there productive.

I should mention briefly the fieldwork I conducted among the North Alaskan Eskimos in the community of Wainwright during 1964–65, the summer of 1966, and the spring of 1971. Data from this investigation forms a partial basis for comparative discussions of Eskimos and Athapaskans near the end of this book. The Eskimo research followed essentially the same design and was carried out through the same field techniques as the present study. Much of the original data, which deals specifically with Eskimo exploitation of the sea-ice environment, is easily available for comparison with the information presented here (Nelson 1966a,b, 1969). A concerted effort was made to collect information on the Kutchin that would be strictly comparable to that already gathered from the Eskimos.

2 The Setting

The Western Kutchin

The Kutchin Indians (correctly pronounced *Gwich'in*) are an Athapaskan-speaking people who occupy a fairly large territory, from the Yukon Flats and Chandalar River in the west to the Mackenzie Flats and Peel River in the east. The first contact between Europeans and Kutchin was made by Sir Alexander Mackenzie, who followed the Mackenzie River to its mouth in 1789. Further contacts with the eastern Kutchin were made by Sir John Franklin, Thomas Simpson, and Sir John Richardson in the first half of the nineteenth century. A fur-trading post was set up at Old Fort Good Hope in about 1810. Changes in the material culture of the Kutchin were noted immediately from the time of first contact.

In 1839 a trading post was established at Fort McPherson, on the Peel River. The first contact with Alaskan Kutchin occurred in 1847, when Alexander Hunter Murray left Fort McPherson, crossed over the Richardson Mountains, and traveled by boat all the way down the Porcupine River. When he reached the Yukon River, he traveled several miles upstream from its confluence with the Porcupine and there established Fort Yukon on behalf of the Hudson's Bay Company. Murray spent several years at Fort Yukon, and he left the earliest descriptions and drawings of the Yukon Flats Kutchin. Since this time there has been a steady

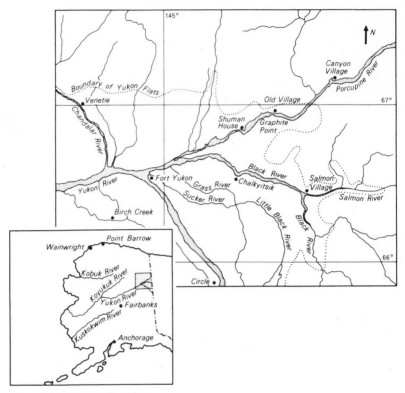

Map of the Chalkyitsik region.

increase in European and American influence. In 1867, when the United States purchased Alaska from the Russians, the Hudson's Bay Company left Fort Yukon. The company remained in the region, however, establishing a station just across the American-Canadian border at Rampart House.

The first missionary at Fort Yukon was the Reverend W. W. Kirby, an Episcopalian, who stayed only for the summer of 1862. Kirby left behind a brief description of the Kutchin. The area was later visited by Archdeacon Robert McDonald, who headquartered on the Peel River. McDonald translated the Bible and the Book of Common Prayer into the Kutchin Language, and his translations are still in use. Thus the Kutchin Indians have been exposed to Christian influence for over a hundred years. (A more detailed account of early historical contacts is found in Osgood [1936*b*, pp. 17–18], the source for much of the information above.)

The Kutchin divide themselves into nine "tribes" or geographic units (Osgood 1934, p. 178; McKennan 1965, p. 23). These are often referred to by the area they inhabit, as follows: Yukon Flats (*Kutchakutchin*), Birch Creek (*Tennuthkutchin*), Chandalar River (*Natsitkutchin*), Koyukuk River headwaters (*Dihaikutchin*), Black River (*Tranjikkutchin*), Crow River (*Vuntakutchin*), Upper Porcupine River (*Tukkuthkutchin*), Peel River (*Tatlitkutchin*), and Mackenzie Flats (*Nakotchokutchin*).

It is difficult to estimate the population of Kutchin people because until rather recently they lived widely scattered across the land. In 1858 the Hudson's Bay Company census at Fort Yukon, including Kutchin of six tribes, totaled 842 persons. Another 337 were counted at Peel River and LaPierre's House, on the Canadian side. Using these figures as a base, Osgood (1936*b*, p. 15) takes a figure of about 1,200 to represent the total Kutchin population at contact. This population was scattered over a territory roughly the size of New England (Osgood 1936*a*, p. 170).

Shimkin (1955, p. 223) estimates the population of Fort Yukon and the entire surrounding area, including Venetie, Chalkyitsik, Birch Creek, and all outlying settlements, at 500 in 1850. The number plunged just after white contact, to about 230 in 1879, then recovered to 500 again by 1930, and in 1947 rose to 600.

This study is concerned with only a limited portion of this area. Chalkyitsik (pronounced Chal-kēēt-sik), where the fieldwork was carried out, is the only modern settlement of the Black River Kutchin. The settlements which are significant to the Chalkyitsik Kutchin are Fort Yukon—by far the most important—Venetie, Birch Creek, Arctic Village, and to a much lesser extent, Beaver, Old Crow, and Circle.

The only one of these villages with which they regularly exchange visits is Fort Yukon. This settlement, just a half-hour's flight away (half a day by snowmobile or two days by boat), is the major intermediary between Chalkyitsik and the outside world. In Fort Yukon, besides a multitude of relatives to visit, there are sometimes jobs and always good times. There are also large, well-stocked stores where furs can be sold and supplies purchased. And for some it is a stopover on the way to Fairbanks, Anchorage, or the "lower forty-eight.'' It is here, too, that Chalkyitsik people see their relatives from the other Kutchin settlements, who gravitate to Fort Yukon for similar reasons. A search of the literature dealing with Kutchin peoples reveals some very good accounts for certain of the tribes and almost nothing beyond mention of a name for others. The best early descriptions of the Kutchin are those of the fur traders—Murray (1910), Jones (1866), and Hardisty (1866), all dealing with the Yukon Flats people. Additional accounts were left by the early explorers—Simpson (1843), Richardson (1852), and Franklin (1828)—and by Dall (1870), Kirby (1864), and Kennicott (1869). Somewhat later writers who described the Kutchin are Stuck (1914) and Mason (1924). The principal ethnographic studies are those of Osgood (1936b) on the Crow River and Peel River Kutchin, McKennan (1965) on the Chandalar Kutchin, Balikci (1963a, b) and Leechman (1954) on the Old Crow Kutchin, and Slobodin (1962) on the Peel River Kutchin.

The Chalkyitsik Kutchin

The Tranjik Kutchin, who now comprise the settlement of Chalkyitsik, have received only brief mention in existing sources. In 1866, Hardisty listed "Tran-jik-koo-chin" with the other tribes; and they were never noted again in the literature until Cadzow left the following description. This, to my knowledge, is the longest account in the literature dealing with the Tranjik Kutchin, and so I quote it in full:

along the headwaters of the Black River, are found the Tranjik-kutchin, the "Cache River People," who take their name from the number of caches or stages built along the stream on which they live. It was on the headwaters of this river that representatives of the bands met in council every few years in ancient times, and while there built caches upon which they stored their food and belongings. The Tranjik-kutchin are famed as snarers of moose, building pounds similar to those used by the Vuntit-kutchin for capturing caribou on the barren grounds. [Cadzow 1925a, pp. 176–77]

The Tranjik Kutchin do not give this translation of their name today, but imply that the meaning of Tranjik is lost. (The term "Kutchin" is a suffix meaning "those who dwell," very similar to the ending "-miut" in Eskimo.) There are very few people living in Chalkyitsik who claim to be real Tranjik Kutchin, in the sense of having been born and raised on the Black River. Most of the older people came originally from other Kutchin groups, specifically from the Yukon Flats, Porcupine River (including the Crow River tribe), and Chandalar River. In any case, whatever distinctness may have characterized the Black River people has now long disappeared as a result of intermixture with other Kutchin, non-Kutchin Athapaskans, and whites.

Until a time well within the memory of the oldest Tranjik Kutchin, the Black River people lived in small, mobile, and scattered groups. When asked where they were born, the old people point up the river and say "up there someplace." They followed a pattern which is common to many Athapaskan groups, traveling far up to the headwaters in fall, staying in the upriver country until spring, then floating down the river and spending the summer fishing in the downriver regions.

Although the picture is not clear, the Black River people apparently began concentrating in somewhat larger and more permanent settlements during the first quarter of this century. The principal settlement, called Salmon Village, was situated near the confluence of the swift and clear Salmon River and the sluggish Black River, some sixty or seventy miles upriver from Chalkyitsik. A few people lived in Salmon Village most of the year, and a few more lived there when they were not out in their line cabins or down at Fort Yukon.

At this same time there were some people who lived downriver at Chalkyitsik. The name, which means something like "fish-hooking place," comes from an excellent fishing spot just outside the mouth of a creek which enters the Black River across from the village. Chalkyitsik was essentially a fish camp, a place where people congregated to exploit prodigious runs of whitefish that descended the little creek each fall. By 1937 there were four cabins at this place.

In 1940 or 1941, a boat came up the Black River loaded with supplies for the construction of a school at Salmon Village. But shallow water stopped the boat short of its destination, and at Chalkyitsik, about 110 miles above Fort Yukon, they unloaded the materials. The people wanted a school, so they came to this place in 1941 and built it. This year marked the real beginning of Chalkyitsik, or Fishhook as it was known then, and signaled the decline of Salmon Village. For some years the cabins at Salmon Village were occupied much as before, but eventually fewer and fewer people stayed there. And then one spring the river cut a new course, leaving the settlement far back on a slough so shallow that it often would not float a boat. So the people moved away, and all that remain there today are rotting log houses with open doors and fallen roofs.

Chalkyitsik must have grown up very quickly, as all the families with children built cabins there. But it was a brief florescence, because after the first year there was no teacher for the school and many of the people moved back out on the trapline in the winters that followed. But some years later another teacher came in, and there have been teachers every year since. More and more people abandoned wintering out on the line, until today all of the Black River Kutchin live permanently in the village.

Ask the old-timers why Chalkyitsik is situated in this place, and they will give three reasons: fish in the creek, fish in the river, and abundant waterfowl close by. Chalkyitsik is an ideal place for a year-round settlement, well situated for access to these important resources. As I have noted, the main reason for the aboriginal settlement here was the presence of an abundant source of whitefish, which run down the nearby creek during the fall. The village is also on a sharp and very deep bend in the Black River, which the people say is about the best fish-netting spot along its entire course. Waterfowl hunting is excellent at Chalkyitsik because it is situated amid an ideal combination of lakes and other features of the landscape, which creates exceptionally good conditions for shooting ducks and geese during their spring and fall migrations.

Chalkyitsik is situated at 66°33′ north latitude, 7 miles above the Arctic Circle, and at 144°20′ west longitude. Some of the village cabins are at the top of the high river bank, but the major portion of the settlement stretches along parallel to the west bank of a large slough that branches off at a right angle from the river. At the south end of Chalkyitsik, just beyond the last house, there is a ridge called Marten Hill, and on top of it are the new school buildings and the airstrip. From Marten Hill the people can look westward over the featureless Yukon Flats country and eastward to the forested hills up the Black River.

Chalkyitsik is thus bounded on three sides by the hill, the slough,

The village of Chalkyitsik, Alaska. Photograph taken from Marten Hill, with the Black River visible beyond the farthest houses.

and the river. The west side, where the newest cabins are situated, is flat and is forested in birch, young spruce, and alders. The birches finger into the village, lending it a particular beauty. All of the houses are log cabins scattered well apart except for the oldest ones, which are built in a row along the slough bank. Like most interior settlements, this one is very picturesque. At the time of this fieldwork there were twenty-six houses, a store, two churches, a community hall, and many caches and outbuildings scattered around between. A network of paths runs among all the houses. The cabins that have been built in recent years are semisecluded in the forest edge at the west side of town, a physical indicator of centrifugal social tendencies which have emerged here. The population fluctuates, but it generally remains around ninety-five persons.

Most of the houses in Chalkyitsik have more than one room.

Rooms vary in size and shape, but average 15 to 20 feet square.
An effort is made to have a main room, used for cooking, eating,
playing, and visiting, and a second room or partitioned area for
sleeping and resting. The door always opens into the main room
and is seldom protected with a porch or hallway. The house is
kept well heated by a wood-burning stove in the main room. Some
of the larger houses have a smaller stove to heat the sleeping room.
Temperatures inside the house are kept comfortable throughout the
day, never excessively hot or cold, although they tend to cool off
when the stove is banked for the night. Houses have several windows, usually covered by an extra layer of clear plastic in wintertime. The people try to have highly transparent windows in order
to keep track of goings-on outside.

Most houses have an elevated cache, which is used for meat
and a wide variety of miscellaneous goods. And most people have
a drying rack, a roofed structure with fencing or slats for walls,
in which fish and meat are hung to dry. There is usually a privy
nearby, and perhaps a shed of some kind for additional storage.
The dogs are kept somewhere near their owner's cabin, usually
chained to trees or bushes but sometimes in small log or board
houses. There is a growing tendency for each house to have a snowmobile parked outside the door.

Athapaskan villages tend to be fairly neat and well maintained.
Garbage and junk are hauled to a designated spot outside the settlement, and each person makes an effort to keep his own area clean.
This holds true inside the house as well as outside. Although they
tend to be scantily furnished, most Indian houses are pleasant and
neat. Life in a village such as Chalkyitsik is usually tranquil and
quiet, pervaded with the beauty of the surrounding country.

The most important communal building in Chalkyitsik is the
school, a large and modern complex of buildings on Marten Hill.
The school has two classrooms and a teacher's quarters next door.
The village has two stores, one privately owned and the other a
village-owned cooperative. Neither store is large or well stocked,
so most of the people order merchandise from Fort Yukon or Fairbanks and pay the air freight costs to have it shipped in. They
depend very heavily upon the outside world for a variety of food
items, clothing, tools, and the like. They have even acquired a taste
for chicken, beef, and pork chops, which add variety to the staple

meats and fish the land provides. Local stores are used primarily to supplement what is not obtained by mail or by hunting.

Chalkyitsik has a rather large community hall which the people built with money received from the government. The hall is used for a variety of purposes: meetings, potlatches (feasts), dances, and a temporary clinic for periodic visits by the public health doctor. There are also two churches, Episcopalian and Baptist. The people are Episcopalians, and a man from the village serves as lay reader for the church. They are periodically visited by the native priest or lay reader from Fort Yukon. The Baptist church was built a few years ago. A minister occasionally arrives to hold services there, and some people attend out of curiosity. There is little interest in the practice of religion, although everyone seems to accept what he feels are some essential religious beliefs.

The population of Chalkyitsik is drawn from various sources. As was noted earlier, there are few "real" Tranjik Kutchin families, ones in which either the grandfather or the grandmother came from the Black River country. Only two families can trace such ancestry. Many families originated, in this or the preceding generation, in the Fort Yukon area. Some others have moved in recently from Venetie, the Chandalar Region, and Birch Creek. An important element comes from the Porcupine River, north and northeast of Chalkyitsik. Then there are persons with more divergent ancestry. One man was born in Tanana, another had a white father and a Canadian Indian mother, and another a white father and part-Indian mother. Many people say that they have some white blood in their ancestry. This is undoubtedly true, since white men have been scattered over this country since before the turn of the century, trapping, trading, and prospecting. A good number of these men found the Indians pleasant company, married in, and settled down.

By and large, the people who live in Chalkyitsik place a high value on things which can be had only in larger settlements. They want electric lights instead of the kerosene and gasoline lanterns they use now; they want to have running water or at least a well, instead of hand-carrying their water from the river; and they want jobs, recreation facilities, good stores, and services.

Why, then, do they stay here? Why does this small, isolated, and technologically backward community exist? I do not pretend to know the full answer, but I can give a few reasons. First, a

good number of the inhabitants were born somewhere in the area
or have spent much of their lives trapping in the surrounding country, and when they decided to move into a permanent village Chalkyitsik was the closest one. From here they could easily reach their
traplines and could hunt in the country they knew best. It was
the most convenient way to continue living off the land and still
take advantage of new living patterns. After moving to the village,
these people have simply chosen to continue here as long as it
remains comfortable, even though there now are greater "opportunities" elsewhere.

Many people who live here also prefer to be where the hunting
and trapping are good, away from settlements like Fort Yukon,
where a large population overexploits the surrounding country. In
the large settlements or cities life is too expensive, because the
people depend so heavily on stores for their food. Unless a good
job is available there is no economic gain in leaving the village.

Another reason, and this one is very important, is a tendency
for the larger settlements to be centers of drinking and violence.
People want to stay away from these influences, which they regard
as both evil and highly tempting. Many feel that if they move to
a town like Fort Yukon or Fairbanks they will be unable to resist
the daily temptation to drink, and they would rather restrict their
indulgence to the times when they visit there. They also feel that
their children are better off away from such places. Alcoholic bever-
ages are prohibited, at least ideally, in Chalkyitsik.

The Country

Chalkyitsik is at the eastern edge of the great Yukon Flats. The
country downstream stretches flat and featureless to the horizon,
a maze of twisting rivers and creeks, sloughs, and thousands of
lakes, ponds, and wet meadows. Upstream the terrain becomes
more irregular, first small hills, then low mountains, and finally some
fairly rugged mountainous country. Most of the region exploited
by the villagers is either flat or hilly, and the modern people rarely
see the larger mountains.

Their land is a true wilderness. About 50 miles to the west is
the settlement of Fort Yukon, 75 miles south is the small community
of Circle, and the village of Old Crow is some 130 miles to the
northeast. The country north and east of Chalkyitsik is a vast

uninhabited wilderness, one of the largest in North America. To the north is empty mountain and tundra country extending for 250 miles to the Arctic Ocean. In the east, forest and mountains stretch 300 miles to the Peel River, then another 200 miles to the Mackenzie. In the old days there were cabins and camps here and there; today, there is no one. It is the fringe of this wilderness, north along the Porcupine River and east up the Black River, that the men of Chalkyitsik enter when they hunt and trap.

These two rivers are of preeminent importance to the Chalkyitsik people. The Black River follows an extraordinarily meandering course beginning some 100 miles straight-line distance to the southeast of the village, flowing almost north and then turning west toward the Yukon. I have no idea of its length if all the bends are included. It is very shallow except during brief periods of high water following the spring thaw and after heavy rains. Traveling on it by boat usually involves scraping and pushing over one shallow riffle after another. Yet the current is sluggish, almost nonexistent in the deeper spots.

The river is of great importance for the people. First, it is a major source of food, from the fish and ducks of its waters to the bear and moose that are often hunted along it. The village water supply comes from the river, though it is discolored and locally impure. And the river is a major avenue for travel in both summer and winter. Besides all this, the Black River is something more. It is the essence of their country. It is a living entity on which they depend, and its constant changeability gives them something to watch and to talk about. The old men, who have lived along it since a very different time, often sit for hours at the bank just watching it flow by.

The Porcupine River is much larger, originating far to the east in Canada, rolling clear and swift through alternately flat and rugged terrain. Several Chalkyitsik people have lived on the Porcupine for most of their lives and still do most of their hunting and trapping there. In wintertime, it is a short 20 miles by overland trail to the Porcupine, but it is perhaps 200 miles to the same place by boat during the summer. The Black River flows into the Porcupine just above its confluence with the Yukon. The Porcupine is much richer in fish than the Black, and it runs through country which is excellent for trapping and moose hunting.

There are countless other small rivers and creeks which are of some importance to the Chalkyitsik Kutchin. Each has its own character and its own resources. The same can be said of the sloughs and lakes which cover this country in such abundance that there may well be as much water as land. The remarkable fact is that each one is different, and to be effective in exploiting his environment the Kutchin must know what it does or does not offer.

Most of the country exploited by the Chalkyitsik Kutchin has a diverse forest cover. Dense, mature stands of towering white spruce are scattered across the land, especially along the rivers. Much of the region has been burned over at various times and is thus covered by subclimax forests of birch and aspen. At the edges of lakes and sloughs and along the sandbars of the rivers there are dense thickets of willow. The stunted black spruce grows in moist habitats, and large grass or sedge meadows are common throughout the country.

The fauna includes most species typical of the boreal forest in the northern hemisphere. The major big game species are moose and black bear; small game includes snowshoe hare, porcupine, and arctic ground squirrel; and the most important fur species are mink, marten, lynx, wolf, red fox, beaver, and muskrat. Waterfowl, including several species of ducks and geese, are abundant during the ice-free seasons. Other birds of importance are the willow ptarmigan and three species of grouse. Rivers and lakes contain a variety of fishes, including salmon, sheefish, whitefish, and northern pike.

As one would expect, the climate is almost as important to the Chalkyitsik people as the land and animals. The continental subarctic climate which characterizes the vast boreal regions of the North is particularly intensified in the Yukon Flats. There are great seasonal extremes, from the warm sunshine of summer to the clear, bitter cold of winter. Summer temperatures reach or exceed 90° F. almost every year. At Fort Yukon, where the climate is practically identical to Chalkyitsik, the average temperature in July (the warmest month) is 61°. The mean maximum for this month is 72°, and the mean minimum is 50°. Prolonged daylight, with the sun continuously above the horizon for approximately a month, maintains fairly high temperature levels (U.S. Department of Commerce 1959, p. 6).

The coldest month at Fort Yukon is December, with an average

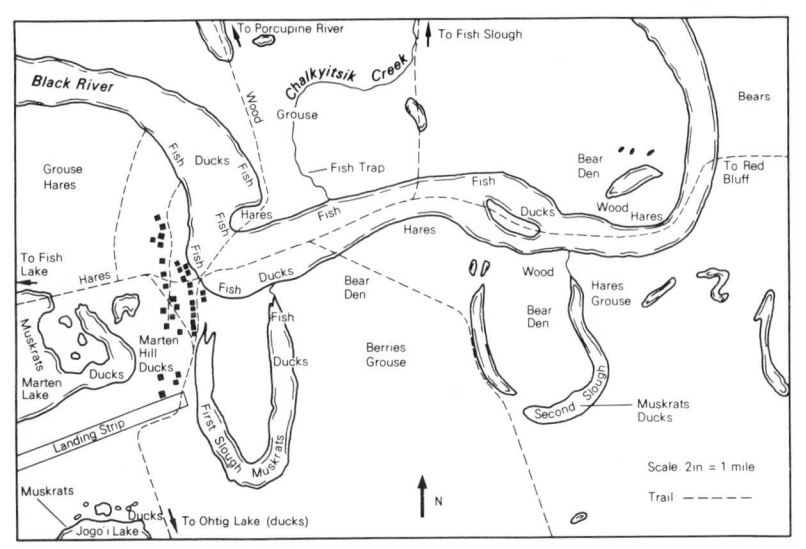

A map of Chalkyitsik and the immediate vicinity, indicating localized resources and major features of the landscape.

temperature of $-19°$, a mean maximum of $-11°$, and a mean minimum of $-27°$. Winter temperatures of $-50°$ to $-60°$ are not uncommon. Fort Yukon holds the record high temperature for all of Alaska at $100°$ F. It also comes within a degree of the record low for the state, at $-75°$, making an overall temperature range of $175°$ (U.S. Department of Commerce, pp. 27, 29).

Another important feature of the climate from the human standpoint is wind. In winter, the wind multiplies the effect of low temperature many times over. It also influences the movements and approachability of game and hardens and drifts the snow. In summer, it influences travel on rivers and lakes. The boreal forest is often supposed to be a land of still, calm waters in summer and dead, frozen quiet in winter; but this is only partly true. Winds, sometimes rather strong, blow almost daily in summer, and the winter alternates between calm or near-calm and gale-force storms.

Northern interior forests receive less precipitation than most of the world's deserts, and the Yukon Flats is a particularly dry area. Most rainfall comes in the form of summer showers so localized that you can often watch rain falling around the area all day long and never feel a drop. Winter snowfall also tends to be light, but it comes in storms of longer duration and accumulates to a fair depth because thaws are so rare. The mean annual snowfall at Fort Yukon is 45.6 inches. The average total precipitation is 6.53 inches, about an inch less than Phoenix, Arizona. But the north country stays wet because of its low evaporation rate. (Statistics from U.S. Department of Commerce 1963, pp. 8, 25).

The sun plays a major role in determining man's activities in the north, not only by influencing the temperature but also by controlling the relative lengths of day and night. In summer the people are completely free from night, with the sun circling endlessly in the sky. From about April 15 until August 15, there is no real darkness because the sun remains near enough to the horizon to leave a twilight glow even at midnight. On the other hand, night is very long in midwinter, when the sun climbs above the horizon for only an hour. But even then there is a long twilight, so that a man can see his way from about 8:30 A.M. until 3:30 P.M. In winter, the length of a day often depends upon cloud cover. When it is clear, the twilight creates a long day, but heavy clouds can shorten it by several hours.

Through the darkest winter months the moon can act almost as a second sun when it is full and high. Each month the moon appears for fourteen to twenty days, and for about ten of these days it is bright enough to illuminate distant landscapes, even so bright that a man can see the sights on his rifle well enough to take aim. Some Indians run their traplines in the light of a full moon. The high moon, extremely clear night air, and the reflectivity of the snow-covered land all combine to brighten the effect of moonlight. And during the periods when the moon is absent, auroral bands, the northern lights, may cast a glow sufficient to travel by.

The Annual Cycle

The physical and biological aspects of this interior subarctic environment determine the annual cycle of the Chalkyitsik Kutchin. In the chapters that follow, the seasonal aspects of each exploitative activity will be described, but the relative position of each activity in the annual round can be made clearer by some introductory comments.

Fall

About the end of August, men who have been away doing wage labor usually return to the village to begin preparations for the fall. Fishing is one of the most important fall activities. Salmon generally appear in the river sometime in July or early August and continue until about mid-October. Nets are set in the river for salmon, pike, and whitefish. After freeze-up, nets are put under the river and lake ice for pike and whitefish. Whitefish run in Chalkyitsik Creek early in September, and if the run is good the people are kept busy cutting and drying them for several weeks.

Moose hunting is the second important fall activity. Some men go up the Black River or Salmon River for moose as early as August, but most wait until the time of the rut, from about September 10 until the end of the month. Moose congregate along the river at this time, and lucky hunters may also encounter bears walking along the banks. Cold weather and the threat of freeze-up on the river bring the season to a close. Bears are hunted in October by finding them inside their dens.

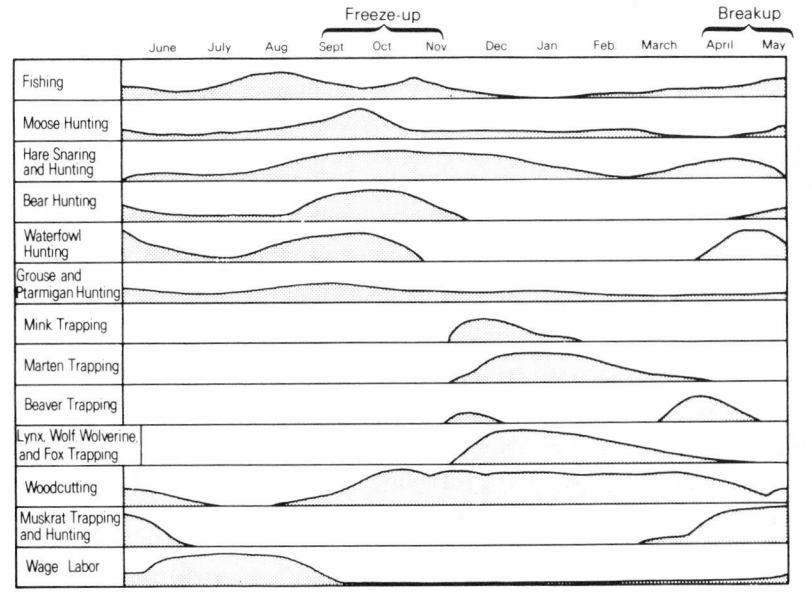

Annual activity cycle, Chalkyitsik, Alaska.

Waterfowl are hunted on lakes and on the rivers throughout the fall. They are especially abundant on nearby Ohtig Lake, where they are hunted from boats. Freeze-up usually ends the season early in October. Snowshoe hares are hunted and snared throughout the fall, but activity increases just before the early snows. Ruffed and sharp-tailed grouse are also hunted at this time, especially when they are abundant. Another fall activity is berry picking.

Some men put considerable effort into cutting wood and hauling it with boats in September and in early October until the river freezes. Between the time of freeze-up and the first snowfall there is no way to haul wood, so people must stock up beforehand. Some men cut wood at this time to be picked up after it snows. September and October are the months for getting toboggans and other equipment ready for the snow season.

Winter

For our purposes, the winter season begins after the early snows, in October or about the first of November, and lasts until the first thaws in April. The amount of activity during this period varies largely with the weather. When it is warm men leave the village for their traplines, but when it is cold there may be little activity for weeks at a time.

Cutting and hauling wood is a major wintertime occupation. People rarely stockpile more than one or two weeks' supply, so they are usually out after wood during the most intense cold spells. Cutting and hauling wood is an almost daily activity around Chalkyitsik throughout the winter season.

Trapping is almost as pervasive in daily life throughout the snow season. It actually includes a number of subseasons, largely determined by game laws. Mink trapping is best in November, trails off in December, and closes at the end of January. After their early efforts for mink, the trappers start setting out for "winter fur," including marten, lynx, wolverine, and wolf. The winter fur season usually begins around November 15 and continues until sometime in March, except for marten season, which ends February 28. Some of the Kutchin start trapping beaver and muskrat as early as February or the first part of March, but these activities are mostly pursued after the beginning of warmer weather in late March.

Snowshoe hares are snared throughout the winter, but the most intensive snaring takes place after the early snowfalls when the "rabbits" are needed to fatten up the dog teams. Hares are too well camouflaged to be shot during the winter. Grouse and ptarmigan are hunted, however, during years when they are common. Moose hunting goes on through the winter. A special effort is made to take moose late in the winter before the spring thaw curtails snowmobile and dog team travel.

Spring

Winter and spring merge into each other as the Indians' activities cut across the turn of the seasons. Trapping efforts shift from "winter fur" to beaver and muskrat as the snow begins to thaw, the last winter moose hunting is done while travel is still easy, and people begin thinking of the open-water season just ahead. Beaver season lasts until April 15, but trappers usually fill their limits or stop because of thaw weather before this time. Muskrat trapping parallels the beaver season but continues into the breakup and open-water seasons. Muskrat hunting on the lakes, in light canoes, was always a very important springtime activity until a law was passed against it in 1969.

Snowshoe hares appear with the first warm weather, usually in April or May. They are easy to hunt as they sit basking in the warm afternoon sun. About the latter part of April, black bears emerge from their dens and wander widely in search of food. Bears are hunted while the lakes are still frozen, and later from boats traveling on the rivers and lakes.

Spring is the most important season for waterfowl, which are hunted on the early-opening lakes, on the river, and as they wing low over the village itself. Ducks and geese begin arriving in April, the exact time depending on the progress of the thaw. Duck hunting continues into early June, then diminishes.

Ice fishing begins when the days lengthen in late winter and early spring, but is especially good just before breakup. Rod-and-reel fishing starts after the ice is gone and continues through the summer. Right after breakup people set fishnets in the river, and some make good catches of pike and whitefish.

Summer

There is little economic activity in Chalkyitsik during the summer. Some minor hunting is done, for hares, grouse, and waterfowl. Fishnets are sometimes put out before the salmon arrive. And occasionally someone travels up the Black River to get some fresh moose meat for those who remain in the village.

But for the most part summer has become the season for wage labor. Many families move to Fort Yukon, where employment may be available, and some men travel as far as Anchorage, Fairbanks, or canneries along the coast. In recent years there has been employment fighting forest fires, but this is available only irregularly. Men usually try to find a job that will last until about September, when most of them will want to start back to the village to prepare for the fall and winter ahead.

II HUNTING, FISHING, AND GATHERING

3

Vegetation
and Its Uses

White Spruce

The white spruce (*Picea glauca*) dominates the boreal forest environment in which the Tranjik Kutchin live. It is by far the largest tree, reaching a height of 30 to 50 feet and a trunk diameter of from 6 to 24 inches, and it is probably the most common as well. And of all the kinds of vegetation which play a role in the Indians' lives, none even approaches the importance of *tsiivii,* the spruce. Wood from spruce trees is used to build houses, caches, canoes, and a variety of other things from net shuttles to radio antenna poles; spruce wood is used in stoves and campfires; its pitch is a good medicine and chewing gum; the old people used its roots for lashings and its bark to cover houses and make canoes. But beyond this, the spruce forest is the country of the Tranjik Kutchin, and the mountain tundra outside its limits is considered a land of danger. In a treeless landscape, there are few ways for a man to find his direction, there is no shelter against the wind and blowing snow, and there is no wood to build a fire when camp is made. Chalkyitsik is surrounded by extensive stands of timber, except in the region toward the west destroyed by the fire of 1969. The forest is hardly a monotype, however, and even the densest stands of spruce have deciduous trees growing in and around them. Many areas which burned sometime in the past have few if any spruce.

By far the most important use of the white spruce is for firewood.

The only other kind of wood brought to the village for firewood is birch, and this is used so rarely that it is insignificant. Spruce grow large, and are often in dense stands so that a man can cut a good supply of wood in one spot. They have a single large trunk, without sizeable branches to make cutting more difficult for the amount of wood obtained. Spruce splits easily into even pieces. And, unlike any other kind of tree, dead, dry spruce is fairly easy to find.

Woodcutting is concentrated, as one would expect, in the colder periods of the year. Few people worry about cutting wood during the summer, when stoves are usually lighted only for cooking. But as fall approaches men start traveling in boats up the Black River, felling dry spruce along its banks and hauling the wood down to the village. This is also done to a lesser extent right after breakup in the spring. But the amount of wood brought into the village in this way is small compared to what is hauled over the snow in winter.

As soon as the first snow is on the ground, snowmobiles begin droning back and forth between Chalkyitsik and the surrounding woodlots. Activity is not continuous, however, because to some degree the people stockpile their firewood. On any given day a few men will probably go out to cut and haul wood, but the really intensive activity comes when the temperature drops to its seasonal lows. When it becomes extremely cold the rate of wood consumption increases tremendously, and woodpiles dwindle rapidly. People admit that they often run out of wood during prolonged cold spells; yet they seldom lay in good supplies against these periods. There is some advantage in waiting until cold weather to cut wood, however, because green spruce is much easier to cut and split when the temperature is very low.

The following notes were written during a cold snap in November of 1969:

With the arrival of really cold weather there is essentially one village activity—getting wood. Nearly everyone except the woodcutters and wood haulers stayed in the village. All day long the buzzing of chain saws rang out from the surrounding forest, and snowmobiles came and went with their loads of wood. With the temperature remaining 40° to 50° below, considerable effort is required just to keep pace with consumption.

Firewood is taken not from just anyplace in the woods around

Chalkyitsik, but from certain areas or woodyards where spruce grow in dense stands and where dead, dry trees are common. It is always preferable, of course, to find a little group of spruce trees growing very close together, since this lets a man build up a good pile of wood in one place with a minimum of effort. This holds both for green and dry wood, although it is much harder to find many dry trees in one spot.

In the days before steel axes and saws were brought into Kutchin country, trees were cut down with a kind of stone adze. The method was described by one man as "beaver style," since the cutter circled around the trunk taking chips out until it became thin enough to fell the tree. Needless to say, steel tools made tree cutting a much simpler task. For many years the people depended upon large cross-cut saws, but within the past ten years they have changed over completely to motorized chain saws. Almost every man owns a chain saw today and is expert in its use. The other essential tool for woodcutting is a good double-bitted ax. Some men work alone, but most prefer to have a companion to make the job faster and easier. This is a dangerous occupation, and having another man or a boy along insures that someone will be around to give assistance in case of an accident.

When they go to the woodyard areas, the men first look for a place where a good number of large spruce trees grow (or have died and become dry) as close together as possible. Once they find a good spot, they go to work. They cut the trees down, remove their limbs, and cut them into sections small enough to haul with a toboggan or wood sled. The techniques of woodcutting are identical to those used throughout North America today, and so they need not be described in detail here.

Once they have cut wood, people try to haul it to the village as soon as possible, using either a snowmobile or a dog team. The machines are much preferred because they are many times faster with a heavy load, they can haul two or three times as much on each trip, and they never get tired. After two or three heavy loads, dogs will almost refuse to turn around and head for the woodpile again, but the snowmobile is never unwilling to go as long as it is mechanically sound.

Once the wood is in the village, stacked next to someone's house, the next job is to split it. Splitting wood is most often a task for the man of the house, but it is also done by the wife or older sons. The Chalkyitsik Kutchin usually split wood with a double-bitted ax, but I have also seen wedges used for this at Huslia. Dry wood splits fairly easily, regardless of temperature, particularly if it is cut into short lengths. Green wood, on the other hand, is very hard to split when the temperature is much over 0° to 10° above. When it is cold, especially at −30° to −50°, green wood splits with almost no effort at all.

Most able-bodied men cut their own wood, but there is an active and profitable business in selling wood to the old, infirm, and indolent members of the community. A cord sells for thirty to thirty-five dollars at Chalkyitsik, delivered to the buyer. Old people must also hire someone to split wood for them, which costs perhaps five to ten dollars a cord. Some are fortunate in having sons or grandsons who will do this for nothing. Old-timers frequently complain that the traditional ethic of care for the elders has fallen out of custom. They are undoubtedly correct, though it should be remembered that in former years aged and infirm members of the group were sometimes left behind to die when they could no longer contribute to the economy.

The total amount of wood consumed in a winter will depend upon how large the house is, how well it insulates against the cold, and what proportions of dry and green wood are used. Herbert John said that for his large two-room house, with two stoves, he needs about ten cords of dry wood and three cords of green wood per year (one cord = 128 cubic feet). A small, tight cabin could probably do with five cords of dry wood.

During the summer months people burn dry wood because they generally keep the fire going only briefly when they want quick heat for cooking. In wintertime they mix green and dry wood together. Green wood, saturated with juice and sap, makes a very hot fire but burns much more slowly than dry wood, and is therefore more economical than dry wood alone. But it cannot be started unless a hot fire is already going, and it will not hold fire well unless it is mixed with an equal amount of dry wood. It is also best to have dry wood under the green so that its flames keep the green wood burning.

People in this area have been using wood-burning stoves for

perhaps seventy or eighty years. The oldest living Tranjik Kutchin, a man about eighty-eight years of age, said he saw his first stove when he was a young boy. A number of different kinds of stoves are in use today. These include small manufactured heaters, homemade types made from gasoline drums laid on their sides and fitted with a door at one end, and the familiar wood-burning stove with a large cast-iron top for cooking and an oven next to the firebox.

The second major use for white spruce is in building cabins, caches, smokehouses, and outbuildings. Spruce is the only locally available wood that is suited for use in structures of this type, since all other species are too small and do not grow straight enough. A detailed consideration of design and construction is beyond the scope of this book, but some general descriptions are included in a later chapter.

Spruce wood is also used for making canoe frames, which are covered with canvas. Its flexibility and lightness make it ideal for this. The paddles used with such canoes are also made from straight-grained spruce. Spruce wood has countless other uses around the village and out in the bush. From it the Indians make tent frames, radio antenna poles, beaver snare toggles, temporary bridges, poles for pushing boats in shallow water, drying racks, various kinds of handles, and many other things. Rotten spruce wood is used for smudge fires underneath drying racks (to keep flies away and speed drying) and for smoking hides.

Spruce boughs are used for soft and insulative beds when the Indians camp in the woods. They often remark that they like the smell of spruce inside a tent. Boughs also make beds for the dogs during trips away from the village, instead of the grass that is used for this at home. In the old days the Kutchin made small canoes from spruce bark and also used bark to cover their dwellings; fiber from under the bark was eaten (Osgood 1936b, p. 37), and thin, supple spruce roots were used for lashings.

The modern Chalkyitsik Kutchin collect spruce pitch in a can or jar and keep it in the house for a medicine. Clear spruce pitch, used alone or melted together with an ointment, is put on infections and sores. The people feel very strongly about the effectiveness of spruce pitch for "drawing out" the soreness of wounds and infections. It can also be boiled, apparently in water, to make a drink which they say is good for tuberculosis. Spruce gum—pitch which has hardened and turned an amber color—is chewed from time to time. It has little taste.

Deciduous Trees and Shrubs

The paper birch (*Betula papyrifera*), called *aat'oo* in Tranjik Kutchin, is a distant second in importance to white spruce. Birch trees are common throughout the Black River country, growing in open stands or scattered within the various plant communities. They can reach a height of 30 to 50 feet, with a trunk diameter of 6 to 12 inches (Taylor 1950, p. 45), but in this region most are smaller, immature trees. The distinctive white bark of birch trees makes them stand out clearly, especially along the high river banks, and they lend a particular beauty to the land.

Birch is highly regarded as firewood, because it burns slowly and will not go out as green spruce will. It is very dense and hard, and so a log will keep its fire for a long time. The Indians say that birch is the best firewood, except that it puts out a sooty black smoke. But despite its good qualities they very rarely cut it, probably because birch trees tend to grow far apart rather than in dense stands like spruce, which makes for considerable extra work. It is very easy to cut and split birch during cold weather but much more difficult when it is warm. Finally, birch is very heavy and therefore harder to handle than the lighter spruce.

Probably the most important use for birch wood is in making toboggans, hardwood sleds, and snowshoe frames. During the fall men take their boats up the river searching for straight birch trees. Each promising tree is inspected closely and checked for straight grain. When a suitable one is found, a 9- to 12-foot section is taken from the trunk and transported back to the village. With a chain saw (formerly with a long ripsaw) it is then ripped into boards which are fashioned into a toboggan. Birch withstands hard wear, bends well, and runs easily on most kinds of snow. It is also well suited for hardwood or basket sleds and makes strong frames for Kutchin snowshoes.

Birch bark (*k'ii*) is widely known as a material for canoes. The traditional Athapaskan canoe, quite distinct from the better-known

Algonkian canoes, consisted of a spruce frame with birch bark skin formed around it. The bark has now been replaced by canvas, but the basic design remains unchanged. Athapaskans also made a variety of containers from folded and sewn birch bark, but these have disappeared entirely in Chalkyitsik and are remembered only by the oldest people. They are still made by the Koyukon, however.

The quaking aspen (*Populus tremuloides*) and balsam polar (*Populus tacamahaca*) are both common around Chalkyitsik, where the people usually call them "cottonwood." Some large areas north and south of the village are covered with dense stands of young aspens, 15 to 30 feet tall, which came in after a fire sometime in the past. These stands have a distinct appearance because the trees grow only a few feet apart and they have peculiarly twisted and bent whitish trunks. Balsam poplar is a larger tree, up to 50 feet tall, with a straight, thick trunk. It is found thinly scattered in most of the forest communities around Chalkyitsik but sometimes occurs in groves along the river banks.

Neither aspen or poplar is important to the Chalkyitsik Kutchin because their wood is of poor quality. They are occasionally used as firewood but are not preferred because they do not burn well, leave too much ash, and in any case are either too small or too widely scattered to be worth cutting. They are used when a household runs low on kindling while the man is away somewhere and children are sent out to the surrounding forest to gather dead wood. Aspen and poplar seem to make good campfires, however, if the wood is dry.

Much of the forest and scrub country along the Black and Porcupine rivers is covered by thick underbrush dominated by willows (*Salix* sp.) and alders (*Alnus* sp.). These slender trees are often 6 to 10 feet high, but range up to 20 and 30 feet in height. They do much to give this country its brushy character, which makes it virtually impossible to travel overland without following well-maintained trails. The larger willows and alders are sometimes used for firewood in the village when the preferred woods are temporarily unavailable, and they make suitable campfires if the wood is dry. The inner fiber of willow bark was formerly twisted to make line, and during periods of starvation it was used as an emergency food (Osgood 1936*b*, p. 37).

Other Plants

It is difficult to obtain good information on the uses of minor plant species by the Tranjik Kutchin, because they are infrequently utilized today. During the period of fieldwork there was almost no opportunity to observe the collection and use of medicinal and food plants, and information from verbal accounts was scanty because it was difficult to identify the species in question. In addition, during this year the berry crop failed almost completely, which severely curtailed my ability to gain information on the important species and their use.

The lowbush cranberry (*Vaccinium vitis*) grows in profusion around Chalkyitsik, especially in the wet sphagnum beneath mature stands of spruce. In normal years these berries are gathered during the fall at certain places where they are especially common. The best of these spots were destroyed in the fire of 1969, but some remained unspoiled. Cranberries are sometimes mixed with fat (or lard) and meat or fish to make what is called "Indian ice cream."

Blueberries (*Vaccinium uliginosum*) are found widely in interior Alaska but are virtually absent around the Chalkyitsik–Fort Yukon region. They do occur at Venetie and Arctic Village, according to native account, and they are used in those areas. The nagoon-berry (*Rubus arcticus*) and highbush cranberry (*Viburnum edule*) are also found in the Chalkyitsik area, but excessive dryness apparently prevented their appearance during this study. The people mention using these species.

The only fruit that was readily available in 1969 was that of the wild rose (*Rosa acicularis*). Rose bushes grow everywhere in the woods and scrub, and their thorny stems are a considerable barrier to walking through the country. Around middle to late August rose hips (as the fruits are called) become red and start to soften, indicating that they are ripe. No concerted effort is made to gather the juicy but very bland rose hips, and apparently they are merely munched during walks in the forest. In the past, when they were probably sought after more enthusiastically, rose hips could have been an important source of vitamin C during the winter months. They sometimes cling to the bush all winter long and remain edible despite their softness (Heller 1966, p. 45).

The Chalkyitsik people occasionally use Labrador tea (*Ledum palustre*), which they call *ledii-masket*. The undried leaves and seeds are added to boiling water, making a tea which is considered very tasty and healthful. The variety which is found in the flats (subspecies *groenlandicum*) has large leaves and is considered inferior to the small-leaved variety (subspecies *decumbens*) that grows in the high hills. McKennan (1965, p. 30) states that the use of Labrador tea does not antedate white contact.

During the spring and early summer, the Chalkyitsik people collect wild rhubarb (*Polygonum alaskanum*), which grows along river and slough banks. Only the young plants, about 6 to 10 inches high, are gathered, and only the stems are eaten. After the roots and leaves are removed, the skin is stripped from the stems and they are boiled in water and vinegar.

An old Chalkyitsik Indian said that one of the best medicines for colds or other aches and pains is an infusion made by boiling the berries (and apparently also the boughs) of a juniper (*Juniperus* sp.) which grows on dry slopes. The Chandalar Kutchin recommend eating juniper berries for colds (McKennan 1965, p. 71).

There are undoubtedly many kinds of native plant medicines, known especially by the older people, which are sought out when they are needed or are sometimes kept in the house. Although all Tranjik Kutchin use native medicine today, feeling that it is as good as any kind of introduced remedy, they also accept the white man's medicines. Both types are considered effective in their own right. Most people will utilize both native and western medicines, often to help cure the same malady. On one occasion I injured my hand and Herbert John prepared a spruce pitch application for it. After he finished with this he suggested that I go to the village health aid for some pills to help it further.

Other plants are used for different purposes. There is a tall marsh grass or sedge that grows in thick stands along the margins of sloughs and lakes, where spring flooding takes place. This grass is cut in large quantities and hauled to the village, to be used as bedding for dogs through the winter months. The same kind of grass is used for insulative bedding in winter camps, usually along with spruce boughs.

Sphagnum moss (*Sphagnum* sp.) which is found everywhere in the spruce-birch forests, has several uses. Most important, it is packed between the logs of the cabins as a sort of chinking. Only in the past few years have some people substituted commercial insulation for moss. Sphagnum is also used on the roofs of some cabins, as an insulative layer beneath an overlying cover of dirt. In former times moss was probably used for diapers (cf. Helm and Lurie 1962, p. 51). Hunters pull wads of sphagnum and use it to clean blood and offal from their hands when they butcher game.

Finally, there is an anemone (*Anemone patens*) that is placed on top of a fire inside the house to create smoke that kills mosquitoes and other flying insects. This plant, which grows in profusion on the dry southeastern slope of Marten Hill behind Chalkyitsik, is seldom gathered today, but was used extensively in the past.

Plants may never have been important in the lives of the Tranjik Kutchin, except for trees such as spruce, birch, and willow. McKennan states that vegetable foods were not an important element of the Chandalar Kutchin diet (1965, p. 30), and this probably holds for the Black River people as well. Certainly the use of medicinal and food plants is minimal today, and in the near future these last usages will also disappear.

4   Summer Travel: The Logistics of Hunting

Introduction

This chapter describes the knowledge and techniques used in summer travel and camping, and provides background information which is essential for understanding the logistics of hunting and fishing throughout the open-water season. Virtually all summer travel is done by boat, and walking, the only other way to get around at this time of year, is restricted to outings in the immediate vicinity of Chalkyitsik. The chapter begins by describing the boats used by the Kutchin, then discusses river travel and summer camping procedures.

Hunting Canoes

The hunting canoe is an essential part of the Indians' equipment for pursuing game in the rivers and lakes. It is also an important means of summer transportation, since its small size and light weight permit easy portaging from lake to lake. Traveling through the lakes is the only way to reach much of the country surrounding Chalkyitsik during the warm season. Thus the Kutchin still depend heavily on their little boats, much as they did in aboriginal times.

The Kutchin hunting canoe belongs to a general type called the "kayak-form canoe," which occurs in strikingly similar form among practically all northern Athapaskan peoples (McKennan 1959, p. 93).

The kayak-form canoe was widely employed in the northwest and was highly developed in both model and construction. It was essentially a portage and hunting craft, ranging in length from 12 to 18 feet and in beam from 24 to 27 inches, with a depth between 9 and 12 inches. In areas where the kayak-form was used as a family and cargo canoe, the length would be as great as 20 or 25 feet and the beam might reach 30 inches. [Adney and Chapelle 1964, p. 158]

The kayak-form canoe is a distinct type, different from the typical "Indian" canoe characteristic of the Algonkian-speaking peoples to the east. The latter are the prototype for commercial canoes widely used in the United States today. As the name implies, the kayak-form canoe closely resembles an Eskimo kayak, but with only a partial deck or no deck at all. It is wholly confined to Athapaskan groups except for some overlap into Eskimo territory in Alaska (e.g., Kobuk River, lower Yukon, lower Kuskokwim).

Before the white man brought canvas into this region canoes were covered with birch bark, first bent to shape and then provided with a spruce-wood frame. The older Tranjik Kutchin grew up using bark canoes, and they offer differing opinions on their performance. One man said that birch-bark canoes were heavy and difficult to make, and it was especially hard to find just the right trees from which to take the bark. This difficulty was very likely the reason canvas replaced bark as the covering. Another old-timer was more complimentary about the traditional covering and said that bark canoes were much better than today's canvas version. Canvas tears very easily on snags, and when this happens the canoe sinks. Birch bark is much tougher, and if it is punctured or if the canoe tips over it still has enough buoyancy to support a man.

The modern hunting canoes in Chalkyitsik, where there are about ten in usable condition today, range between 13½ and 14 feet in length. They have sloping sides, so that the maximum width across the bottom (between 15½ and 18 inches) is considerably less than across the gunwale (ranging from 26½ to 28 inches). The depth is somewhat less at the center (8 to 9½ inches) than at the stem and stern (9 to 11½ inches). A short canvas deck covers the forward 3 to 3½ feet of the boat, but the stern portion is entirely open.

The stem and stern may be nearly vertical or gently sloped, but the angle is usually the same at both ends. Single-bladed paddles about 6½ feet long are used. The blade is about 2 feet long and 5 inches wide, with a ridge down the middle of one side. The ridge faces toward the stern during paddling.

When they use their little canoes, Tranjik Kutchin hunters kneel in the middle, hams on heels. Some old men, whose age has taken away their balancing skill, sit with legs outstretched. This lowers their center of gravity, making the craft much less tippy. Paddlers usually take two or three strokes on one side, then on the other. When they cross shallow riffles, canoers use two sticks to push along the bottom, a much more effective technique than paddling through the low, swift water.

The Indian canoes are ideally suited for the environment in which they are used, because they are fairly swift and are easily paddled over long distances, present a low profile for easy approach to birds or mammals, and are extremely light for easy carrying. Much of their use involves portaging from one lake to the next or through portages which cut across looping bends in the river. The canoe, weighing only 25 to 35 pounds, is carried with its gunwale on the hunter's shoulder. The limited decking makes for light and easy portaging, increases loading capacity, and allows easy entry and exit. Getting in or out, the Indian steps into the middle of the canoe, holding one gunwale and bracing his paddle against the shore.

There are two major disadvantages to the design of this canoe. With little deck and a very low profile, it is a veritable death trap in rough water, and so hunters must avoid being caught out on large lakes when there is a wind. Second, the canoe is very unstable, and it is made more so because paddlers elevate their center of gravity by kneeling rather than sitting in the bottom. Kneeling allows greater leverage for paddling, however, and makes it easier to handle rifles and game. Canoe hunters are always careful to shoot straight ahead and not toward the side, because the kick of a rifle or shotgun could easily upset them. Several persons mentioned having tipped over in their canoes, and within the past few years one young man drowned when his boat was apparently swamped by rough water. Some of the Chalkyitsik people can swim, but it is unlikely that they all know how. Apparently very few Kutchin were able to swim in the past (Kennicott 1869, p. 178).

River Boats

The modern Chalkyitsik Indians use large wooden boats with outboard engines to travel on the river for various kinds of hunting, woodcutting, and transporting game. In the old days, however, most hunting was done with the small bark canoes described above. These were adequate as hunting vehicles, but left unsolved the problem of transporting hundreds of pounds of meat back to the camp or settlement.

In those days the Kutchin also had a slightly larger version of the bark canoe, usually over 20 feet long, which was paddled by two women. This was a traveling canoe, made for hauling loads while the men went on ahead in their little hunting canoes. When the men wanted to camp, they went ashore and left a mark, then hunted on ahead and returned after camp was set up. The women's canoe might be used to transport some game killed by the men, perhaps dried on the spot to make it lighter.

But usually a different method was used. Until the past twenty years or so, men paddled their little canoes upriver, alone or in pairs. When they shot moose, they built a boat right on the spot to haul the heavy meat back to their settlement. The boat, which could be made in one day, consisted of a wooden frame covered with the skin (or skins) of the moose. All of the older Tranjik Kutchin have used such boats, and the younger adults have seen them.

If one moose was killed, a small canoe 6 or 7 feet long and about 18 inches deep could be made. Once finished, the meat was loaded inside, and the moosehide boat was paddled downstream with the empty hunting canoe tied on behind. If several moose were killed, one man sewed their skins together in a waterproof seam while another built the frame. The skin was then lashed on, the seams were smeared with moose fat to seal them, and the boat was tested for leaks in the water. The meat was loaded on top of willows thrown in the bottom. A three-moose canoe was some 12 feet or more in length with a depth of 24 to 30 inches.

Larger moose-skin boats might be covered with 6 or 7 hides. These boats, measuring 20 to 25 feet long and 4 to 5 feet wide, were used to haul people and their goods down from the headwaters each spring. Several might be made for this purpose by a group. The moose-skin boat was built by many northern Athapaskan groups, and the mode of construction was basically like that of the birch-bark canoe. The skin covering was essential for holding the wooden frame together, a fundamental difference from the Eskimo skin umiak, which has a rigid framework capable of standing without its covering (Adney and Chapelle 1964, p. 219).

It is hard to say, when the first American or European boats were used in the Black River country, but it must have been before the turn of the century. Wooden boats coexisted with traditional craft for many years before the latter began disappearing. In the early days there were no engines, and so boats were either poled along the river or "lined" by men on shore pulling them by long ropes. It took ten to twelve days to reach Chalkyitsik from Fort Yukon in this way. The Koyukon Indians harnessed dogs to lines and let them do the pulling, but this was never done on the Black River. At the same time there was still considerable canoe travel, and the moosehide boat remained important for moose hunting.

In 1926 the first inboard-powered boats came to the Black River,

A typical river boat with a hunting canoe inside.

and the outboard engine arrived a few years later. Despite their early introduction, motorboats were owned by very few Indians until the past ten years. In the late 1950s there were about three in Chalkyitsik, but by 1970 there were seventeen. The acquisition of motor-powered boats led to hunting by boat crews, a change from the more individualistic canoe hunting. When there were few boats, crews were rather large. The trend has reversed today, as more and more people get boats, but crews of two to four men are the rule.

The boats used today in Chalkyitsik are typical interior Alaskan river craft. They range from 18 to 24 feet long and 4 to 5 feet wide, with a flat bottom and square bow. The older ones are made with planks, the newer ones with plywood. Most are built by their owners. Outboard engines, usually between 15 and 25 horsepower, are used on all the boats. The engines are sometimes mounted on "lifters," devices which can hoist them to whatever depth is necessary to cross shallow riffles.

River Travel

The ease or difficulty of boat travel on the Black River is determined by the weather and the condition of the river itself. The first concern of river travelers is the wind. A brisk wind, 15 to 20 miles per hour, raises fair-sized waves when it blows up or down a long stretch of the river. This is especially true on the Black River, which has little current to help flatten the water. Furthermore, a strong wind can slow a boat down substantially, especially on the long upwind stretches, or on shallow riffles where the engine gets little "bite" in the water. Men are therefore reluctant to leave the village to go upriver when it is windy. A steady rain will also keep them home, since traveling all day in the wet and cold is a miserable experience.

Boats cannot simply be driven up the Black River; they must be carefully navigated. Upstream from Chalkyitsik the river becomes an endless succession of shallow riffles, each with its own deepest channel which must be found and negotiated. Unless the water is unusually high, a novice will have considerable difficulty getting up the river. Even the experts often find no channel deeper than a few inches, and the only way to continue upstream is to pole or pull the boat over the shallow spots. So boats cannot just follow the twisting course of the river; they must wind back and forth within the river itself. In effect, the channel meanders within the river's meanders, adding insult to injury.

As the river becomes shallower upstream, it also becomes more rocky, increasing the probability of damage to outboard engines. The most troublesome and dangerous riffles, the ones with no real channel, are usually given names. These places—Deadman Riffle, Pete Nelson Riffle, and so on—are major reference points along the river's course. It is not surprising that when men talk of traveling up the river their conversation often turns to outboard motor trouble. And most frequently the problems result from damage caused by hitting rocks in the shallow spots. Many a traveler has drifted home from upriver, and some have walked back from downriver as well.

The older, more experienced boatmen know the location of every riffle along the river and have a good idea where the channel will be (if there is one). The water level is important in navigating these places, so men try to travel when the river is highest. Seasonally, the water is highest at breakup time and remains fairly high through June. But it drops after that and usually stays low for the summer, unless the weather is especially rainy. The river is watched closely during the fall moose-hunting season. If rain comes, the water may rise before freezing temperatures hit the headwaters. When the tributaries in the hills freeze, however, the water level drops sharply.

After a rain the river is watched closely to see if it creeps up or down the banks. Rising water is sometimes a signal to get up a crew and go after moose. When they camp upriver, men try to note the water level at night, so they can tell in the morning if it has changed. Falling water level could make it difficult to return downriver if the boat is heavily loaded. A good indicator of rising water is sticks and debris floating with the current.

There are several methods, in addition to foreknowledge, by which navigators find the deepest places to cross shallow riffles. The Black and Salmon rivers seem to descend by "steps." Every few hundred yards to a mile there is an abrupt slope in the bottom, where the current is fast and the water is shallow. These places are marked by swift, rippling water. Most riffles have a definite channel, sometimes two feet or more deep, sometimes just a few inches deep. The channel is marked by a distinct convergence of the swiftly flowing water through a definite place, generally indicated by markedly higher ripples and darker water. Channels can be anywhere—in the middle of the river or right along the bank. With a little practice, however, they are fairly easy to locate. It is harder to see the indicators of a channel while traveling into the sun than with the sun behind.

In the very swift Salmon River, shallow water is combined with the real danger of upsetting in certain places. Many of the powerful riffles here have their channels where fast water runs right along the outside of a sharp bend. In these places a boat traveling downstream may be swept into the bank and upset, thrown into a "sweeper" (a tree or log hanging out from the bank), or pushed up onto a snag where it can swamp or tip over.

On the way upriver, shallow areas can often be negotiated by running slowly up through the channel, or by lifting the engine somewhat so that it clears the bottom. Many times, however, the water is so shallow that the motor has to be lifted until it loses most of its power. Then it can become very difficult to move against the swift current. When the boat slows too much, it may barely hold its own or may start drifting downstream with the current. Then it is time to start poling.

As long as there is some water for the propeller, the helmsman keeps the engine running, while the other men use 6- to 9-foot poles with their heavy ends sharpened to push the boat forward. This often requires great effort against the current before there is finally enough water for the engine to move the boat again. Coming downstream is easy, since the engine can be lifted while the boat drifts over shallow places, unless the load is heavy and the bottom scrapes. Then the poles are brought out quickly and used hard, because if a loaded boat gets stuck the fast water may rush over the stern and swamp it.

When the water is really shallow, so that the boat scrapes heavily, the men jump ashore and pull the boat across with ropes. Sometimes they have to get in the water to lift and pull the boat across a riffle. This is a last resort, however, because it means wet, cold feet. Some years the water is so shallow that hunters must pole across almost every riffle, which is extremely laborious but necessary if they are to get moose.

The difficulty of navigating on the Black River is increased by constant shifting in the channels crossing the riffles. This happens every year, especially in spring, so a man has to relearn the channels at least once a year. In fact the rivers themselves are constantly changing course, and last year's mainstream may now be a slough, or vice versa, or the deep channel passing an island may change from one side to the other. These changes are particularly common in the upper Black and Salmon rivers, and they force travelers to keep up to date in their knowledge.

But despite its changes, the Indians who have traveled up and down the Black River all their lives know exactly where to expect riffles, how to locate their channels, and just how long it will take to get from one place to another. I have seen them navigate flawlessly by dim moonlight, when the usual indicators were lost in darkness. An important part of navigation is long-term experience in the area, so that a knowledge of the local "landscape" is acquired. This is a recurrent and dominant theme in environmental exploitation here, where an intimate familiarity with localized resources and detailed geographical knowledge is fundamental to success.

Camping

Camping is an important part of summer and fall travel, especially during moose hunting. The boat crew must stop to camp at least once on their way to moose country, and they camp for a number of days while they travel along the Salmon River or upper Black River searching for moose.

Travelers prefer to find a good camping place before it gets dark, because if they wait too long it is hard to find dry, flat ground with plenty of firewood close at hand. These conditions, plus a river bank that is fairly easy to climb, are the main criteria for a campsite. Stopping early is also preferable because it is difficult to travel on the river in darkness, and there is no point in passing good game areas when the light is too poor for shooting.

When they find a good camping spot, the Indians immediately start unloading their gear from the boat, usually while one man gathers wood for a fire. Once their gear is up the bank and a fire has been built, they sit around the warm blaze removing their heavy clothes and heating a pot of water for tea. A pot of meat is prepared and set on the fire to cook while the men drink tea and eat bread.

When the meat is ready they eat, keeping the fire high for warmth. As they finish eating and the fire burns down, the hunters may spend some time working on equipment and talking; then each man removes some of his clothing and retires inside his sleeping bag.

In the morning one man gets up and makes a fire, piling the logs high for a good warming blaze. Tea is made, and some meat from the previous night is eaten. Usually this is all done rather quickly, because the men are in a hurry to be out cruising the river for game while it is early. When they have finished eating, they roll up their sleeping bags, get their things together and load them into the boat, and begin the day's traveling.

One of the most important aspects of camping in this environment is fire-making. A good fire is essential for a pleasant, energy-restoring camp in the summer and fall, but during the colder seasons being able to make a fire can mean the difference between life and death. Several times when I was slow getting a fire started a man would comment, "If it's fifty below maybe your hand frozen by now."

It is much easier to build a fire today than it was before people had matches. The old-timers describe a method of starting fires by using flint to strike sparks into a birch fungus (*Fomes igniarius*) that had been split to expose combustible material inside. Another man said that pieces of this fungus were shredded together with fragments of birch bark by rubbing them between the palms. Once a spark caught in this finely shredded material, the man blew on it until it ignited.

To start a fire today's Kutchin first pick up some kind of tinder. This may be a piece of birch bark (which burns very strongly), a bundle of dried grass, some paper, or a handful of the little dry, twiggy branches usually found at the base of living spruce trees. A small pile of tinder may be set between two parallel dry poles to protect it from the wind. Small sticks are placed on the tinder before it is lit (with a match these days), and larger sticks, then poles or logs, are added as the flames grow. Sometimes the hunters save time and effort by making a pile of fair-sized sticks and lighting it with kerosene or gasoline. This is especially handy when it is very cold, when the wind is strong, or when the men are in a hurry.

The Indians have a characteristic way of building fires. They always lay the sticks and logs parallel, so that they burn in the middle but their ends extend beyond the edge of the flames. When the middle of the log burns away, they push the pieces inward from both ends to rekindle the blaze. This technique minimizes the amount of woodcutting. Fairly long pieces of wood can be placed on the fire, and when the flames "cut" them the two halves are put back onto the fire to be halved again. The Kutchin often want a big fire when they camp, and so they pile the logs high and add heavy pieces to the blaze. Sometimes the fire burns 4 or 5 feet wide in the logs, hot flames leaping, and the men stay warm even though it may be intensely cold. Heavy logs also hold fire all night, so that it is easy to start the blaze again in the morning.

Each man brings his own selection of food for camping, but when meals are prepared there is a fair amount of sharing. One man might supply the tea and sugar and another the bread, and the meat is usually from the immediate proceeds of the hunt. Foods carried include tea, coffee, sugar, bread, crackers, butter, dried moose meat, salt, pepper, and some canned items. "White man grub" has been important here for many years, but the oldest men can remember when they ate only meat and drank cold water in the morning before going out.

The main meals, usually three a day, are generally composed of game killed during the trip. This includes fish, waterfowl, hare, porcupine, or moose. The meat generally is boiled, along with plenty of fat if it is available. Sometimes it is roasted, usually until a well-charred crust covers it. All kinds of meat are cooked thoroughly, whether boiled, roasted, or fried. The idea of eating raw meat is completely repulsive to the Kutchin, although the Koyukon enjoy raw fish.

Shelters are not very important for summer and fall camping unless it starts to rain. Tents and tarpaulins are carried along, but there is little need to bother with them unless a steady rain seems probable. If it sprinkles or showers now and then, hunters may throw tarps over their sleeping bags or make simple shelters with poles and canvas. Sleeping places are usually right at the base of large, sheltering spruce trees, which provide good protection from sprinkles.

When a man prepares his bed, he cuts spruce boughs if they are available. These may be the ends of long branches on large trees or the branches of little saplings. When young trees 5 to 7 feet tall are available, they are cut down and stripped of their branches with a knife or ax. This is quicker than cutting the ends of large boughs, and the young branches are quite soft. Sometimes the Indians do not bother with boughs, but put a ground cloth down with their heavy clothes on top of it for a mattress. The sleeping bags are usually army-surplus down-filled mummy bags, used singly or doubled. The Kutchin sleep with most of their clothes on, in camp as well as at home.

If the weather turns really cold or if a hunter is caught with no sleeping bag, there is a good way to make a warm sleeping place. A big fire is built and kept burning for perhaps as long as two hours, then the coals are swept away, spruce boughs are placed on the warmed earth, and the man sleeps there. This method is often said to be too warm for comfortable sleeping. If no sleeping bag is available a man also might wrap himself in canvas, or an emergency blanket can be made from a fresh moose hide dried in front of a big fire.

One other camping problem should be mentioned. During the summer and early fall hunters may be plagued by clouds of mosquitoes. In the days before mosquito repellent and protective netting the people were forced to stay inside closed shelters or make large smudge fires around the camp to keep the insects away. Today the Chalkyitsik Kutchin cope with these pests in several ways. Mosquito netting, often made from cheesecloth, is hung on wooden frames over their sleeping places. A commercial product made from *Pyrethrum* plant is burned inside houses or tents to kill all the insects. Insect repellent is used outdoors. Smudge fires are used in camps and sometimes around the village.

The abundance of mosquitoes varies from year to year depending on how dry it is. In a wet year they fairly cloud the air, but dry years may be nearly free of them. Some men say they have seen dogs killed by mosquitoes, and this is not difficult to believe. They usually appear around late May, become thick in June, diminish in July, and disappear sometime in August or early September. Gnats also appear in summertime, and their bite is much worse than the mosquito's. They are not abundant at Chalkyitsik, but they can be so thick at Huslia that people can hardly go outside their houses. Hundreds of them swarm on those who do venture out, and repellents are ineffective. Head nets are the only real defense against them.

5   Fish

Introduction

Of all the food resources exploited by the Tranjik Kutchin, fish are one of the richest and most reliable. In fact, it is reasonable to speculate that fish were the most important single resource during the aboriginal past, and in some years this is probably still true. The Yukon Flats people exploit the river runs of salmon in summer and early fall, as well as fair numbers of whitefish, pike, and other species. Great numbers of fish may also be taken in smaller creeks, and some lakes are well stocked, providing an important winter food source.

As was noted earlier, Chalkyitsik is uniquely situated for exploiting several very good fish resources. Most important is the usually prolific fall run of whitefish that descends Chalkyitsik Creek, which enters the Black River near the village. A much smaller run ascends the creek in spring. Second, there is the large, deep bend of the Black River which provides an excellent spot for fish-netting during the summer, fall, and, to a lesser extent, spring. In the fall of 1969 the net farthest from the village was some 500 yards upstream. This contrasts to some interior settlements, where people travel several miles to find eddies suitable for netting. And finally, Chalkyitsik is near some good fishing lakes, particularly one called *Ch'atritt,* where pike and whitefish are usually available in large numbers.

The species of fish which are regularly taken at Chalkyitsik and are significant in the local economy include the following: chum or dog salmon (*Oncorhynchus keta*), sockeye salmon (*Oncorhynchus nerka*), whitefish (*Coregonus* sp.), sheefish or inconnu (*Stenodus leucichthys*), louche or burbot (*Lota lota*), northern pike (*Esox luscius*), and grayling (*Thymallus arcticus*).

Hook and Line Fishing

During the months of open water, northern pike and grayling are taken with commercially made spin-casting equipment which is purchased through the mail. Children often use a homemade rig consisting of a coffee can with line and lure attached to it. The line is tossed out into the water and then reeled in by wrapping it around the can, which is held by making a fist inside. This method works very well—large fish can be taken if the line is strong. For pike a red and white spoon lure is used, and for grayling a "spinner" lure is most effective. This kind of fishing is done mostly by women and children; men seldom take part even though it can be quite productive.

Northern pike, or *eltin*, are found almost anywhere in the Black River, but they congregate in places where there is little current, such as eddies, backwaters, or deep spots like the bend at Chalkyitsik. Pike can always be caught in dead water. The best spots are where a creek or slough empties into the river. In about two hours' fishing at the mouth of a slough near Chalkyitsik, a party of four fishermen took some 100 to 150 pounds of pike. These fish are abundant in some of the lakes, but they are difficult to reach during the summer months. Grayling (*shriijaa*), a small trout common in northern waters, are found mostly in swift places with a gravel bottom. They occur around Chalkyitsik during the fall but are common year-round in the upper Black and Salmon rivers. Grayling are generally caught by casting from shore, and pike are most often taken from a boat.

Another kind of open-water fishing is carried out with small hunting canoes. This is most frequently done by the men, who paddle to good fishing spots near the village and use small hand lines consisting of a stick about 18 inches long, 3 to 5 feet of heavy cord for line, a wire leader, and a spoon lure with a piece of pike belly-skin attached to one of the hooks. Hand-line fishing is done in the daytime for pike, but for louche it must be carried out in the darkness.

Instead of using a hook and line, the Chalkyitsik Kutchin sometimes catch fish with gaff hooks. This was formerly done at a place called Fish Hole, far up the Salmon River. Salmon congregated by the thousands here to spawn and were easily taken by men standing on the shore and using long-handled gaff hooks. The only fish taken this way today are louche, which congregate around the mouth of Chalkyitsik Creek during the fall. Men go out late at night, when louche swim into the shallow water near the creek. The fish are easily seen with a flashlight as they swim or lie sluggishly, waiting for small fish to prey upon. The gaff hook, on the end of an 8-foot pole, is simply eased into the water and jerked suddenly to snag a fish. In good years hundreds of louche congregate here every night, and large numbers are taken.

Fish Traps

Perhaps the most important aboriginal means of catching fish involved various kinds of traps, which were set in rivers and streams. All of these traps have been out of use for many years, except for one which will be described shortly. The fish trap is fairly complicated, but consists basically of a barrier or partial barrier of poles driven into the stream bottom, which channels fish into a box or basket. The trap itself usually has a cone-shaped entry protruding into it, so that the fish cannot find an escape. Some of the old men at Chalkyitsik know how to make certain kinds of fish traps, but their accounts are vague. Several types of Kutchin fish traps have been expertly described by Osgood (1936*b*, pp. 33, 35, 68–69, 73–74), and therefore need not be reconsidered here.

Fish traps began to disappear after commercial fishnets were introduced to the Kutchin. During aboriginal times some Kutchin tribes apparently made fishnets out of babiche (rawhide) and twisted willow bark (Osgood 1936*b*, pp. 67, 72). These nets would have needed regular drying, they probably wore out quickly, and they may have been rather ineffective as well. But when long-lasting and highly effective cotton and (later) nylon nets became available, most kinds of fish traps gradually fell out of use. Fishnets replaced traps, I think, because they were more productive, required much less effort to use, and could be handled by one or two persons. Fish traps were generally large and elaborate, often requiring communal effort by a number of men to build and sometimes to operate as well. A trend toward individualism during the postcontact era also favored the use of nets. In addition, nets could be set anywhere—in rivers, streams, lakes, and sloughs, in open or ice-covered water—with little difference in the effort required.

One kind of fish trapping survives today at Chalkyitsik in the form of a sluice trap set each year in Chalkyitsik Creek. This is a small creek, usually just a yard or two wide, which connects a series of four or five lakes northeast of the village. Each of these lakes contains a large population of whitefish, and the fish run down the creek in fall and up in the spring. The size of the run varies greatly from year to year, and is usually best when fall rains cause a heavy flow of water in the creek before freeze-up.

About the first week in September, people start watching the creek for the first whitefish. Sometimes they set a net across its mouth or make a small, temporary sluice trap to intercept the first fish. Once the fish appear some men build a full-sized trap. The creek is narrowed with gravel dikes or gates of wood and wire screening. A long, narrow wooden sluice box is set into the creek bed, and the sluice spills into another box or enclosure which is several inches lower. This box has cracks between its boards and a screen at its downstream end, so the creek water flows right through. The height and length of the trap vary according to the depth and flow of the water. In 1969, the creek was only a few inches deep and about a yard wide. The trap that year was about 12 feet long, 20 inches high, and 20 inches wide.

Whitefish swimming downstream are carried into the box of the sluice trap. They may be able to swim out against the current over the spillway from the sluice into the box, but most do not. When the trap is checked, one man goes upstream and drives fish into it, while another uses a small flat-sided net to scoop out the catch. In years when the fish run heavily there are too many for the people to handle, so they apparently let some of the fish through by opening the lower end of the trap. Drying racks and cutting tables are set up right by the trap, and the fish are cleaned and hung up to dry on the spot. Whitefish taken here are small, up to a foot or so in length, but are fat and delicious. Besides being important in the human diet, they are a major source of dog food for the Chalkyitsik Kutchin.

A man who spent most of his life on the upper Black River described another related fish trap, which is set at beaver dams in the deep tributaries that flow out of the hills. First, the men break a hole about 2½ feet wide and 2½ feet deep in the dam; then they set a square fish trap made of chicken wire in the opening so the water pours through it. The trap is angled downward along the outside slope of the dam and the water runs through it so fast that the fish cannot escape once they have entered it. Someone has to stay close by or the beaver will patch the hole in its dam and ruin the trap-set.

The most important modern fish trap is the widely used fish wheel. This is a kind of water wheel, with two very large scoops or "baskets" that are turned by the current. Salmon swimming upstream during their annual run are lifted from the water by the turning scoops and dropped into a trough which empties into a box. The design of fish wheels is well known and is too complex for a detailed description here. And they are not regularly used by the Tranjik Kutchin.

The Black River has too little current to turn a wheel, at least in spots where enough salmon congregate to make it worth the effort to build and operate fish wheels. They have been tried, but until recently they always failed to produce. Then several years ago a young, energetic man decided to build a fish wheel despite the old-timers' insistence that he was foolish. Nobody would help him, because they said it was not worth the effort. Finally someone helped him put it in the water, and when he found the right spot for it he took some three thousand salmon, an outstanding season's catch.

Netting

The importance of fish netting among the aboriginal Kutchin is little known, but it is certain that commercial fishnets made this a major productive technique. And it is important to note that nets and the fish they take can be handled effectively by women, old people, and children. William Sam, a seventy-five-year-old Tranjik Kutchin, said that when he was a boy the women did nearly all the summer fishing while men hunted or traveled to Fort Yukon in their canoes. Women must have carried a major economic burden in the past, because the fish and small game mainly procured by them were the most stable and reliable food sources. With the advent of the fur trade and wage labor, plus a continuing dependence on big game, men assumed a heavily dominant position in the postcontact economy.

Fish netting is most importantly correlated with the annual salmon run. Salmon usually appear at Chalkyitsik about the end of July or the first half of August. The size of the run varies from year to year. As soon as people begin to catch salmon in fair numbers, many nets are put into the river in front of Chalkyitsik. Dog salmon (*khii*) usually appear first. A second species, the sockeye, begins running early in October and continues through November, usually after dog salmon have become scarce. Other species are taken throughout this time, including sheefish, whitefish, pike, and a few louche, sucker, and grayling.

Sometime early in October the river begins to freeze, starting in deep, still places such as the bend at Chalkyitsik. When ice starts forming, people take their nets out to prevent their being frozen in. Then as soon as the ice is about 2 inches thick, they walk onto it and set their nets beneath the ice. This kind of netting continues until thick ice, poor catches, and cold weather force a halt, usually sometime in November.

Some time before the river freezes (around the first of October) ice forms on the lakes around Chalkyitsik. The people watch one large lake, called *Ch'atritt,* with special interest because this is their fishing lake. As soon as it has solid ice and there is enough frost or snow on the ground to make a trip there, people take their nets and head for the fishing area. Some other lakes and sloughs are also fished, but none can produce pike and whitefish as *Ch'atritt* does. Ice thickens fast on the lakes, and so the season is not long. After a month or so, depending on the weather, the nets are pulled out. The fishing season must have been longer in the past when people were willing to put more effort into it.

The final netting season comes after the river ice breaks up in spring, usually in early May. Sometimes people rush the season a bit, setting their nets in the open water that forms between the shore and the edge of the river ice. After the ice is gone, more nets are set, for whitefish, pike, and an occasional louche. A few people may keep a fishnet in the water from time to time throughout the summer months.

The fishnets used at Chalkyitsik are commercially made nylon gill nets, which entangle fish that swim into them. In the past, people wove their own nets from cotton line, but today they are purchased at the store in Fort Yukon or ordered through the mail. River nets are approximately 30 to 80 feet long.' It is possible to buy fishnets ready to set—that is, with top and bottom lines, floats, and lead sinkers attached. Most people prefer to save money by "hanging" the net themselves, which involves skillfully stringing a doubled cotton cord along the top and bottom edges.

When it is set, the net itself is suspended loosely between these two lines, which are anchored at each end. Floats were formerly made of wood, as they still are for under-ice netting, but in open water empty plastic containers are used. For sinkers, rocks weigh-

Setting a fishnet in open water with a hunting canoe.

ing about half a pound are tied along the net's lower edge. Nets are washed out occasionally to keep them clean, because fish will not go into them if they are dirty.

The best place for netting fish is in an eddy, a place where some irregularity in the bank or a bend in the river creates a deep, quiet pool. Eddies have a gentle countercurrent, and fish are apparently attracted to them to escape from the swift mainstream. Indians set their fishnets in the larger eddies, those wide enough to accommodate the net, because these are the most productive spots and because it would be difficult to keep a net anchored and clear of debris if it extended out into the current. In the Black River around Chalkyitsik there are seven major eddies in which the people place their nets. Each eddy has its own peculiarities, especially in terms of the kinds of fish that congregate there. Some eddies are attractive to all species, some attract many pike and louche, others are good for salmon, and so on.

In some villages, such as Huslia, people utilize eddies scattered along the river for miles up and downstream. The Chalkyitsik people move their nets around within or between netting places until they find what appears to be a good spot. There is some tendency for the net farthest downstream in a given place to catch the most fish, and the one farthest upstream to catch the fewest. This is not always true, however. People try to set their nets in the least crowded place they can find.

Fishnets are usually set out with large wooden boats. First the net is anchored to a stake driven into the shore or the bottom just offshore. Then while one person paddles or slowly drives the boat outward from shore the other pays the net out into the water. The outer end of the net is attached to a long line with a heavy anchor on it, usually a sack of rocks or a piece of metal. When the net is stretched tightly, this anchor is thrown out to hold it.

When someone wishes to check his fishnet, he takes a large boat or hunting canoe to it, grasps the net at its shoreward end, and pulls up a portion of the netting so he can see if there are any fish tangled in it. He continues to do this, gradually pulling the boat toward the net's outer end. Fish are usually clubbed with a stick to still them as they are untangled from the encircling strands. Removing the fish is not easy, since they are often incredibly wound up in the netting, and no small amount of practice is required to

Setting a fishnet under the Black River ice in the fall. Note the series of holes made in the ice.

take fish quickly from a gill net. Pieces of debris are removed at the same time.

Fishnets can be set and checked without a boat if necessary. Two long poles are cut, laid parallel, and tied together at the end that will be pushed out into the water. The net is then tied along the length of one of these poles. Now the poles are pushed out at a right angle to the shore. Once they are all the way out, the one with the net hanging from it is tethered ashore, while the other is spread apart from it and fastened 10 or 15 feet away. The second pole acts as a brace to keep the net pole straight out from shore. To check the net, the two poles are unfastened and pulled in.

If the fishing is good, nets are checked every day, but if it is poor they are tended less frequently. The best fishermen check regularly, because leaving fish in a net decreases its effectiveness. Some people lose interest, however, and may leave their nets a week or more without looking at them.

Setting fishnets under the ice presents a different problem, but the solution is much simpler than one might expect. In fact, netting fish under fairly thin ice is a good deal easier than with a boat. The procedure is as follows:

1. First the net is stretched out on the ice where it is to be set, and sinkers and floats are attached. Four or five small wooden floats are tied along the top edge, and an equal number of small rocks are fastened with cord to the lower edge. The net will be stretched between two poles which are pushed into the bottom. These poles hold the net suspended in midwater, and the slight buoyancy of the floats cannot raise the net up to the ice. The floats are tied with light string that can be broken easily should a float freeze into the thickening ice above.

2. Now, with the prepared net laid out, six to eight holes are made through the ice along the line where the net will be strung. The first hole is made 10 or 15 feet out from shore, where one end of the net will be anchored. The rest of the holes, 8 to 10 feet apart and about 18 inches square, are now made.

3. This done, a strong cord long enough to reach between the innermost and outermost holes is attached to a 10-foot-long dry pole. This pole is inserted through the first hole, so that it floats up against the bottom of the ice. Then it is pushed along under the ice from one hole to the next until it reaches the outermost

one, where it is pulled up onto the ice. Now a line has been strung under the ice along the entire length of the set.

4. The net is attached to one end of this line, and while one man feeds it into the water, the other pulls the line from the opposite end, stretching the net out beneath the ice.

5. When the net is entirely under the ice, each end is tied to a long, freshly cut willow pole which is then stuck down through the hole and into the bottom. This suspends the net beneath the ice between the two poles. Sometimes the outermost pole cannot reach bottom but is braced with short poles on top of the ice.

6. A day or so later, when the net is checked, the poles have frozen into the ice and must be chopped out. The two end holes

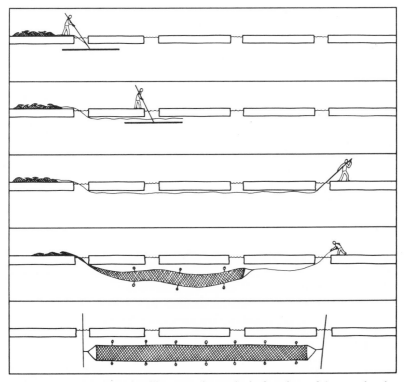

This cross-sectional drawing illustrates the method of setting a fishnet under the ice.

are opened to their original size to allow easy handling of the net. The other holes are no longer used. To check the net, one pole is lifted out onto the ice, the net is untied from it, and a long cord is fastened to the net. Then the man walks to the other end and begins pulling the net, piling it at his feet as he removes fish from it. The line is payed out beneath the ice from the far end, and when he has checked the net he simply pulls it back into the water with line. This can be done by one man but is easier with a partner. When the temperature drops below zero, a man has to work fast lest the net and his bare fingers freeze.

Fish netting is done exactly the same way in the nearby lakes. If a lake or slough is shallow, however, it takes some care to be sure the net and floats do not freeze into the undersurface of the ice. The most important thing to know in lake netting is where to set, and this knowledge comes through generations of experience in the country. Pike and whitefish are the species taken in lakes.

Fish populations in the surrounding lakes are subject to great variation, ranging from abundance to none at all. This apparently relates to the floods that from time to time spread out over the river flats. Moses William, a knowledgeable old-timer, said that when there is no flood for five or six years the fish in the lakes die off, and the lakes have no fish until the next flood. Then the fish reenter the lakes and breed, and in a few years fishing is excellent. The whitefish and pike will be small but plentiful at first, and in succeeding years more and more large fish will be caught until another die-off comes.

Ice Fishing

Netting is not the only way to catch fish after the rivers and lakes are locked in ice. Once they are frozen over, it is easy for the Kutchin to walk to a good fishing place, make a hole in the ice, then sit there and try to catch fish. Ice fishing not only is a profitable occupation, it is also a pleasant diversion for men and women and an adventure for the children. Today ice fishing is done exclusively with hook and line, but in the past fish were also speared through the ice.

Ice fishing season begins as soon as the rivers and lakes freeze in the fall and continues through the winter and spring until the ice is too rotten to walk on. Pike, sheefish, louche, and grayling

An ice fisherman using his jigging stick. The ice chisel and ax are used to make the fishing hole. Note the large pike he has taken. He wears heavy mittens, parka, and flight pants for maximum warmth.

can be taken along both the Black and the Porcupine rivers. Fishing is popular around freeze-up, but it slows down after this time, and little is done in December and January. As the sun begins rising higher in late January, people start fishing for pike at Chalkyitsik. The season peaks when meltwater starts lifting the ice and threatens to carry it away down the river. People say, perhaps optimistically, that a hundred pike can be caught in a day at this time. In the spring of 1970, five was a good day's catch.

Ice fishing is done with a short (about 18-inch) stick with 4 or 5 feet of line attached to it. A spoon lure is generally used, with a small strip of pike skin attached to its hooks. The fisherman chops a hole through the ice with an ax or chisel, and clears slush from it by swishing it out with the ax head. Then he drops his hook down and begins jigging it. Styles differ, but jigging usually consists of repeated short jerks on the line with a longer pull every five or ten seconds. When a fish is caught, it is pulled up through the hole and stunned with the jigging rod or some other piece of wood. If it is cold, the fisherman clears ice from the fishing hole every few minutes by sweeping the end of his rod back and forth over the water.

After freeze-up there may be good fishing for louche near the village, especially where Chalkyitsik Creek enters the river. People, especially women and young boys, go out at night to try their luck. They dress in their warmest clothes and sit on a sled or a mat of insulating grass. Sometimes up to fifteen or twenty louche are taken in a night.

Uses of Fish

It should be clear from what has been said in this chapter that, although fishing can be a highly productive and important activity, it is subject to marked fluctuations. My own impression of its variability is perhaps exaggerated because in 1960–70 every kind of fishing was at a productive minimum. Very few fish were taken during the summer of 1969, and the salmon run in particular was extraordinarily poor. When fall came, the river fishing remained poor, and the annual run of whitefish in Chalkyitsik Creek failed completely. After freeze-up the fears of poor fishing in the lakes were more than realized, and not a single fish was taken. Even the winter ice fishing in the Porcupine River was poor, and the spring pike fishing at Chalkyitsik followed suit. Thus in this one year all the fish resources failed together, surely a very unusual occurrence. But it underscores the sort of fluctuations in resource availability that characterize this environment, something that will come up time and again in succeeding chapters. Any discussion of human ecology in this region, and probably in the boreal forest biome generally, would be incomplete without drawing attention to the rhythmic and nonrhythmic variations in its productivity.

It is no accident that the Tranjik Kutchin are aware of the dynamic nature of their environment, since they are regularly confronted with short- and long-term changes in it. One year there are many salmon, the next there are few. Several years ago the hares seemed to be extinct, now they are everywhere. Fifteen years ago moose were so common that they were hunted just around the nearest bend in the river, and now the men travel 50 miles upriver before they see a track. And there may be changes of longer term than this. One old man said that when he was younger there seemed to be more fish than there are today, both in the rivers and in the lakes. He even feels that the whitefish taken in lakes were larger then. He is undoubtedly correct about fish in the rivers because of the reduction in salmon runs caused by commercial fishing. About the rest, perhaps he is idealizing. Then again, perhaps not.

During a good fishing year, the summer's take is mostly stored by drying. This involves splitting each fish along one side of the backbone to the tail, slicing into the thick meat to allow easier drying, and then hanging it on a drying rack. These racks are small, roofed structures with fencelike walls to admit a flow of air while excluding the marauding dogs. Slow, smoky fires of punky wood are built under the hanging fish to keep the flies away and encourage faster drying. As soon as the fish are sufficiently dried they are stored away in caches for later use. All kinds of fish can be dried; salmon, whitefish, and pike are the most important at Chalkyitsik.

Dried fish are sometimes eaten by people, but this seems less prevalent here than in many interior Alaskan settlements. Most of the dry fish are used for dog food. Fish eggs, from salmon, whitefish, and other species, are also highly regarded as nutritious dog food. They dry easily, do not rot, and are rich in fat. Here again, the Chalkyitsik people seem unusual because they seldom (except in the case of louche) eat fish eggs themselves. Fish meat, on the other hand, is considered excellent eating, particularly fresh, fat whitefish. Some dog salmon caught here are good eating, but others are not. Those with reddish flesh are considered edible, and the rest are strictly dog food. Sockeye salmon, beautiful red fish caught in late fall, are relished by some of the Kutchin, disdained by others.

The "real Indian way" to cook fish, now mostly reserved for camping trips, is to roast them in a fire. Often the fish are simply placed in hot coals with no cleaning or preparation. Another way is to split the fish, skewer them on forked sticks, and plant the sticks at an angle over the heat of the fire. When whole fish are roasted, their entrails and heads are discarded. Whitefish and grayling are most frequently mentioned as good fish to roast.

In addition to salmon, whitefish, and grayling, the Chalkyitsik Kutchin eat sheefish, sucker, northern pike, and louche. Sheefish is well regarded, sucker apparently less so, and pike flesh is considered to be poor-tasting and too low in fat. Fried pike liver and intestines are relished, however. Louche are not eaten except for the liver and eggs. The meat and entrails of fish are most commonly fried or boiled. The Kutchin do not eat fish without cooking it, unless it has been dried.

Fishing has gradually declined over the past years as people have turned away from the land in favor of an increasing dependence upon the world Outside. But the rate of decline increased precipitously in the two or three years preceding this study because of the introduction of snowmobiles and the consequent decrease in the number of pulling dogs. Before this change the Chalkyitsik Kutchin depended heavily upon fish for dog food, and therefore made a considerable fishing effort each year.

Now that reliance on dogs for transportation is fading rapidly, the only really significant summer activity, and one of the major fall occupations, has dwindled to only a fraction of its previous importance. Even though a fair number of dogs remain in the village, people can catch enough fish for them rather quickly if it is a good year. Otherwise they can rely on commercial food and other local resources to keep their dogs alive, or they can kill all but a few of the dogs, as they have little need for them. This is happening or has happened throughout all of Alaska in the past ten years. A major institution of native Alaska, the summer fish camp, has now almost disappeared. And soon the rows of drying racks, heavily laden with thousands of split and drying fish, will exist only in the stories of the old people.

6 Birds

Introduction

The Tranjik Kutchin live on the edge of the huge Yukon Flats, one of the most important waterfowl areas in all of North America. The country is a maze of lakes and rivers, almost as much water as land, and aquatic birds are attracted to it in prodigious numbers. They are particularly abundant during the spring and fall migrations, although they remain fairly common throughout the summer. As one would expect, waterfowl occupy a position of some importance in the Kutchin economy. The only other bird species which are at all significant as food are the various kinds of grouse.

The following list includes those bird species which are of economic significance to the modern Tranjik Kutchin. Many of the Kutchin terms are from Mueller (1964, pp. 39–42).

Mallard (*Anas platyrhynchos*); Kutchin name *neet'ak-chooh:* A common duck, important in the local economy.

Pintail (*Anas acuta*); Kutchin name *ch'iri-njaa:* Another common and important species.

American Widgeon (*Mareca americana*); Kutchin name *chalvii:* This species is very common and almost as important as the mallard and pintail.

Green-winged Teal (*Anas carolinensis*); Kutchin name *ch'idzin:*

This common and easily approached duck is well liked but is too small to be much sought after.

Greater Scaup (*Aythya marila*), Kutchin name *taainchoo'*, and Lesser Scaup (*Aythya affinis*): Apparently both species are found here commonly and are often hunted.

Common Goldeneye (*Bucephala clangula*); Kutchin name *kik'ii:* This duck is fairly common but is seldom hunted because of its small size and rapid flight.

Bufflehead (*Bucephala albeola*); Kutchin name *tł'aandii':* A rather uncommon, small duck which is seldom taken.

White-winged Scoter (*Melanitta deglandi*); Kutchin name *njaa:* This duck is abundant in springtime, when it is enthusiastically hunted.

Canada Goose (*Branta canadensis*); Kutchin name *khee:* A common, important spring and summer bird.

White-fronted Goose (*Anser albifrons*); Kutchin name *deechy'a:* Also quite common in spring and summer, and perhaps more important than the Canada goose.

Snow Goose (*Chen hyperborea*); Kutchin name *gwigeh:* An uncommon spring migrant, seldom shot but highly regarded as food.

Red-breasted Merganser (*Mergus serrator*); Kutchin name *traa:* Abundant in the Black River but very rarely hunted.

Common Loon (*Gavia immer*); Kutchin name *deedrai:* A common river and lake bird but almost never hunted.

Arctic Loon (*Gavia arctica*); Kutchin name *ts'alvit:* Common in the Black River but very rarely hunted.

Spruce Grouse (*Canachites canadensis*); Kutchin name *dai:* Variable or cyclic population but a commonly hunted resident species.

Ruffed Grouse (*Bonasa umbellus*); Kutchin name *tregwat:* Another variable or cyclic species, highly regarded as food and often hunted.

Sharp-tailed Grouse (*Pedioecetes phasianellus*); Kutchin name *ch'aahtal:* Also variable or cyclic in numbers but frequently taken.

Willow Ptarmigan (*Lagopus lagopus*); Kutchin name *daagoo:* A sometimes-common winter resident which is hunted when encountered.

Sandhill Crane (*Grus canadensis*); Kutchin name *jyaa:* A large, fairly common bird, sometimes taken when encountered.

Snow Bunting (*Plectrophenax nivalis*); Kutchin name *gwigee-zuu:*
A common sparrowlike spring migrant, sometimes hunted in the
past.

Raven (*Corvus corax*); Kutchin name *deetry'a:* A ubiquitous
northern bird, not eaten but important because of its depredations
on cached or trapped game.

Gray Jay (*Perisoreus canadensis*); Kutchin name *ch'idingwat'an:*
A common year-round resident. Its local name, "camp robber,"
indicates its only significance, as a marauder that steals cached
meat.

Waterfowl

This section will discuss the three general methods of hunting ducks
and geese. The first is hunting from boats in the Black River, an
important spring and fall activity which is carried out almost daily.
The second method is hunting on land, including overhead shooting
from blinds, hills, or from the village itself, and stalking waterfowl
in the water near shore. Finally, there is lake hunting with canoes
and larger boats.

River Hunting

River hunting for ducks and (to a much lesser degree) geese is carried out during all of the open-water months, from May through
September. In spring the ducks arrive as soon as there are open
places in the river ice, and they are abundant by the time it is
clear enough for boat travel. As summer comes on, waterfowl scatter widely over the lakes and rivers, no longer concentrating on
the Black River. When fall's cool weather arrives the number of
ducks seen along the river increases somewhat, and when the lakes
freeze over they are driven to the unfrozen rivers. Fall and early
spring are the times when motor-powered boats and small hunting
canoes are on the river each morning and evening, and shotgun
blasts ring out so often that people almost stop noticing them.

In the fall, before the lakes are frozen, ducks often fly to the
river from the surrounding lakes during early morning and at evening
to eat the roots of sedges and other plants that grow at the river's
edge and to pick up grit from the sandbars. Kutchin hunters take

their boats and course up and down the river, searching in the dusky light for the shapes of ducks along the banks. During the spring, ducks are very common on the river, and men often hunt them all "night" in the twenty-four-hour daylight.

Kutchin hunters are adept at identifying waterfowl at a distance, even in poor light, a skill which is important for deciding which birds to pursue and which to ignore. The large, slow-flying species such as pintail, mallard, American widgeon, and white-winged scoter are easiest to hit and have the most meat. Small, fast ducks such as the relatively fearless green-winged teal, the bufflehead, and the goldeneye are not hunted much because they are very difficult to hit and offer much less meat. The price of a shotgun shell is the same whether it hits a three-pound mallard or a one-pound teal; so it is wise to save the shell for bigger prey.

In river hunting the idea is to drive or paddle a boat as close as possible to ducks sitting on the water or flying low over it; so hunters ride up and down the river for hours at a time, approaching each duck or group of ducks they see. Usually there are several hunters in a motor boat. They apparently watch for the birds to turn into the wind or to assume a stiff and alert posture indicating they are about to take flight. Birds are easiest to hit while still on the water, but often the boat is not within range until after they have taken flight. Hunters usually fire when they get within 30 to 50 yards, but some take longer shots.

Hunters who go out with canoes use the same technique, but they stay much closer to the village. When they spot ducks on the water, they attempt to paddle or drift as close as possible before shooting. It is strange that whereas some ducks are quite unafraid of canoes others seem more frightened by them than by motorboats. Canoe hunters sometimes paddle to a place where ducks may land, and wait quietly next to the concealing bank vegetation. When dusk has closed over most of the sky, ducks often land or swim within a few yards, to be shot in the near-darkness.

Ducks shot from boats are easily retrieved as they float lifeless on the water. But if only wounded they will dive repeatedly, and the hunters must wait for them to appear, then give chase, wait again, and so on until they manage a killing shot. Shotguns or .22 rifles are used to kill the wounded birds.

In the past, hunters would pursue flightless young and adult geese during the month of July. At this time the fat young geese are not yet able to fly and the adults are undergoing their molt. Hunters chased the geese with boats and shot them in the water or caught them by hand on the bank. They were especially easy to catch along a steep cutbank which they could not climb. Flightless geese are found only in certain places, so hunters had to know just what area of the river or its tributaries they frequent. The Chalkyitsik Kutchin rarely, if ever, go hunting for these geese today.

Land Hunting

The second general type of waterfowl hunting, which I call land hunting, is done primarily during the springtime. The Indians hunt waterfowl at this season because they have a genuine need for meat. The arrival of ducks often breaks a lean period in which little game of any kind can be taken. Although this hunting is not in accord with the white man's regulatory custom, the Kutchin feel that it is a necessary part of their existence and that any interference with it would be a violation of their rights. It is worth noting here that they very rarely kill any animal without genuine need.

Normally, waterfowl begin to arrive in the spring as soon as open places appear in the river, usually around middle to late April. From this time until the end of May there is heavy hunting, though it does not go on with equal intensity every day. Migrating waterfowl seem to fly in greatest numbers when they are aided by a tailwind from the south, and they become uncommon when a stiff breeze blows from the north. The Kutchin feel that the temperature, not the wind, has the greatest influence on waterfowl migrations. This is certainly true to the extent that temperature determines the presence of open water in the early spring. If the open places freeze over again in a spring cold snap, waterfowl must find their way south to a suitable habitat. The people say that when it turns warm in late April, the ducks and geese will fail to show up if there is to be another cold wind before the final warmth appears.

The first places to have open water in the spring are the small muskeg ponds, which are usually surrounded by sedges and willow thickets. These little ponds thaw quickly, and ducks fly in to feed and rest on them. Hunters can stalk to within range of a shotgun or .22 rifle if there are willows around such a pond. It is easy to retrieve birds from such places by using a long stick or by waiting for the wind to blow them to shore. The same hunting technique can be used at open spots in the river, where men wait concealed in the brush.

A good number of the waterfowl shot by Chalkyitsik hunters are taken within the village itself. During the month or so of the migration, many people keep a shotgun near the door of the house. Anyone who is outside—man, woman, or child—keeps an eye toward the south, watching for ducks or geese flying toward the village. When someone calls out or when a shot is heard at the south end of the settlement, the men head for the door and grab their shotguns. If birds fly low enough over Chalkyitsik, there is a fair chance that one or two will be hit.

The people who are really after ducks walk up on Marten Hill, along the south and west sides of the village, an especially good place because all the country south of Marten Hill is flat wetland which the ducks pass over at low altitude. When they reach the hill they must gain elevation, but they pass within easy shotgun range of its crest. Hunting from Marten Hill and the village is best in early May when most of the waterfowl arrive. It reaches a second peak about the first of June, when the long, strung-out flocks of white-winged scoters come in. The scoters are large, slow-flying, and not very clever ducks that come low over the hill and the village.

Waterfowl seem to rest during midday, then take to the air during the low-sun period. In the spring this means that hunters watch especially around dusk, which starts between 7:00 and 9:00 P.M., depending on the date. By late April there is twilight all night long, and they can keep a long vigil until the bright sunshine comes at 2:00 or 3:00 A.M. Sometimes two or three men, and perhaps their wives, go up on the hill to sit and talk through the evening as they wait for ducks.

Hunters with long experience know many spots where ducks and geese tend to fly back and forth between lakes, from river to lake, or across a portage at a bend in the river. One such spot, for example, is a small island in the Black River about 5 miles above Chalkyitsik. There is quiet water and good feeding in a narrow channel separating the island from the shore, making it attractive for ducks. It is also situated on a sharp, looping bend, where ducks and geese fly overland from one part of the river to another, and there are several good lakes nearby, which they regularly fly in and out of. Hunters wait at the edge of some willow thickets and shoot birds as they fly along the various aerial pathways.

Another desirable area, especially for hunting geese, is on any of the hundreds of sandbars along the Yukon or Porcupine rivers. When geese follow the rivers they are almost forced to land on a sandbar if they are to land at all. When they come in they fly low over one end or the other, and so the hunter makes a little blind there and waits. When the water is rising in spring the hunting is especially good, because only a few high bars remain exposed and the geese congregate on them.

Another important kind of land hunting, especially for geese, is done in certain places where extensive sedge or grass meadows surround shallow lakes. Two species, the Canada goose and the white-fronted goose, are abundant here for several weeks in spring. Both are hunted enthusiastically. Snow geese are occasionally taken, but they are uncommon and are difficult to approach.

When they arrive at a meadow-lake, hunters first locate a good place for a blind. Points that extend into the water, or areas which geese frequently pass over as they fly from lake to lake, are the best places for close shots. The blind is a semicircular framework of sticks, covered with the long marsh grass that abounds at the margins of good waterfowl lakes. It looks like a mound in the sur-rounding grass and makes a highly effective cover for the hunter. Occasionally a willow thicket is growing in the right spot and so he need not build a blind.

Once the hunter has a blind he waits until he hears and sees a flight of geese coming. The Kutchin attract geese by imitating their high-pitched calls. The call of the Canada goose is fairly easy to mimic, and the technique works about equally well on both Canada and white-fronted geese. But the call of the latter is much harder to imitate, and many hunters use only the Canada goose call. These mimics can be a very effective way to bring the big birds in for a close shot.

Geese are usually hunted with 12-gauge shotguns, using shells with fairly heavy shot; 20-gauge shotguns can also kill geese, but are less effective. These gauges, plus 16-gauge, are also used for duck hunting. It takes considerable skill to shoot waterfowl in flight, and an important part of this skill is being able to judge exactly when the birds are as close as they are going to come so the closest possible shot can be taken. A hunter often gets two or three shots at a flock of slow-flying geese before they are out of range.

After he has killed geese the hunter can use them as realistic decoys by simply posing them on bare ground or the lakeshore, with forked sticks 8 to 12 inches long stuck in the ground to hold their heads in a lifelike position. The decoys should be placed 30 to 50 yards from the blind in a place near water, where geese might ordinarily land. I have seen geese wheel and drift in to land near such decoys, completely unsuspecting until the hunter's shotgun caught them. One man mentioned using simple paper decoys until some geese are shot and can be set up for this purpose.

Early morning and evening are the best periods for hunting from blinds. At these times ducks and geese become restless and leave their feeding and resting places to fly around. The more they move around the better it is for stationary hunters. For this reason, one man may be sent around a lake to keep the birds flying. The birds along shore will fly up at his approach, and those far out on the water can be frightened into the air by shooting toward them with a .22 rifle. A number of men can hunt together quite effectively, setting up blinds at several places around a lake and having one of their number drive the birds up.

Waterfowl are often difficult to stalk when it is windy, because at such times they tend to stay well out from shore. Perhaps they do this to avoid being caught by predators, whose approach would be concealed by the sounds of wind. The only chance a hunter has is to follow the upwind shore of the lake, where ducks and geese sometimes congregate in the still, protected waters. This can sometimes be highly effective, especially along timbered lakes where ducks such as mallards, widgeons, and teal may feed right at the water's edge. A careful hunter, walking very slowly along the forested shore, may get some very close shots at ducks in the shallow water.

It is not easy to hunt geese. They are unusually wary, keep away from the lakeshore once frightened, and tend to fly high and watch closely what is on the ground beneath them; and even when hit they are difficult to fell. On one spring hunting trip three men spent two days out and came home with ten geese and a duck. "I wonder how many years since anybody brought that many geese home from one hunt?'' a man commented. There are thousands of geese in the country, but only a few are killed.

Lake Hunting

The Yukon Flats are covered with lakes, but most are not connected and must be reached on foot during the open-water season. To hunt on these small lakes, the Indian must have his light canoe, which he can carry easily from one lake to the next. The basic method of lake hunting consists of moving through a series of lakes and sloughs and perhaps paddling some distance on the river. The hunter skirts or paddles across each lake in search of ducks. Little needs to be said of the hunting method—locating, approaching, identifying, shooting, and retrieving the waterfowl—because it is essentially identical to the river hunting described earlier. As in every form of economic activity here, the resources are localized; so the hunter must know which lakes are best for waterfowl and which seldom have any birds at all. The most important lake in this region is Ohtig Lake, about 4 miles south of Chalkyitsik. This large, shallow lake attracts thousands of migrating waterfowl during August and September, and to a lesser degree in spring.

In the past, canoe hunters went to Ohtig Lake throughout the late summer and fall, but especially during the period when the ducks were molting and unable to fly. At this time they could be "herded" by large numbers of people in canoes. Large flocks were driven into narrow places, where many ducks would just sit on the surface looking around in confusion while the hunters shot them with bow and arrow or shotgun. Hundreds were said to have been taken in a single day by this technique. Duck hunting, particularly the fall hunting on Ohtig Lake, is the last activity for which the bow and arrow was used. All the men over seventy have used the bow and arrow, but only for ducks or small game.

Today the drives are all but gone. Men go down to Ohtig Lake to hunt alone or in pairs, but people do not seem able to organize for communal hunts. Occasionally a motorboat is hauled to the lake and hunters cruise around shooting ducks. Takes can run up to a hundred ducks or more in a day. Of course these large bags are impressive, but they are always divided among several hunters, who then divide them around the village. A hundred ducks may, in fact, end up as ten ducks apiece for ten families. During the spring there is a fair amount of lake hunting with canoes, especially when the white-winged scoters or "black ducks" appear. These ducks usually arrive in fairly large numbers during the last week of May and remain common for about two weeks. The Kutchin love scoters because they are the only fat spring ducks. Scoters have certain predictable behavior patterns that make them easy to shoot; they are reluctant to take flight as a canoe approaches, and swim away instead. On a big lake they can just keep swimming, but on small lakes the hunter attempts to drive them to a brushy shore where they cannot take off away from him. Scoters cannot jump right up off the water, but must run briefly into the wind, then slowly gain altitude. A good hunter tries to approach them from upwind, so that when they take flight they will come toward him where he can get the closest possible shot.

The Kutchin usually cook ducks and geese as a thin stew, boiling the meat in water with rice or macaroni, vegetables, and condiments added. Hunters sometimes roast ducks over a campfire while they are away from the village. The bird's sternum and breast muscles are cut so its body cavity can be opened, then it is spread flat and skewered on a stick set into the ground next to the fire so it can cook easily inside and out.

Waterfowl are an important supplement to the diet of the modern Chalkyitsik Kutchin, but they do not make up a large proportion of the total meat intake. It is important to note, however, that unlike practically every other species of animal utilized by the Kutchin, waterfowl do not appear to fluctuate greatly in numbers. Surely there are differences in the number of ducks and geese that appear each year, but there is little to indicate that their population varies like that of fish, mammals, and some other bird species.

Grouse and Ptarmigan

All species of grouse and ptarmigan are subject to wide variations in abundance. For ruffed grouse, this variation apparently follows a regular eight-to-eleven-year cyclic pattern, and fluctuations in the other species may or may not be cyclic (Keith 1963, p. 61). Ruffed grouse are probably the most common; all four species are highly regarded as food.

Ptarmigan, which migrate southward from the tundra into the forest after the early snows, were formerly caught with snares set by making little stick fences in places where flocks of ptarmigan were often seen. Snares, most recently made by pulling one thin wire strand from braided picture wire, were placed in small openings in the fence. The ptarmigan were caught in the snares as they tried to walk through the openings, and they would die very quickly. They could be decoyed by simply setting up chunks of snow in the surrounding willows. Quite possibly some kind of bait was placed inside the fence. Similar snaring arrangements were probably used for the forest-dwelling grouse.

An interesting snare technique, widely distributed among northern Athapaskans and Algonkians, is the pole snare. This device, probably used only for spruce grouse, consists of a long, slender pole with a snare on one end. It is usually made on the spot, and the length of the pole depends on how high the grouse are roosting. Spruce grouse are usually quite unafraid, so they can be approached from in front or behind. The noose is carefully maneuvered until it is above and in front of the bird, lowered until it is level with its head, then jerked backward and pulled tight around its neck (Cooper 1938, pp. 15–16).

Most grouse hunting today is done with small-caliber rifles. Spruce grouse are most often encountered by trappers running their lines; as the name implies, they are birds of the timber. They tend to roost and feed in little flocks, sometimes up to fifteen together, and so when one is seen there is a good chance that others will be in the same tree or another tree close by. They are so fearless that often several can be shot before the rest take flight. Head or neck shots are preferred, because they do not spoil the good breast meat.

The most productive grouse hunting is done close to the village by men, women, and young boys who go out with .22 rifles or light-gauge shotguns. These outings are usually combined with "rabbit" hunting. Ruffed, spruce, or sharp-tailed grouse are sometimes seen as they walk through the thick underbrush, but more often are spotted near the tops of tall willows or alders. They are especially common in the willow thickets that line sandbars or islands along the rivers and are easiest to find during the morning and evening. Another way to locate them is to listen for their call. Once the hunter sees grouse he walks quietly to within range and tries to shoot them in the head or heart. Any that he kills are plucked on the spot, because the feathers are most easily removed while the bird is still warm.

Other Birds

We have now covered all the species of birds that are really significant in the modern economy of Chalkyitsik. A few other species, however, assume minor roles in the people's economic lives.

Sandhill Crane

The sandhill crane is a very large bird with a 6- or 7-foot wingspan. It is fairly common around Chalkyitsik, especially during the spring. The Kutchin sometimes eat crane, but most have tried it only a few times. Some say it tastes good, others say it tastes bad; some claim that cranes are too skinny to be good eating, whereas others say that they look skinny but there is fat all through their flesh. Very few cranes are shot, though occasionally somebody stalks close enough to kill one.

Snow Bunting

We go from the largest to the smallest bird utilized by the Black River people. The snow bunting is a white, sparrow-size bird that migrates through this region around late March and early April on its way north to the tundra. One man said that despite their small size "snow birds" were used in the recent past to make a tasty stew. They were caught with a fence snare like the one described for grouse. Cornmeal or oatmeal was scattered inside and outside a circular fence. The birds hopped around eating and eventually went into one of the openings, where they were snared. "Snow birds are bigger than they look; they got fat round bodies and good meat."

Raven and Gray Jay

Both of these common birds are classified as "varmints" by the Kutchin, who feel no love at all toward them. When people check their rabbit snares they often find that ravens have been there before them, leaving nothing but a few bones. When moose or bear meat is left behind to be picked up later, it must be covered with thick brush or the ravens and jays will peck at it. What is worse, their excrements often foul whatever they land on. Fish-drying racks away from the village must always be guarded against their thievery. Jays are seldom shot, except by young boys, but ravens are frequently killed by men, who do not like their scavenging. Jays can be caught by setting a string snare in the narrow entryway to a small house made of sticks. They are caught when they try to hop inside after a bait of meat or fat. They are not eaten.

In the past, birds have probably saved many a Kutchin from starvation. At these times they would eat any bird that could be killed, except perhaps eagles, ravens, and woodpeckers (Osgood 1936*b*, p. 28). And there were undoubtedly some species, such as swans, cranes, and perhaps shorebirds, that assumed a role in the economy not even hinted at today. When the Kutchin ran out of food it is likely that birds were one animal they always had a fair chance of finding. Thus, their role in the economy might have been much more important than is evident at first glance, because they could be a crucial resource for getting the people through lean periods.

7   Moose

Introduction

The moose (*Alces alces*), which the Tranjik Kutchin call *dinjik,* is the largest animal found in the Black River country. Adult males in prime condition reach a weight of 1,000 to 1,600 pounds, and females reach 800 to 1,200 pounds. Even the calves grow to over 300 pounds during their first five months. Moose are found over much of Alaska and the boreal regions of North America. They are most abundant in second-growth birch forests that come in after fires or logging, on the timberline plateaus, and along the larger rivers of the interior country (Rausch n.d., p. 1).

Moose are browsing animals, feeding especially on the shoots and leaves of willow, birch, and aspen. In the country around Chalkyitsik their favorite spots are willow thickets, which occur along the rivers, around lakes and meadows, and in other wet places. In spring moose do considerable grazing, especially on sedges, horsetail, pond weeds, and grasses, all of which attract them to meadow areas. In some regions they feed on aquatic vegetation in the small lakes during the summer, and in others they feed on leaves of birch, willow, and aspen (Rausch, n.d., p. 2).

It is impossible to say just how vital a role moose played in the traditional Kutchin economy, but there is little question about its importance to the people today. The Chalkyitsik Kutchin consider

moose *the* game in their country. They always want to have moose
meat on hand, and if they run out they think and talk about how
they will get more. 'Meat'' is almost synonymous with moose.
Whereas other animals may be considered delicacies or treats,
moose is probably the one meat they could least think of doing
without. During some years the volume of other foods, such as
fish, may exceed the volume of moose, but the people still seem
to consider it the most important.

Most of the twenty-two adult males living in Chalkyitsik (total
population ninety-five) did some moose hunting during 1969–70, but
of these only eight hunted frequently throughout the year. Thus
a small number of hunters supplied the village with most of its
moose. This is partly due to people's growing disinterest in hunting
in recent years and to their willingness to take advantage of the
sharing custom by which they can usually obtain some meat. About
thirty-six moose were taken during the period of this study, a little
over one moose for every three persons. This is a lot of meat considering the size of a moose and that about half these people were
children. But a greater effort could probably have produced twice
this amount, which underscores the productive potential of this
resource.

As we will see in this chapter, moose hunting involves an
elaborate body of knowledge and a variety of techniques. Chalkyitsik is an ideal place to see a wide range of modern hunting methods,
since moose are "scarce" here by comparison with much of interior
Alaska. This means that the people have to use their abilities to
the fullest to find and kill enough of them. In places where moose
are abundant, they are so easily taken that the more difficult and
subtle hunting techniques are never used.

The complexities of moose hunting were brought home to me
during my first winter hunt, along the Porcupine River in late
November. I made the following note:

> Today's hunt was one of the first hunting experiences I have had where
> I could not figure out what was going on. All of the reasons behind the
> hunters' movements—their locating the moose, their circling around, their
> waiting here or stopping there—all of these things were complete mysteries
> to me while they were taking place. I was as completely "lost" as I might
> have been in unfamiliar country without a compass or trail to follow. In
> the end, after I asked questions and heard explanations, it began to make
> sense; but I realized that moose hunting is anything but simple. It requires

great knowledge of the moose, of tracking and stalking, of the country, and of certain techniques for locating, driving, and intercepting the animal. A novice could fortuitously kill one now and then, but he would not be a real moose hunter until he had learned a great deal indeed. There is a difference between being able to kill an animal and being able to hunt it, one involving a large measure of luck and the other being principally based on skill and knowledge.

The Koyukon Athapaskans sometimes hunt with their neighbors, the Kobuk River Eskimos. They praise the Eskimos' ability as hunters and outdoorsmen except when it comes to moose hunting. Here the Eskimos, without experience in hunting this alert and wary animal, find themselves distinctly inferior to the Athapaskans, who can draw on many generations of accumulated experience when they hunt moose. The elaboration of moose-hunting techniques is one of the unique developments of northern Athapaskan culture.

Moose and the Seasons

Moose undertake local movements and alter their behavior in accordance with seasonal phenomena. The Chalkyitsik Kutchin are quite aware of these patterns and utilize this knowledge in their hunting activities.

Fall

The principal season for moose hunting is during the fall rut, which begins about September 10, is in full swing by the 20th, and lasts into October. Before this time some moose have been down along the river, but many of them have been back in the hills or flats. When the rut begins they gravitate toward the river, especially to the long willow-covered bars that curve along the inner margins of its bends. This tendency to gather along the river, plus a general fearlessness among the bulls, makes for good hunting.

The last two weeks in September usually see a great flurry of hunting activity in Chalkyitsik, because it is the best time of year to get moose and because moose shot at this time can be kept without drying them to prevent spoilage. The people must also hunt quickly before cold weather sets in and freezes the river, bringing the season to a close.

Winter

After the rut is over, moose apparently scatter again, some remaining along the rivers and others moving back into the hills and flats. They tend to remain in bunches of three to five at least until midwinter. When the first snow falls after freeze-up it is a good time to go north to the Porcupine River or south to some large meadows to look for these groups of moose.

Sometime between January 1 and the end of February, moose which have gone up into the hills are driven back down toward the river valleys. The Indians say that deep snow or heavy hoarfrost causes them to move. At this time the moose tend to separate, although some remain together in the willows and meadows around lakes. Cows and their calves, of course, do not separate until spring. If the snow gets very deep, so that the moose drag their bellies in it as they walk, they tend to find a good feed patch and stay there. They can then establish a network of trails and use them repeatedly as they move around feeding, instead of wading through the deep snow whenever they go from place to place. They also tend to stay in the river valleys when the snow is deep.

Spring

About the end of March, when the snow softens and begins to melt, moose start traveling around the country. Sometimes their tracks go for miles in one direction, as if toward a definite goal, but if there actually is a goal it is not evident. Well before the breakup and its floods moose are said to be up in the hills away from the rivers. Some hunters try to get out after moose in March, before the animals start moving and before wet snow makes travel difficult. Later on, when the snow disappears and the rivers are still frozen, moose are difficult to find and sled travel is impossible.

Summer

Summertime can be said to begin when the ice breaks up and disappears from the rivers and to continue until the beginning of fall hunting in September. During this season moose are said to be "all over the country," feeding in the lakes and marshes, in the upland brush, and down along the rivers. One thing that is said

to bring moose to the river in numbers is an abundance of mosquitos. When mosquitos are thick moose can escape them by taking
to the water and frequenting the open sandbars where the pests
are less common. The chances of finding moose along the Black River during the
summer, however, are generally not considered good enough to
justify the long boat trip that is necessary. Sometimes men hunt
in early summer just after breakup, when the water is high and
most people are out of moose meat. The Black River usually breaks
up around the second week in May, and the Porcupine somewhat
later.

River Hunting

Preparing for the Hunt

Before Chalkyitsik hunters can reach moose country they must
make preparations at the village, then travel up the long and twisting
course of the Black River, camping at least once on the way. Thus
it is several days before the men reach the upriver country to start
hunting for moose.

It is usually a man who owns a boat and motor who decides
that he would like to go after moose around a certain date. He
may then talk it over with close friends or relatives who often hunt
or trap with him to see if they are interested. Eventually it becomes
known that so-and-so is "going up," and interested persons will
approach him to see exactly what his plans are and perhaps to ask
if they may go along. The crew may be only two men, but generally
there are three or four.

The plans for leaving are made several days beforehand, but are
always contingent on the weather. Each man has to prepare his
own gear, but the crew members work together if anything must
be done to get the boat and motor ready. There is always gasoline
to be poured into 5-gallon cans, usually ten or fifteen of them, and
oil must be purchased. The cost of these items is shared equally
among the crew members, but of course the boat owner pays more
in the long run because he must purchase and maintain the equipment. He receives no extra share of the meat to compensate for
this.

On the day of the proposed departure the men rise early. The boat owner is the "boss," and he decides in consultation with the others when and if they will leave. If the weather looks good each man gets his gear and carries it to the boat. When all are present the boat is carefully loaded so it rides level in the water, and they head upriver.

The equipment carried by each moose hunter includes a heavy rifle, usually 30/06 or 30/30 caliber, a shotgun for shooting ducks along the way, hunting knife and sharpening stone for butchering game, flashlight, moose scapula for attracting bull moose, file for sharpening axes and knives, watch, sleeping bag, ground cloth, and matches. Each man also carries a food box containing his food and cigarettes, a teapot or kettle, plate, cup, spoon, and fork. Communal equipment includes axes, a lantern, candles, tent, some large tarps, and sometimes an extra outboard engine.

Summer and fall boat travel, even when the weather is mild, is surprisingly cold, and the men wear their winter gear most of the time. A typical hunter uses long underwear and heavy socks, cotton or wool pants, wool or flannel shirt, waterproof leather or rubber boots, and a warm cloth jacket. When he is traveling he wears a heavy cloth parka over this, unless it is very warm. Usually the parka is his winter coat. When it is cool, as at dawn and dusk, he also puts on heavy cloth flight pants or coveralls. But with all this clothing, he is still likely to be chilled to the bone if it is especially windy or cold.

Locating and Approaching Moose

When the Chalkyitsik Kutchin hunt moose in the summer and fall, they always go up the Black River and sometimes into its tributary, the Salmon. Before 1969 they did some hunting downriver from Chalkyitsik, but after the forest fire that year there were few moose in that country. All the land between Chalkyitsik and Fort Yukon burned, destroying at least 80 percent of the vegetation. Scattered stands of brush and timber remained, but the area was unattractive to game. Hunters from Chalkyitsik take most of their fall moose in areas at least 35 miles up the Black River, which is more than a day's travel. Moose are occasionally seen below this point, but are much more common farther upstream. Most hunting is done from here to a point 35 or 40 miles up the Salmon River and about the same distance up the Black River beyond Salmon Village.

The first thing the Kutchin consider in locating moose, then, is the general territory in which they can hope to find them. Once the hunters enter this country, they follow other more specific principles. The experienced hunters know this region intimately. They know where every likely habitat is to be found: a long willow stand on a bend in the river, a slough lined with brush, a grassy meadow or a small shallow lake that can be seen by climbing the bank in a certain place. Some of these spots are always good for moose. For example, a place called Rotten Fish Creek is often chosen for the first night's camp because it is a favorite moose haunt.

Another good indicator of moose is the reports of other hunters who have been up the river within the past week or so. If they noticed moose sign at a particular place they will perhaps tell others, who are sure to check carefully there. The Indians always keep careful note of where tracks are seen, and may pass this information along.

In the fall, especially after the leaves have begun to drop, making it easy to see into the thickets, moose hunters may climb any of several hills on the way upriver to scan the surrounding countryside. The best way to find moose, however, is to travel along the river and watch, particularly in any of the hundreds of areas where there are willow stands. An apron of willows grows along the inside of almost every bend, usually with small brush on its outer fringes and tall thickets away from the river. In some places the willows are extensive, running hundreds of yards—perhaps up to half a mile—along a sandbar. These large stands are very good places for moose, and in certain of them there are more likely to be moose than not.

Moose are best hunted at dawn and dusk, when they come out along the river to feed or to rake their antlers in the brush as a challenge to any other bull moose that might be nearby. But these are also the times when moose are hard to see in the brush and when rifles are difficult to aim. In the last two weeks of September conditions for spotting moose steadily improve because of the falling leaves.

While hunting with the Kutchin I found that they were remarkably adept at picking out game from a distance with the unaided eye. They seem to focus upon minute details of the scene that confronts them rather than viewing the landscape more generally, as an Outsider does. This ability to pick out subtleties in the environment probably comes from practice; at least it seems that Outsiders are able to improve their perceptiveness greatly over a period of time. I found that the Eskimos in north Alaska, for example, would point out "hills" in what looked like perfectly flat tundra. After months of hunting and traveling with them, however, I could see these "hills" quite easily. In the same way, one learns to identify animals by fleeting glimpses of their shape or behavior, as some persons in our own society can identify birds from a distant or very brief sighting. There is nothing mystical involved, though in our amazement we sometimes think so. It is a matter of practice and interest.

Another means of locating moose is sound. This method is used not while traveling along in a boat, but while standing quietly along the river bank on a still day. If the wind is blowing there is little chance to hear moose, because it will drown out their sounds. In the fall and early winter bull moose make noise with their antlers as they run through the willows. During the rut, bulls also rake their antlers noisily in the brush to challenge other males in the area, and they utter a low call associated with breeding. If a moose is near, it may also be detected by the sound of twigs breaking as it walks. An unusual way to find bull moose is to smell their musky odor on the river bars during the fall rut. This odor is so heavy that sometimes a man can easily smell one that is nearby or has been in the area within a half hour or so.

Finally, one of the most important methods of locating moose at any season is tracking. As hunters travel along the river they watch all the sandy and muddy areas closely for tracks. Moose often cross the river, leaving tracks on both banks, or walk along the river in soft ground where tracks are visible. The Indian knows that he has much less chance of seeing an animal than the tracks it leaves behind; thus he often watches more closely for tracks than for game itself, playing the better probabilities.

When they land on a sandbar or other suitable place, the first thing Kutchin hunters do is look for tracks. If they find some they follow them up and down, looking for indicators of their age and for other signs. Bull moose often scrape the bark from short bushes when they rake their antlers, and they paw the ground in places, sometimes plowing it up extensively. Moose tend to travel a great deal at this season, however, and if their tracks are not very fresh there is a good chance they have moved on. Conversely, a moose can appear anywhere, regardless of whether there are tracks around.

The Tranjik Kutchin are masterly trackers. They are able to see the faintest sign and can read the age of a track and the sex, size, and condition of the animal that made it. Judging the age of tracks in mud or sand is more difficult than in snow, and it comes only with long experience. As one would expect, a fresh track is sharp in outline and remains as moist as the surrounding earth. As time passes it will start to dry out around its edges, especially where there are thin fragments of dirt. But unless the weather is warm and sunny, a track in mud may not begin to look dry for a week or more; old tracks often look quite fresh. One good way to tell the age of spoor where moose enter the water is to look for water-filled tracks. In muddy places the water will remain cloudy for about half a day, then become clear.

In spite of their many techniques for finding moose, hunters frequently just happen onto them as they stand along the river. The bulls, and to a lesser extent the cows, have little fear of boats, especially during the fall. Many bulls will stand unmoving until hunters get within range and start firing. A majority of the fall kills are made from the boat in this way, without any careful stalk. The noise of engines does not seem to bother moose at any season, perhaps because they are so accustomed to the sound of airplanes flying harmlessly overhead. Hunters are not particularly careful about mechanical sounds of any type, such as banging things inside the boat, but they always talk very softly. Speaking is the worst sound to make while hunting, according to the Kutchin, because it identifies man to his prey more certainly than anything else. The aggressive bulls are not likely to run from any noise, however, especially during the night.

The following account from field notes written September 11, 1969, illustrates some aspects of fall moose hunting:

About a mile or two up the Salmon River we spotted two moose feeding in the willows. Though we saw them well before they seemed to detect us, Robert surprised me by heading right toward them with the boat. They soon looked up and started to run. Herbert started shooting right then, but all of his shots missed and the animals vanished.

When the moose ran, the boat was immediately taken to shore. Herbert ran to where the moose had been standing and quickly examined their tracks. He followed a track into the birch woods behind the willows, but saw no moose. He then backtracked almost to the place where they were originally seen. As he stood there looking at the tracks, he heard a moose calling softly from where they were first spotted. He looked up and smiled, then half-ran very quietly toward the low sound. There among the willows stood a cow moose, ears up, staring at him. He leveled and shot her in the chest. Just then he saw a young bull moose beyond the dying cow. He ran up a few yards past her, mimicked the cow's call to get the bull's attention, and killed him with one shot from ten yards.

Herbert said later that when moose separate they often return to meet at the place where they were last together. The cow and bull had circled to within thirty yards of him in less than a minute's time without making a sound until the cow's calling gave them away.

This account illustrates the kind of knowledge, alertness, and ability to make quick predictions which characterize a good hunter. Animals often have stylized, highly predictable behavior patterns which hunters learn from tradition and experience. Once the animal is located, a thorough understanding of its limited behavioral repertory can make a kill almost inevitable if the hunter knows the correct responses. This kind of behavioral interaction, whereby the man capitalizes upon predictable activities or reactions of game species, is the key factor in human predation.

Attracting Moose

There are also ways of attracting moose during the rut by a method that has been used since traditional times: "in the fall, when the moose are rutting, the hunter provides himself with a shoulder blade of the same animal; he then approaches the male as close as possible, and rubs the bone against the trees. The moose charges at once, mistaking the sound for that made by another male rubbing his horns against the trees" (Jones 1866, p. 322). Although it did not always have such an immediate effect, the method was undoubtedly one of the best for bringing moose within bow and arrow range.

The Chalkyitsik Kutchin still use a device made from a moose scapula for hunting during the fall rut. It usually consists of a well-dried cow moose scapula, with the dorsal spine cut down to a low ridge and its articulating process carved to a narrow handle. The cartilage is left along its bladelike end, so that it comes to a sharp edge. Bull moose scapulae are seldom used because they are too heavy. A fresh bone can be used if necessary but does not resonate properly.

When the hunters stop their boat in a place where moose sign is found, one of them may use a scapula in an effort to attract a bull. He scrapes the bone up and down on a bush, briskly but rather gently, letting it ride along the branches. He allows his wrist to flex with it, as if the bone were a brush and the bush a wall he is painting. When hunters find a clump of bushes which has been raked and scraped of its bark, someone will surely use a scapula on it. Long periods of silent listening always follow each use. Sometimes a hunter rakes the device along on the brush as he walks, and occasionally he may scrape it on a log or tree. In the evening when they camp, some hunters scrape with a bone at varying intervals of fifteen to thirty minutes, then listen intently. The same thing may be done in the morning.

The Kutchin say it takes great skill to attract bull moose in this way, and that the old-timers were much better at it than today's hunters. The idea is to "act just like moose"—to imitate closely the sound they make. Old men say it is best to hear a moose first, listen to his sound, then mimic that noise exactly. If the animal detects anything wrong about it, he will stop and listen, then run away. It appears, however, that some bulls are more belligerent than cautious. An old Kutchin said, "When I hear a moose rake his horns, that's my moose. No way to miss it if I got a moose bone with me."

Most of the time a moose scapula is used "in the blind," that is, when there is spoor around but the animal has not actually been heard. It is a means of attracting a bull moose to a certain place or getting him to reveal himself. This device works until the rut has ended, sometime after mid-October. But from that time until the moose shed their antlers, it is a useful item to carry. It will not usually attract a moose after the rut, but if a hunter scrapes it gently in the brush while attempting a stalk he may fool the animal into believing he is another of its own kind so it will not run away. Sometimes it will even move toward the sound.

There is one other way to attract moose, also used only during the fall rut. Cow moose make a distinctive very low grunting sound. Hunters can locate moose by listening carefully for this call. Whenever a cow's call is heard, it is almost certain a bull will be nearby. Both calling and antler-raking are most likely to be heard when dusk is becoming night and at dawn. Sometimes a hunter will mimic the call as the boat passes spots where moose are likely to be. If a bull moose is in the brush he may suddenly charge out into the open. The call is also used to get the attention of a moose which has been seen, to bring it closer or make it move a bit for a better target. Some people imitate the call well, others have the wrong voice for it and find it difficult to produce the correct sound.

The bull moose is a huge, formidable animal with awesome antlers and a very bad temperament during the rutting season. The thought naturally occurs that such an animal might be dangerous to the men who hunt it. But the evidence indicates that although moose can be dangerous, they rarely present a threat to the Indians and have seldom been known to injure anyone. These statements require some qualification, however.

The Chalkyitsik Kutchin emphatically do not consider the moose a dangerous animal. Sometimes a bull moose in the rut will chase a man, especially during the night, but moose are easy to deal with if a person knows what he is doing. One very knowledgeable old-timer said, "If he see you he's going to run for his life every time." It may not be quite that way, but in this area there is little evidence that bull moose are highly aggressive toward humans. Many Chalkyitsik people were asked, but not one knew a single case of a moose injuring a man, not even from stories their fathers and grandfathers told. But all were aware of the potential bellicosity of a large bull moose.

The Huslia and Hughes Indians give a different account of moose temperament. In the Koyukuk River country, especially in the large flats surrounding Huslia, it is difficult to travel anywhere without constantly encountering moose. The Huslia people say that bull moose are a serious problem during the fall. They never use a moose scapula for hunting because too many bulls would be attracted. Indeed, even if they wish to build a fire, they have to pick up branches very quietly and be careful not to break them; and in spite of these precautions they are frequently driven away by bull moose. All during the rut the Huslia people move quietly in the woods. The contrast to Chalkyitsik is certainly remarkable—days of hard work just to find moose in one place and perpetual caution to avoid them in another.

Moose are also dangerous during the winter around Huslia and Hughes because they sometimes attack dog teams, using defensive aggression as they would against wolves. The situation is especially bad when the snow is very deep, because then moose prefer to travel around on sled trails. If they encounter a dog team they are often reluctant to give up the right-of-way. Many such encounters occur during winter travel, even within a few hundred yards of the village.

It is obvious, I think, that the difference in moose behavior between the Black River and Koyukuk River areas is a function of population density. If the Tranjik Kutchin were encountering moose at every turn they would have more problems with them. Part of the difference is one of probability—the more moose encountered the greater the chances of meeting belligerent ones. But the Koyukuk River moose may be more aggressive because of their extremely dense population.

Despite the behavior of moose in the Koyukuk area, there appear to be no recent cases of injury to men. This certainly attests to the Indians' ability to respond effectively to advances or attacks, and to their general efforts to avoid encounters with them during the rut. A Huslia man said he heard of someone being killed by a bull moose, probably long ago, after he had walked in the urine of a cow moose he was butchering.

Shooting Moose

Rifles of one kind or another have been used by the Kutchin since before the Hudson's Bay Company established Fort Yukon in 1847. Today the Chalkyitsik Kutchin use heavy rifles for hunting moose, 30/06 being the most popular caliber. Some other calibers are used, such as .303, or approximately equal foreign models. The 30/30 is owned by many hunters and is fairly effective for killing moose.

River hunting requires many very difficult shots. Men often hunt in poor light at dawn and dusk when it is hard to see the sights on a rifle, and much shooting is done from a moving boat. Telescopic sights would be very useful in the dim light, but the Indians do not own them. Incidentally, the Kutchin feel that left-handed shooting (like all left-handedness) is no good. Moses William, who is left-handed, was told, "You got that from the Devil."

The Tranjik Kutchin prefer heart shots for any kind of game, in marked contrast to the Koyukon and Eskimo, who say that shoulder shots are best. When they shoot moose, the Kutchin aim just behind the leg from the side or right into the center of the chest from the front. Heart shots will cause many kinds of animals to run, but I never saw this happen with moose. When they are wounded at all seriously, they generally stand still or move around just a little. Chalkyitsik hunters avoid shoulder shots because they are likely to spoil some good meat. They say that neck shots are very effective, but it is difficult to judge exactly where the vertebrae are for a killing shot. This is especially true in the fall, when bull moose swell up in the neck region.

Big moose are hard to kill, even with heavy rifles. They are often hit several times before they fall mortally wounded. River hunters seem to average five or six shots for every kill but about half of these miss the animal entirely. Wounded moose generally cannot move far, which is lucky for the hunters who must carry the meat from wherever they fall. When a moose is dying the Kutchin rarely attempt to finish it off, preferring to let it die in its own time. They look at it for a moment, say "It will die," then leave it until it is still. Cripples with much life in them are shot in the neck.

The Chalkyitsik Kutchin get so few moose that they cannot be selective about the ones they shoot. Any moose is meat, and they hunt the toughest, thinnest old bulls and the fat, tender young with equal enthusiasm. The Indians are very good at judging age and sex, and often refer to "a two-year-old cow," "a three-year-old bull," and so on. They are aware that certain kinds of moose are better than others, and generally prefer two-year-old animals.

The Kutchin language has a series of terms denoting the various kinds of moose (Mueller 1964, p. 26):

dinjik	moose
ch'izhir'	largest bull
ditii'dho'neehee-chik	second largest bull
dijii	third largest bull
jyaagoo	fourth largest bull
dachan-chik	fifth largest bull
ja'aɬkhok	young bull
dizhuu-viditsik-kwaa	barren or old cow

dizhuu	cow (can bear calves)
kheedeetsik	young cow
ditsik	calf

As one might expect, the Koyukuk River Athapaskans, with their abundance of moose, are very selective about the animals they kill. During the summer they prefer a young bull. In the fall they usually shoot a barren cow or a two-year-old bull. In early fall before the rut they will also kill large bulls. In winter an adult cow, preferably without a calf, is best; and during the late winter they may also shoot a young bull (G. R. Bane, personal communication).

Butchering, Caching, and Transporting Moose

Once an animal has been killed the real work begins, especially when a huge bull moose is shot. As soon as the men start butchering they cut a good pile of brush and lay it on the ground so they can place the meat on top to keep it out of the dirt. Skinning and butchering is a skill requiring long practice and a thorough acquaintance with the anatomy of the animal. Some men are much better at butchering than others, and consequently they do a better job in less time.

Butchering an animal essentially involves cutting it into natural sections or parts, much like dismantling a machine. If a man knows where to cut, where the joints and weak points are, he can cut a moose into relatively small pieces with a knife alone. Usually, however, an ax is used to cut through bones in difficult places, largely because it saves time.

Instead of tracing out the details of butchering a moose, I will simply list the parts into which the animal is cut. First, the skin is removed by slitting it down the belly and up the insides of the legs. The carcass is then cut into approximately fourteen pieces, including the two hind legs, two forelegs (including scapulae), head, neck, two rib sections (right and left side), brisket (sternum), three backbone sections, and two strips of meat cut from along either side of the vertebral spines. The lower legs are usually cut away and discarded or cooked on the spot for marrow. Some of these pieces may be cut into smaller sections, depending on how they are to be transported. For example, the scapulae may be severed from the rest of the forelimbs to make them easier to handle. Some internal organs are kept and others are discarded. The liver, lungs, and most of the stomach are thrown away, as are the intestines. The heart, mesenteries, colon, and part of the stomach are saved. When the load is heavy, the head (except the tongue), neck, skin, and lower vertebrae are discarded.

Butchering is not difficult, but it takes a great deal of time. If the animal dies far from the water much labor is required to haul the meat to the boat. But this is no problem at all compared with the work required when a moose dies in the water. When this happens the animal is pulled to shore and gradually dragged higher as more parts are removed. If a wounded moose runs into the water, hunters try to drive it up on shore. Conversely, if a moose runs far from the water they try to drive it toward the bank before killing it.

After hunters kill their first moose they usually plan to go farther upstream, but they do not wish to haul the meat with them. So they cache it temporarily, which usually means simply throwing a thick layer of willows over it to keep ravens and jays away. This type of cache is good for a day or two, since wolves or bears are unlikely to come across it in so short a time. If meat is to be left longer it is hung up in trees, where there is less chance it will be bothered by large animals. But if it is to be left for a week or so, ravens will eat too much to make a tree cache effective. Long-term caching has to be done in log structures built like small rectangular cabins. Caches of this type are rarely, if ever, used today because game is killed only if it can be hauled to the village within a few days.

When moose meat is transported by boat it must be loaded so that the boat does not list or ride too low in the bow or stern. Willows, canvas, or plastic sheeting are spread under the meat to keep it clean. I have seen five full-grown moose and a calf carried in one 24-foot river boat, but usually three or four are considered a full load. Occasionally an empty boat is towed along upriver to increase the crew's carrying capacity. The number of moose that can be hauled depends as much on the amount of water a boat will draw as on its load capacity, because it is usually necessary to get across riffles where the water is less than a foot deep.

When a river hunting crew returns home, the meat is usually

divided among its members according to need, not on an equal basis. Thus, although all members contribute equally for gasoline and the boat owner furnishes his equipment in addition to an equal share of fuel, everyone benefits according to the size of his family. This concept of distribution according to need even carries over into the Indians' view of how wage money should be allotted. They feel that workers should be paid according to the size of their families rather than on an equal-work, equal-pay basis.

Although a given hunter might take a large amount of meat home, he must distribute a fair share of it to close relatives. A successful hunter is also likely to be visited by people who indicate by subtle or not-so-subtle means that they could use some meat. Occasionally meat is bought and sold. There is a definite tendency for meat to be distributed much more widely when game is in short supply than when it is common.

Winter and Spring Hunting

During the short three-week fall season, Chalkyitsik hunters kill almost half the year's take of moose. Nearly all the rest are brought in one now, one then throughout the winter season. In winter the trappers are traveling widely over the country, no longer bound by the narrow river courses, free to go wherever they please on the snow-covered ground and the frozen lakes and rivers. It is surprising at first glance that they do not take more moose during the cold months, since the animals leave a trail that records every move they make and men are free to follow. But in winter the moose are wise, usually wiser than a man. The Kutchin are also preoccupied with trapping throughout this season and often pass by even the freshest moose tracks.

Locating Moose

When the winter storms blow clouds of snow along the river and even build drifts in the forest, few of the Kutchin move outside their houses. But if men are seen bundled to clumsiness, driving out of the village on snowmobiles, they are almost certainly moose hunters. Wind is the greatest ally of the winter hunters, though it makes travel utter misery. Luckily for the hunters, the temperature usually rises during winter storms (to between 0° and 15° above in midwinter and to freezing or above toward spring). It is the moderation in temperature that allows them to go out and face only extreme discomfort rather than grave danger. There are two reasons for hunting at these times: First, the rush of wind in the trees and the ceaseless clack and clatter of willow bushes covers the sound of a hunter as he approaches his game. Second, relatively warm temperatures soften the snow so that it makes little noise when a man walks through it.

The ideal conditions for hunting moose in winter occur right after a new snow which shows only the freshest tracks, on a warm day with a wind blowing. The temperature is as important as the wind. When it is −15° to −20° or colder there is little chance to hunt moose unless a roaring gale covers all sound. This is because the snow at cold temperatures squeaks and crunches loudly underfoot. When it is really warm, somewhere above zero, a man can walk almost soundlessly through the snow. The warmer it is the less need there is for an accompanying wind.

The Chalkyitsik Kutchin especially like to hunt in November, when moose often gather in bunches of three or four. Since the Porcupine River country has the largest number of moose in this region and the chances for finding game are best there, hunters travel some 20 miles north to that river as soon as there is snow, and they go there from time to time during the winter thereafter. Many specific localities are good for hunting moose year after year, and are usually known by the man whose trapline runs nearby. These include certain willow stands along the rivers, lakes, meadows, or trails. If a man sees tracks at a given spot, he can often predict the animal's destination because of his familiarity with the surrounding territory.

During his trapping activities the Indian may notice moose sign in one area on several different occasions. Some animals tend to stay within a very limited area all winter, and a hunter can predict with some assurance that they will be found near the place where their tracks have been sighted repeatedly. They sometimes grow accustomed to the sound of a snowmobile or dog team passing by and do not run away. This can make them easy prey.

Moose are often located by following fresh sign encountered during a hunt or while running a trapline. Fresh tracks are the best sign, especially if they are only a few hours old. Broken willows are another very good sign of moose, and they are often visible from a distance or while traveling rapidly on a snowmobile. Moose break down the willows to get at the young shoots, and the white inner wood of the broken stems is very easy to see. When a man sees this he watches for tracks, which indicate how recently the feeding occurred. The Chalkyitsik Kutchin usually do not consider it worthwhile to follow tracks more than two days old if no sign has previously been seen in the area.

Moose are sometimes encountered by chance, but such luck is rare. When it does happen, very fast action is needed to make a kill. Trappers usually tie their rifles loosely on top of their loaded toboggans so they can be pulled out quickly should they come across a moose unexpectedly while traveling. This is especially important in early morning, when moose are out feeding.

Stalking

Most winter hunts require tracking or stalking moose on foot through the snow. Effective tracking involves great skill and long experience. The knowledge and techniques in this account make up a general background sufficient as a basis for learning the more subtle skills that come only with time.

The easiest conditions for pursuit of moose in winter occur when the snow is unusually deep or when a hard crust forms on the snow's surface after a thaw. This makes it very difficult for the animals to move, and so they are confined to a limited area where they follow their own trails. If moose sink into the snow up to their bellies, all a man on snowshoes has to do is follow a track until he catches up with the animal. The Indians often speak of "running down" a moose, which means shuffling along quickly on snowshoes at a pace much faster than the animal can maintain.

A deep, crusted snow is very hard on moose. It is almost impossible for them to move around because the ice crust cuts and scrapes their skin. They are easy prey for wolves if the crust is strong enough so the wolves can run on top of it. The Indians also take advantage of this condition and, perhaps following the wolves' example, use their dogs to assist in the chase. While the hunter follows on snowshoes, his dogs run ahead and corner the moose until he arrives to shoot it (cf. Jones 1866, p. 322). This technique has probably been used since the precontact era, when the Kutchin used their dogs mostly for hunting rather than for pulling sleds. But it continued, at least occasionally, into the recent past.

When the snow is not deep and the moose are free to run and evade pursuit, hunting becomes much more difficult. If a hunter sees moose tracks he first must find out how old they are. During the cold winter months any disturbance of the snow will cause it to harden. A track an hour or so old will be as soft as the snow around it. After a few hours the snow inside a track starts to get crusty and hard, first around the top and later near the bottom. A track made the previous night will have a thin crust inside so that some hardening is easy to feel, although the crust breaks easily.

Hardness is usually tested by stepping inside several tracks and finding out how much pressure is required to break through the crust. Some men get a quick idea of freshness simply by dragging their foot across a track as they pass by on a snowmobile or dog sled. If a track is really fresh it cannot be felt at all; if it is fairly fresh (e.g., the previous night) it is distinctly harder than the surrounding snow; and if it is two days or more old it is very hard and registers as a sharp bump when a man drags his foot through it. Careful checking has to be made by walking along in the tracks or standing and gently pushing one foot inside.

Hunters are usually not interested in tracks that are over two days old, and they especially want to find tracks made the previous night. Thus they look for thinly crusted tracks. The ones that are frozen solid, sometimes clear to the ground underneath, interest them very little. Even tracks that have filled up with drifted snow will reveal their age this way, although they look older than they are because of the snow in them. When late winter comes it is more difficult to age tracks because of the wind and warmer temperatures. At this time hunters will carefully check a number of footprints along a given track to judge the age accurately.

When a moose is feeding or moving along slowly, several piles of its droppings are likely to be found within a fairly short distance. If a trail is very fresh the pellets of excrement will be soft and dark brown in color. Then, as they freeze, they become hard and change to a much lighter brown. The amount of time it takes for them to freeze will of course depend on the temperature.

Sometimes a moose trail will be lightly crusted, with frozen excrement along it; then farther on the tracks become soft and the droppings dark brown and partially frozen. A trail like this indicates a slowly moving animal which is probably close by.

A hunter wants to find signs that the moose is feeding and resting in a certain area, as indicated by a very crooked, wandering trail with beds in the snow, broken willows, and perhaps areas where the snow has been pawed to get at the vegetation underneath. The more tracks he finds the better. On the other hand, a straight trail through the forest is a bad sign, because it probably means that the animal was on the move and is now far away.

When an Indian has found a promising fresh trail he sets out to follow it, usually having a fair idea where the moose might be from his knowledge of local geography. Moose are easiest to stalk in the early morning before sunrise, because they are making considerable noise feeding and moving around in the brush. This leads a hunter to the moose and covers the sound of his approach. After they feed, moose sleep soundly for a while in early morning and are relatively easy to approach. After this sleep, they only lie down during the rest of the day and are very difficult to stalk. Around evening they start to feed again.

Kutchin moose hunters try to avoid using nylon or slick cotton clothing which makes noise when it rubs against itself or the brush. Wool clothing is best because it is almost noiseless. Snowshoes are never used for tracking moose, except in deep snow as discussed above, because they always squeak. If the weather is right, however, these sounds make little difference. On days when the temperature is near freezing and a gale wind blows, the Chalkyitsik Indians often say, "I guess any man can kill moose today."

One of the most important things a hunter knows is that when moose lie down or sleep they usually double back downwind from their own trail so that if any animal follows them its scent will drift to where they are resting. This is why hunters tracking moose often find that the animal has gotten their scent first and disappeared into the brush. The Athapaskans' best-known hunting technique, semicircular tracking, is a means of compensating for this defensive behavior.

Instead of following directly in the animal's track, the Indian makes semicircular detours or loops downwind away from the trail, returning to it at intervals. If he circles back and does not find the trail where it should be he knows the moose has doubled back. At this point he makes a series of smaller semicircles back in the direction from which he came until he finds the animal's doubling-back trail, which he then follows (see diagram). If there is a good wind the hunter can almost walk right up to a moose, but usually the animal attempts to escape before the hunter gets close, so he must shoot fast and well.

Ideally, the moose would make a straight trail through the forest, then double back on it and sleep. Unfortunately, it is rarely so simple. When moose feed their trails wander everywhere through the brush, and such trails are very difficult to follow. The hunter is liable to encounter a jumble of tracks going in all directions, and he must decipher which way the animal actually went. Furthermore, moose do not always double back on their trail—many of them sleep right in the midst of their feed patches. One man said that bull moose rarely seem to bother with this defensive pattern. This is why Chalkyitsik hunters seldom use semicircular tracking nowadays, preferring to take their chances on a direct stalk when there is a good wind blowing. This approach is nearly always combined with putting men in "stands" around the area or making drives, as we will see shortly.

On any moose hunt one man usually acts as a tracker. This man follows the trail into the brush, trying to locate the freshest sign and places where the animal has fed and rested in one area. When he finds these spots, the tracker moves very slowly and quietly because the moose could appear at any moment. He pokes each pile of excrement and tests every bed to see if it is frozen. When the tracks get very thick and confusing, the only thing to do is find the outside edge of the trampled area and circle it to locate the trail leading from it. To do this a man obviously has to know the direction of each footprint so that he does not track backward. The best indicator is the imprint of the dewclaws, which are in back of each foot. They do not show in every print, but a little following will turn up good tracks. Trackers also watch for snow that is kicked out of the footprint when the moose lifts its leg. This snow scatters ahead of the track, and the area behind the track remains generally clean. The deepest part of a footprint is also in the front.

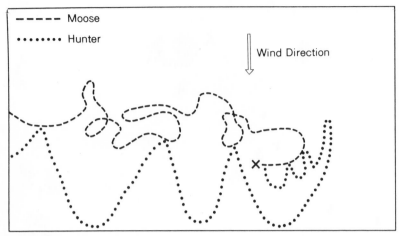

Diagram of semicircular hunting for a moose which has doubled back downwind of its own trail after feeding.

Moose are clever at escaping when being tracked. When they hear a sound, they usually circle away to get downwind where they can identify the intruder by scent. Hunters thus often search downwind for a moose they have frightened. During the winter of this study one trapper encountered the same moose several times, and on each occasion it ran off into the brush, circled behind him, and crossed his trail back in the direction from which he had come. This is a clever evasive tactic, since most animals run directly away from their pursuer's approach. A second hunter stationed back along the trail, however, can sometimes kill such a moose. A cow and calf moose will often separate when pursued but usually return to the place where they separated to reunite. The hunter waits for them there.

Man is a very wise hunter. Consider the following example: An Indian was traveling by dog team along the Sucker River. This river meanders a great deal but has such high steep banks that men usually have to stay right on the river instead of cutting across short portages. This man came upon a moose standing in the river, and it ran away ahead of him, unable to climb the steep banks. When he reached a short portage the hunter got off his sled with his rifle, let his team chase the moose, and ran across the portage to wait for the moose to come around the meander. A short time later it appeared, with dogs still following, and he killed it.

Driving Moose

A major proportion of winter-killed moose are taken in communal hunts, primarily along the Porcupine River. This is an aboriginal technique which has been carried over into modern times. Cooperative hunts are generally made by three or four men, but sometimes ten or more will go along. One man usually acts as a leader, deciding the area and the specific places to hunt according to his special familiarity with the country.

First the hunters travel along the river checking islands, peninsulas, or other isolated stands of willow for moose tracks leading into them. When tracks are found they circle the island with their snowmobiles, checking to see if there are tracks coming out somewhere else, to determine if the moose are still there. Sometimes there are no tracks around a good island, so someone walks straight back into it, checking for signs of moose that may have been there for a long time.

When they find an island with moose on it, the hunters station themselves around it, at places where animals are known to come out or where fresh tracks lead onto it. A hunter with long experience hunting at each island knows where the best places are, and so he instructs the others where to stand. Some general principles are followed as well. Most islands are near one side of the river, and moose usually enter and leave by crossing the narrowest place. Thus, hunters station themselves mostly along the narrow channel and pay less attention to the river side.

Men also are stationed in places which afford the longest possible view, such as at the middle of a bend, where they can see along both sides of it, or in the middle of a long straight area. The fewer hunters there are, the more crucial it is that they be stationed in the best places. Of course if there are so many hunters that they can cover all of the island's shoreline it makes little difference if the best spots are known. But this is rarely possible, since many islands are a mile or more in length.

When the hunters are all at their stands, one or two men go onto the island, following the animal's tracks. These men have the best chance to get the moose, and are also lucky because they do not have to stand quietly in the cold. Men on the stands cannot build fires, and so they are usually chilled to the bone when the hunt is over. When a moose is driven from an island, men on stands

shoot it immediately if it is within range. If it is too far away they
either walk or drive their snowmobiles closer. Moose usually show
little fear of a snowmobile, especially when the headlight is on. It
is quite another situation with a dog team, which they perhaps mistake for a pack of wolves.

Drives can be made wherever there is a limited area of good
habitat with lakes or rivers on two or more sides, or in any place
where hunters know from experience that moose tend to run out
to open places when chased. I have seen drives made through willow stands along the Porcupine, with only one side open to the
river. More often than not, of course, these drives fail, but whenever
there is more than one hunter the drive technique is certain to be
used. There is always a fair chance that a moose will either be
shot by a tracker or will run toward a spot where an experienced
leader has placed someone to watch. As one would expect, an island
is by far the best location for driving moose.

Transporting and Caching

In winter, as in summer, hunters prefer to shoot moose where
they can easily be loaded for transportation to the village. This
is not always possible, and when moose are killed far back in the
brush there is no choice but to cut a trail to them. Sometimes men
can hold their fire until the animal reaches a good spot, then kill
it. Wounded moose can also be chased out of the brush toward
open areas which a dog team or snowmobile can reach easily. I
have seen Indians attempt to move a badly wounded bull moose
by hurling sticks at it.

Sometimes hunters encounter moose when their toboggans are
already fully loaded or shoot more than they can carry at one time.
In this case they butcher the animals according to the usual procedure, then bury them completely under mounds of snow. The snow
conceals them from ravens and jays, and retards the scent of fresh
meat so that it does not attract foxes, wolves, or wolverines. Of
course if scavengers walk near the meat they will probably find
it and eat all they can.

Snowmobiles can carry much larger loads than dog teams, and
so when a machine is used meat is butchered into the same large

pieces as for boat hauling. If dogs are used, the small toboggan and limited pulling strength makes it advantageous to cut the meat into small chunks of a few pounds each and leave the bones behind. If these chunks are placed on the ground to freeze separately overnight, they can be piled together without solidifying into a single mass. A full load is carried home and the remainder is buried under mounds of snow to be picked up whenever needed.

Moose Snaring

Snares are as effective for taking game and fur animals as they are simple in design and use. In our own society, which equates hunting with guns, bows and arrows, and spears, we do not appreciate the remarkable efficacy of trapping devices. Athapaskan culture, however, testifies to their effectiveness.

I believe that the importance of the big-game snare in the Athapaskan culture pattern is not fully appreciated. In the days of the bow and arrow it was the most effective method for securing game. According to Upper Tanana natives, the bow and arrow was practically never used during extremely cold weather, for should the first arrow miss the mark, the twang of the bowstring was so loud as to be sure to frighten the animal. Among the Kutchin, moose were likewise more generally snared than shot. [McKennan 1959, p. 48]

The key factor in moose snaring is knowing the right place to make a set. Moose snares are set in spots where the animals are known to come year after year, or where tracks show that they are currently staying around a certain place. In the latter case a snare is set where an abundance of tracks indicate that moose have passed through a narrow place several times. For example, moose often stay near lakes during the winter, following their own trails between the best willow patches. They also tend to use man-made trails, which permit easy travel through heavy brush. The essential consideration in moose snaring is that the noose must be located in a narrow opening through the undergrowth, where the animals will walk into a set rather than around it.

Once a suitable place has been found, the Indian prepares his snare set. The snare itself has been made with flexible steel cable since the traditional babiche snare was given up. Rope heavy enough to hold a moose is usually so thick that the animal would see it easily. The snare is first attached to a heavy log which is placed in the brush alongside the trail or to a slender tree growing there. Snares that are fastened to loose toggles are less apt to be broken than those attached to a solid tether. The snare cable itself has a running noose with a special slipknot that tightens when pulled and will not loosen again. This helps to kill the animal and prevents escapes.

After the snare is tethered securely to the toggle, slender pieces of willow or other brush are stuck into the ground or snow on either side of the loop, leaving only a narrow space about 2 feet wide for the animal to pass through. These sticks are 5 or 6 feet long and angle outward so they just reach the outer edges of the snare. The noose is then opened to about a 30- to 48-inch diameter and is held open by tying it to the side sticks with bits of thin string or grass, or by hooking it onto twigs on these sticks. An important shorter stick is placed vertically beneath the middle of the snare, reaching almost to its lower edge, to keep the moose from ducking underneath.

People vary in their opinions on the correct height of a snare. Apparently moose often walk with their heads low, because the bottom edge of a snare should be from 30 to 45 inches above the ground. The most knowledgeable Kutchin seemed to agree that 30 to 36 inches is best. This puts the top of the snare a respectable 6 to 7 feet above the ground, but moose are very tall animals. However, the fact that men have captured moose in small snares set for wolf attests to their habit of walking with the head toward the ground. Perhaps they do this because they detect human scent around snare sets.

The frequency with which moose snares are checked depends on many circumstances. In some places they might be seen only a few times during the winter, perhaps once a month. In good spots where fresh tracks are found, fairly regular checks would be made. Snared moose generally die and freeze, presenting a difficult problem for the man who butchers them. The people say that these frozen carcasses should be cut up with old-fashioned crosscut saws. With these big saws the method of cutting makes little difference—"You cut any way you want to." Butchering can also be done with an ax, in which case the cuts follow joints and anatomical separation points just as with freshly killed animals.

Some people say that moose found dead in snares are unfit for human consumption because the meat is spoiled by the viscera before it freezes. Of course a moose found live in the snare is edible. A snare-killed moose is said to be useful mostly for dog food, although one man said that the heavy meat of the hind legs can be eaten by humans. In any case, today moose are snared very rarely, if at all.

Uses of Moose

Chalkyitsik hunters no longer put forth anything like a maximum effort to take moose, partly because there are now government assistance programs that they can depend on when necessary. Another factor lowering takes is the sheer difficulty of finding moose in the Chalkyitsik region. They are not common and they seem much more wary of man than the animals in the Koyukuk River area. During the fall of 1969, one crew of hunters searched for eleven days before sighting their first moose.

I have a definite record of thirty-three moose taken by Chalkyitsik hunters during a ten-month period in 1969–70, but there were probably several I never heard about. The total kill for this village of some ninety-five people was therefore about thrity-six moose, perhaps as high as forty. About half of these were killed during the fall season, and the remainder were taken throughout the rest of the year. Each moose that is brought into the village is eventually distributed among a number of households, and the hunter is probably lucky if he saves half of his take for himself.

The Chalkyitsik Kutchin regard certain parts of a moose as delicacies. These are usually small parts, like the brisket (meat from around the sternum), short sections of ribs, the heart, the tongue, a small saclike digestive organ, marrow, and any kind of fat. Most of these are prepared by boiling. The liver is not eaten. Of the larger meat sections, the hindquarters and heavy shoulder meat are preferred. When they get a moose fetus, which is not often, they give it to old people, who relish the very soft and tasty meat.

Moose heads are sometimes brought home to be made into a great delicacy called "moosehead soup," a kind of stew that includes vegetables, macaroni, and a variety of little meat tidbits from the head of a moose. Today the bones are only used to get marrow, but in former times the people were careful to save them because when hard times came they could be crushed up and boiled into a fatty broth.

In the old days nearly every part of the moose was used, but today certain parts (e.g., the stomach) are either left behind or fed to the dogs. Even the skin, formerly one of the most important parts of the animal, is frequently discarded. Women no longer want to tan moosehides, and so they often order them from fur companies outside Alaska. This is "carrying coals to Newcastle," to say the least.

Most meat that cannot be consumed immediately during the warm months must be dried. This is hardly a sacrifice, since people thoroughly enjoy "dry meat." It is prepared by cutting the meat into strips about ¼ inch thick, 2 to 3 inches wide, and 12 to 24 inches long. An effort is made to have fat on these strips. The strips are hung up inside a roofed drying rack, with a smudge usually kept going beneath them to keep insects away and speed the drying. Meat can be dried in fall or winter by hanging the strips inside the house near the ceiling, but this is not often done.

The Kutchin generally prefer to cook moose meat by boiling. At home, meat is cut up and boiled in kettles, or in shallow pans with vegetables and thick sauce. Frying thin meat slices is also popular, and the grease is made into a gravy by adding flour. Roasting is primarily an outdoor technique and rarely is done in the home. Almost all Athapaskan dishes are tasty and agreeable to the white man's palate. The Indians are fairly particular about their foods, wanting them clean and well cooked. They find many of the white man's meats tasty as well, but say that the only food that makes a Kutchin feel well nourished is wild meat. And of these wild meats, moose is the one that really counts.

Caribou

The caribou (*Rangifer arcticus*) plays a very minor role in the subsistence life of the Black River Kutchin, but it deserves a brief discussion before we move on to the next chapter. Caribou are medium-sized deer, weighing some 100 to 300 pounds, which closely resemble the Old World reindeer. They are found throughout Alaska, especially in treeless or open wooded high country and northern tundra plains. Unlike the moose, these animals gather in large herds and migrate hundreds of miles in response to seasonal changes.

Lowland and riverine peoples such as the Tranjik Kutchin seldom have access to caribou, because these animals seldom penetrate deep into timbered country. Rarely—about once in ten to fifteen years—they have moved southward into the flats around Chalkyitsik. But within the last few decades forest fires have burned much of the territory north of the Black River, and the resultant lack of food plants has ended even these uncommon appearances. In fact, caribou are so rare in this area that few of today's active adults have ever hunted them. In the year of this study a few were killed by Chalkyitsik hunters who were traveling in the Porcupine River country. The people occasionally obtain caribou this way, but more often they get meat and skins from their neighbors in the Chandalar region. This kind of trade is much less common today than it was in the past, however.

Because caribou hunting is so rare, I had no opportunity to observe it; also, few men know enough about it to give useful verbal accounts of techniques, and those who do know are generally not inclined to talk about a subject which has so little relevance today. A few general comments can be made, however, based on the rare discussions of caribou hunts I was able to hear.

Caribou are usually hunted during the fall when the animals are reported crossing the Porcupine River; but they are also occasionally taken during the spring, should they remain in the area until after breakup. In any case, when they are reported by river travelers or airplane pilots some people muster crews and gasoline for the long trip from Fort Yukon to the hunting areas. Hunting is apparently rather simple, especially if caribou are abundant. As they travel along the river, crews of hunters encounter herds or small groups, approach as near as they can, then shoot the animals as they stand or run along the banks. They might also wait at river crossings and kill caribou as they approach. The number taken depends upon the capacity of the boat, because the trip is so long that hunters do not want to return for animals left behind.

Caribou are also hunted during the winter if they move into country that is within range of Chalkyitsik people. Usually a trapper discovers caribou or their tracks in the course of his travels, then tries to kill whatever he can. Winter hunting for caribou is similar to moose hunting, though apparently the gregarious caribou are less difficult to approach. If they hear a man coming they are likely to mistake him for another of their own kind. It is best to hunt them during warm periods, however, when the snow is wet and soft, affording almost noiseless approach. When migrating, caribou are practically without fear and will walk very close to people. They sometimes migrate right through the village of Hughes, on the Koyukuk River, enabling the Indians there to hunt from their doorsteps. But the scattered wintering groups encountered by the Tranjik Kutchin are far more difficult to hunt.

It is very hard to say how frequently the Black River Kutchin are able to obtain caribou meat today. In 1969–70 about eight caribou were brought into Chalkyitsik, and it is likely that each family got a small share. During most years very little caribou meat enters the village. It is therefore not surprising that some people do not care for it, because it is strange to them. The older people, who have all spent time in caribou country, seem to like it very much. In the old days a caribou head roasted by hanging it over a fire was considered a great delicacy, and unborn calves were also relished.

Even though the Tranjik Kutchin have never relied heavily on the caribou for food, they apparently needed its skin for winter clothing. Today a few have caribou skins which they use as mattresses under their sleeping bags. All northern Indians and Eskimos are aware of the remarkable warmth of caribou fur, and before the white man's arrival it was the major element in much of their clothing.

In former times an active hunter was likely to need a new outfit of caribou hide clothing each year, though occasionally one would last longer. Calf skin was the best material, though it was not always available. Sinew from the caribou was used for sewing. The skins might also be tanned and cut into thin strips to make lines or cords. Caribou parkas remained in use along the Black River until the 1940s, but now caribou-hide clothing has disappeared entirely.

8 Bears

Introduction

Two species of bear are found in the Black River country, the black
bear or *shooh-zhraii* (*Ursus americanus*) and the grizzly bear or
shiih-tthoo (*Ursus arctos*). The black bear is by far the most common and is the only one hunted for its meat. Bears provide a relatively small volume of food in the Chalkyitsik Kutchin economy,
but they occupy a major role in the minds of the people. They
are large, relatively fearless, sometimes aggressive animals, and the
Indian hunter must be prepared for their unexpected appearance
whenever he is outdoors.

Black bears are inhabitants of the brushy and forested lowland
country, whereas grizzlies tend to be found in more open upland
areas. Nevertheless, either species may turn up anywhere in the
Black River region. The area right around Chalkyitsik seems especially attractive to black bears, which are perhaps enticed by the
smell of human refuse and the opportunity to filch a meal from
garbage dumps or fish traps. It is not unusual to run across bear
tracks on a trail or sandbar just outside the village.

Bears are of course seasonal animals, hibernating for several
months during the winter. Even during the seasons when they are
active and therefore readily hunted there are only certain periods
when the Kutchin consider them fit for eating. Black bears are

115

hunted especially during the fall, when they build up their thickest fat. They retire to their dens by late September, but remain fat and tasty through the winter. After they emerge from their dens between mid-April and early May, food is scarce and they become lean. By June they are thin, and the Indians do not hunt them.

Snaring

It takes little more than the thought of facing a bear at close range with a bow and arrow or spear to make one understand why snares were an important method of killing these animals in aboriginal times. Snares were highly effective and required almost no risk to the hunter. Today's adult Kutchin are all familiar with bear snaring techniques, but if they still catch bears this way they do not consider it a matter of public information. The best time for snaring bears is during the fall, when they are fat and seem to wander along well-

A cable snare set in a trail for black bear. The stick beneath the snare prevents an animal from ducking under it. Note how inconspicuous the snare is. Bears are rarely, if ever, snared today.

defined trails. They could be snared during the spring as well, but no one ever mentioned doing this.

The aboriginal Kutchin made their snares from braided strands of babiche, but in recent times ⅛-inch or ¼-inch aviation cable was found to be more effective. A homemade cable snare works well unless the bear does not pull it tight and is able to slip it off with its claws. Commercial snares are provided with one-way choking locks and cannot be removed. The human scent is eliminated from a cable snare by boiling it with willow bark or by rubbing it with the tips of spruce boughs.

The bear snare is usually set in a trail, either a man-made trail intended for winter travel or a natural game trail. It is generally placed where a constriction is created by bushes or trees, so that the snare fills the whole trail. Another good place is where a log or tree has fallen over the trail, so that the bear is forced to go underneath. A snare set under a log is very effective, and is easily tethered to the log itself. Instead of using a fixed toggle or anchorage, a bear snare is attached to a flexible young tree, to a sizable log, or to a log placed between the crotches of two trees on opposite sides of the trail. In the last case the anchor is a crosspiece which cannot be dragged off, but the bear may simply chew the log in half and escape. The loose log toggle is dragged away into the brush until the bear finally chokes itself. Many a snare has been broken, however, leaving the bear with a snare collar as a memento of his escape.

A typical snare set for black or grizzly bear would be made along the lines described earlier for moose snares. After finding a suitable place on a trail and selecting a fixed or loose toggle, the Indian tethers his snare so that it hangs in the middle of the pathway. It is opened to a loop varying from 20 to 24 inches in diameter, with its bottom edge 24 to 30 inches above the ground. The cable snare is held open by tying it in several places to slender sticks pushed into the ground beside it. Short pieces of grass or thread are used to make the ties.

The trail is usually wider than the snare's loop, and so a few sticks 4 or 5 feet long are set up on either side of it to block the way around. One or more sticks are also pushed into the ground right under the snare, reaching almost to its lower edge, to keep the animal from going under it.

Den Hunting

Black bears spend approximately seven months of the year hibernating, and grizzlies occupy their dens for four to five months. It is not surprising that over the centuries northern Athapaskans have amassed great knowledge of the bears' denning habits and have developed effective methods of hunting them in their winter quarters. Northern Athapaskans are masters of den hunting, just as they are expert hunters of moose. The Koyukon Indians point out that these are the two skills in which they surpass their neighbors, the Kobuk Eskimos.

Den hunting must have been very important in the aboriginal past, when it afforded an easy means of killing bears with only a spear or bow and arrow. Rifles have replaced traditional weapons, but den hunting is still important. This is especially true among the Koyukon, who live in a country rich in bears. They are highly skilled in den-hunting techniques and enjoy bear meat so much that they put considerable effort into the early winter hunts. Den-killed bears are the fattest and best tasting of all; so it is little wonder that the people want them.

As was noted earlier, black bears go into their dens by late September. The date is variable, depending on the weather. They start working on the dens sometime in September, and occupy them intermittently until really cold weather signals the time for uninterrupted hibernation. Grizzly bears enter their dens much later, in November or December, and may become active during midwinter warm spells. They seem to take hibernation much less seriously than do black bears.

The Koyukon and Kutchin Athapaskans often find bear dens by accident, stumbling onto them when they are traveling through the brush at any time of the year. Once they have discovered a den they check it each fall. The Koyukon usually consider each den a sort of property, "owned" by the man who discovered it or learned of it from his father. Thus people speak of "Sam's den," "Henry's den," and so on (G. R. Bane, personal communication). The Chalkyitsik Kutchin do not formalize ownership in this way. Each hunter knows the location of many dens, and they are hunted on a first-come, first-served basis. The only kind of "ownership" here is established by men who find dens and keep their locations secret, thus ensuring themselves a private potential resource.

Each fall or early winter a hunter is likely to go out and check the dens he "owns" or knows about to see if any are occupied. There are several ways to find previously undiscovered dens or to pinpoint known dens once their general location has been ascertained. In the early fall, when bears have selected a hibernating site but are still active, they will remain in the immediate area digging up the moss and dirt searching for roots. When an Indian comes across this kind of sign in September, he knows that a bear is probably going to hibernate in that area. This is the best indicator that a denning site is nearby, but of course much searching may be required to find the site itself.

Black bears like to make their dens in places where they get some help from nature. Most dens are under partly overturned trees, whose roots have lifted the earth and moss to create a bear-sized cavern underneath. They also like to dig dens in banks, such as along a steep-sided creek bed. Another good place for denning is a sandy knoll or ridge, where caverns are easily dug out. In general, holes beneath upturned spruce trees seem the most likely den sites, and these are perhaps the easiest kind to locate. One such den that I saw was about 5 feet long, 4 feet wide, and 2½ feet high.

A black bear prepares its den by gathering moss and grass from the surrounding area and lining the interior with it. The entrance will be plugged with the same material later on. Thus, if a hunter comes across a place where the moss and grass are freshly dug up and scraped away it is a sure sign that a bear den is nearby. If such a place is discovered before snow falls the bear is likely to be away foraging, and so the hunter remembers its location and returns later. When snow covers the ground, dens are much harder to find. A small hole usually remains open in the snow above a den, however, and heavy frost covers the surface and any vegetation around its opening. The frost is formed by condensation from the bear's moist breath.

Sometimes very special knowledge and alertness leads to the discovery of a bear den. For example, Simon Edwards of Huslia once came upon a set of tracks from a running fox. He followed them a short distance and found a place where the fox had sat down for a while, looking back over its trail. Simon wondered what had frightened it, and why it sat watching back the way it had come, so he followed the trail the opposite way. He found shortly that the fox had encountered a bear den and was frightened away by its occupant. Simon got the bear.

Another time this same man was walking along on snowshoes and came to a place where a marten track crossed the trail. Thinking he might find the marten in a burrow, he sidetracked and followed it. At one point he noticed that the animal had dug into the snow before moving on, and next to the hole he found a single blade of grass the marten had pulled up onto the snow. The grass was a kind that bears use for bedding in their dens, and so he poked around further and discovered that the marten had dug right into an occupied bear den. The reward for his effort was fat black bear.

The Koyukon and Kutchin use different techniques for bear den hunting. The following account of the Koyukon method is based largely on information supplied by G. R. Bane, who has lived among these people for several years.

Having located a denning site, the Koyukon hunter first needs to learn if it is occupied or empty. He finds a long stick which he can shove into the den's opening. It should be curved because bear holes have a tendency to go down, then turn off to one side. He pokes around inside until the stick touches the bear, disturbing it enough so its movement can be felt. If the hunter is not sure, he holds the stick against what he thinks is the bear and its breathing will move the stick back and forth. Listening closely, the hunter may also hear the animal's breathing. Once he has ascertained that a bear is inside, the Indian puts his stick to another use. He takes note of the exact direction the passageway runs, and just how far in the stick goes before it touches the bear. Then he pulls it out and lays it on the ground or snow. Its end should mark a point right above the animal.

After he knows the bear's location, the hunter finds several large poles or logs and plugs the entrance with them. These may be tied securely in place to be sure that the animal cannot escape. This done, he uses his ax to chop into the roof of the den so he will have an opening through which to shoot. This can be quite a job, since he wants an opening about 6 inches in diameter and may have to chop through 2 feet of frozen ground. If it is too dark in the den, he can toss a handful of snow on the bear so that a white dusting makes it clearly visible. Once he sees it well, the Indian shoots it in the head. In former times he would kill it with a spear. After a bear is killed in its den, a rope is used to pull it up through the entrance.

The Black River Kutchin use a simpler but more dangerous method of killing bears in their winter dens. Once they are certain a bear is inside, they start poking and jabbing at it with a long stick. Eventually the animal becomes unsettled enough to come out after whatever is tormenting it. When it starts moving up the entryway the hunters stand ready with their rifles. Black bears come out slowly and are either shot in the head when they first emerge or shot in the heart after they get about halfway out.

This method is much simpler than the Koyukon technique. It requires less physical labor, since there are no holes to chop and the dead bear does not have to be dragged out of the hole. And the method can be used when a den is dug into a bank, where there is no way to chop down into it. It does involve a somewhat greater risk, but so long as the animal is a black bear the Kutchin feel that there is no danger. Herbert John said he once knelt on top of a den and killed the emerging bear with his knife.

Grizzly bears can be killed by driving them from their winter quarters, but the Indians treat them in a different way. Whereas a black bear comes out slowly, not looking for a fight, the grizzly angrily charges out, trying to get anyone it can. The Kutchin say that grizzlies do not really hibernate; "Maybe he don't even go to sleep in there." Thus if a grizzly den is found, the hunter must expect trouble unless he decides to be prudent and leave it alone. One of the first things a Kutchin will do upon locating a den, therefore, is decide whether it belongs to a black bear or a grizzly bear.

Black bear dens have fairly small openings, about 2 feet high and 3 feet wide, whereas grizzly dens are higher and wider by about a foot. There is also a tendency for the black bear to plug the opening of its quarters, or at least narrow its size considerably, whereas grizzly bears leave the opening wide enough to move in and out. A grizzly is also likely to growl when anyone walks near its hole, which black bears apparently never do.

The Chalkyitsik Kutchin say that it is often unnecessary to coax a grizzly from its den, because the animal may charge out before a hunter has a chance to do anything. Otherwise, a grizzly would be hunted in much the same way as a black bear. Actually, the Kutchin fear the grizzly and rarely eat its flesh, and so they seldom take the risk of hunting this animal in its den.

Spring and Summer Hunting

Most bears are killed when encountered by hunters traveling overland during the early spring or going along the river in boats during the summer and fall, or when the animals appear close to an occupied camp or village. Spring is the best season for bears because they still retain some fat from the winter and they are almost completely unafraid of people. In the fall they run if they sense a man nearby.

The black bear usually leaves his hibernating place after the snow disappears in late April. If he is not well fattened when he enters his den, hunger drives him out earlier. During May and June an Indian never goes anywhere without a rifle or shotgun because he knows a bear could turn up unexpectedly. A number of black bears were sighted within 200 yards of Chalkyitsik in the spring of 1970. When the people lived in muskrat-hunting camps during the spring, they could count on frequent visits from bears attracted by the smell of meat. The Indians also know of many areas that are especially good for bears during the spring, and they sometimes go to these places to hunt for them.

Some bears run when they see a snowmobile or dog team, but others will merely stand and watch. The snowmobile hunter can stop and take a shot if he gets within range, but with a dog team things are not so simple. If there is no snow on the lakes, a hunter cruising the ice looking for bears cannot hope to stop his team once the dogs spot an animal. All he can do is let them chase the bear, then jump off the sled and try to shoot before his dogs reach it. When an Indian finds very fresh bear sign but there is not enough snow to track the animal, he may try to attract the animal by using an old technique. He conceals himself and imitates the call of a raven. If the bear is nearby it may think a raven has discovered carrion and come straight to the sound, expecting to find a free meal.

Dogs are sometimes used to run down a bear that escapes into the brush and cannot be caught in any other way. They might be released from the team after a bear is spotted, or a hunter might go out from the village on foot, taking his dogs along to help him. In the old days a man would take several dogs when he hunted, and they would course through the woods searching for a scent. When dogs catch up to a black bear it will climb a tree to escape them. Grizzlies stay on the ground and always stop to defend themselves against the biting dogs. If a hunter hears all of his dogs barking at one place, he knows they have found a bear, moose, or porcupine, and he goes quickly to get whatever game they have brought to bay.

Bears are also hunted from boats during the open-water season. A number are usually taken during the fall moose hunt, when the Indians see them along the river. Some bears are wary enough to run when they see a boat coming, but others are unafraid. Bears are also shot by hunters traveling on the river in spring, often by duck hunters in their little canoes.

The Chalkyitsik Kutchin prefer to shoot bears in the heart, perhaps because this was always the best shot with a bow and arrow. Heart shots can be very dangerous, however, because when an animal is hit in the heart it often runs a fair distance before dying. This could mean a charge at the hunter. The Eskimos and the Koyukon Athapaskans warn against shooting bears in the heart, preferring shoulder or neck shots, which instantly incapacitate the animal. They advise heart shots only if a light rifle such as a .22 is being used, when there is no chance of shattering the animal's shoulder or neck bones.

The Kutchin are aware that neck and head shots are deadly, but correctly point out that these are very small targets. If they are close to a bear, they may shoot for the neck vertebrae or the occipital condyle (where the head and neck join). But only an expert takes these shots, because if they miss the bone the animal is wounded and enraged. If a bear charges or comes straight toward a hunter, he shoots it in the chest between the forelegs, or in the head. The Kutchin prefer heavy rifles, such as 30/06 caliber, for shooting bears. Black bears can be killed with a .22 rifle, but this requires a perfect hit in the occipital condyle or heart. Shotguns afford good protection from bears if they are used at close range and are aimed for the animal's eyes, but they are not good for ordinary hunting.

The Koyukon suggest that the best shot for a big bear angles from the shoulder to the hip. This gives maximum crippling potential and is likely to do considerable internal damage. Like the Eskimos, they prefer shoulder, backbone, or neck shots. They advise shooting a black bear in the ear if a .22 rifle is used. Eskimos prefer ear or heart shots with a .22, and have killed both grizzly bears and polar bears in this way.

It is difficult to understand why the Kutchin prefer heart shots over hits which are more deadly and crippling, particularly in view of the dangers involved. They never mention shoulder shots as the correct way to shoot any animal, and apparently consider them poor because they damage some of the meat. Needless to say, Kutchin hunters must always be alert for a charge, especially if they shoot a grizzly. The Indians say that if a bear charges it is best to stand still and aim at the bear, waiting until it is close enough for a certain shot. Both the Kutchin and Koyukon warn that a wounded black bear or grizzly bear may wait in concealment for a hunter to follow, then attack when he comes along.

Danger from Bears

Although there is no question about the potential danger from bears, it remains to be seen what the *actual* danger is in terms of their usual responses to man and man's responses to them. No matter how great the potential danger of a situation may be, its actual danger depends on the man's ability to respond to it effectively.

The Chalkyitsik Kutchin generally consider black bears little cause for concern, except during the spring. Most of the time black bears are rather timid and harmless, "just like dog." They might come right into a camp at night and steal food without bothering anyone. And usually they will run away when they see a man nearby. But in the spring black bears are best treated with respect, because they may become belligerent. No one at Chalkyitsik remembered any attacks by black bears, but several Huslia men recounted their own disquieting experiences with them.

One very old Koyukon man said that black bears are dangerous in spring because they are hungry—"Nothing to eat now, so he eat anything. If I go out I'll take a dog with me all the time so I know if something come around. I tell the kids not to go far away, too, but they never listen." He then told of an experience when he was camped on a sandbar and a growling black bear walked right up to him. His rifle, already loaded, was beside his sleeping bag. He picked it up and shot the bear point-blank.

The large and notorious grizzly bear has a very different reputation from its smaller relative. The Kutchin have a profound respect for grizzlies and an unconcealed fear of them, although they will try to kill them at almost any opportunity. Of all the bear stories I heard from the Kutchin and Koyukon, however, not one recounted an actual injury or death caused by a grizzly bear. People often commented that in the old days, before there were rifles, grizzlies could kill anyone whenever they pleased, but now they must fear man and keep out of his way. Certainly there have been bear injuries, but seldom in recent times.

Yet the Chalkyitsik Kutchin frequently talk about grizzly bears and always comment on how dangerous they are. Grizzlies will usually run from a man, they say, but if wounded or suddenly startled by a man's approach they might attack. They are apparently very temperamental, unpredictable, and potentially aggressive. Old-timers say that if a grizzly charges it is essential to stand still. The bear will usually stop short, stand on its hind legs and look for a few moments, then suddenly turn and run away. A man should never run from a charging grizzly, because doing so almost insures that the animal will chase him down.

Although the Indians have reason to fear grizzly bears, even today when they can protect themselves with high-powered rifles, sometimes this fear seems out of proportion to the actual danger. One phenomenon that is essential to understanding their fear is the "winter bear." Once in a while, especially in years when the berry crop fails, some bears do not build up enough fat to hibernate. These animals must remain active throughout the winter, eating whatever they can find. They may get into open places in the river, then emerge covered with ice and mud, which freezes on their fur. The Kutchin say that this icy coating makes them very difficult to kill without a powerful rifle. Winter bears are usually grizzlies, but occasionally are black bears.

The Kutchin regard winter bears as bizarre freaks of nature, but above all they consider them dangerous. Because they are starving, they will attack any living thing, including man. They will follow a man on the trail, waiting for a chance to stalk him, or conceal themselves alongside a trail awaiting his arrival. Thus every trapper carries a heavy rifle with him at all times and keeps an eye out for any sign of winter bear. If someone runs across bear tracks in midwinter, it is cause for considerable alarm and uneasiness. Old people warn that a winter bear might walk right into the village, apparently basing their opinion on tales of such happenings long ago.

It is important to note, however, that winter bears are exceedingly rare. I heard only four accounts of actual encounters with such animals by Chalkyitsik Indians. Two of these bears made unprovoked attacks, but in all four cases the animal was killed before harming anyone. Although few men have ever seen a winter bear, most have come across their tracks more than once. It seems, however, that although these animals can be a real danger, they are so rare that they are hardly worth worrying about.

There are a number of ways to safeguard against danger from bears. First, the Indians suggest keeping at least one dog around in bear country. Dogs will bark when a bear approaches, and so they are often kept around camps as a sort of alarm system. It is essential to keep them tied, however, because if they are loose they will pursue and harass a bear, then run back to camp with the animal at their heels. Anyone who is around may have both the dog and the bear upon him. The Kutchin warn that dogs are sometimes too frightened to make a sound when a grizzly approaches, and in this case they may fail to warn their owners.

Another way to avoid bear trouble, especially in the spring, is to keep up a fairly constant noise while out in the brush. When the Indians portage their canoes through narrow lake-to-lake trails they often break twigs, scrape their boats on the brush, or talk aloud to keep from blundering into a bear. If someone meets a bear when unarmed, he stands dead still until it goes away. It is also a good idea to keep away from places where bears are known to be common. The Kutchin know many camping spots, for example, that are especially bad during the spring. And they are always careful not to camp on or near a bear trail. One of the best ways to avoid bears is to camp on islands, where they are unlikely to be found. Finally, the Kutchin never go anywhere without a powerful rifle or a shotgun, especially between the first of April and the end of June.

The Indians consider these precautions very important, but they also know that bears are rarely aggressive and nearly always run at the sight of man. Hunters approach them with confidence and never hesitate to pursue them if they want meat. The main advantage a man has in facing a bear is his knowledge of what it will probably do and of how to take proper action.

Uses of Bear

The number of bears killed each year varies a great deal according to their movements, their occurrence along the river, and the effort put into hunting them. During the period of this study, an extraordinarily poor year for bear, only three or four were killed by Chalkyitsik hunters. In a "normal" year the take is probably ten to twenty bears, but this is still not a large volume of meat. There seem to be more bears along the Koyukuk River, and consequently the people kill more of them. The most bears taken at Huslia in one fall denning season was thirty.

Bear meat is most often cooked by boiling but may also be fried. It is very agreeable to the white man's taste, especially if the meat is from a fat, tender young animal. The Indians feel very strongly that a bear must be fat to be worth eating, and they say that cubs are the best of all. Bears that have been living mainly on fish are not very good eating, nor are the ones that feed heavily on "goose grass" (*Equisetum*) during the summer. When they eat plenty of roots and berries, however, they are very tasty.

The Chalkyitsik Kutchin rarely shoot grizzly bears, and when they do they usually take only the skin and leave the rest behind. Those who have tried grizzly meat, and there are very few who have, say that it tastes good; but they still consider it inedible. Bear skin is useful to the people, both for their own purposes and for sale to fur buyers. The hides are prime in fall, winter, and spring and may be sold at these times. People also use them at home, either for soft, warm mattresses or cut into strips for insulation around doors.

9   Small Game

Porcupine

The porcupine or *ts'it* (*Erethrizon dorsatum*) is found throughout the Black River country and most of interior Alaska. Porcupines are herbivorous animals, living on bark and twigs from a variety of trees and shrubs. They are likely to be encountered almost anywhere, from mature spruce forests to willow and alder thickets, and even in grassy meadows. They wander freely through the country, having little to fear from predators. They are fortunate in having a pincushion defense, since few animals waddle more slowly.

The Kutchin, like other northern Athapaskan people, hunt porcupines enthusiastically at certain times of the year. In fall and winter, from August until February, they are heavy with fat and most of the Indians consider them a real treat. But from March through July they are "nothing but skin and bones," and few people bother to hunt them.

Porcupines probably travel around less than most animals in this environment, but they are not exactly sedentary. They seem to choose a particular area, wander around feeding here and there within it, then move on as the fancy takes them. The Kutchin say that they cover the most ground during the fall and move around relatively little in the winter. The tendency to remain more or less in one place makes them fairly easy to hunt when snow is on the ground. If a traveler comes across fresh porcupine tracks he knows there is a good chance of finding the animal somewhere nearby.

During the summer, porcupines are found only by coming upon them accidentally while traveling on foot or by boat. In the winter there is much more chance to catch porcupines, because their tracks give them away. A porcupine's trail is seen first as a crooked trough about eight inches deep, with closely spaced footprints pushed into the snow inside it. Hunters also find porcupines by watching for white, freshly gnawed patches on the trunks of spruce trees. Sometimes a porcupine can be seen perched on a limb far up in such a tree, gnawing off a patch of bark.

The method of hunting is simple. The only difficult part is following the animals' tracks as they wind aimlessly through the underbrush. The tracks can be confusing because they wind about so much, and a man must watch the footprints carefully lest he start tracking backward. Kutchin hunters sometimes follow a wandering porcupine trail through soft snow for half an hour or more before finding the animal or giving up, exhausted. If a porcupine is up in a tree it may be shot, or the tree may be chopped down and the animal clubbed with a heavy stick. Porcupines are often found waddling along on the ground, however, which simplifies the hunt.

Occasionally a trapper can catch a porcupine with a steel trap. If he runs across a fresh trail and follows it to a burrow, and if he knows he will be coming by again within the next couple of days, he sets a trap in the opening of the hole and toggles it to a large stick. This is almost a sure way to get the animal, because chances are good that it will step into the trap on its way out.

The first thing to do after killing a porcupine is to make a good fire and singe off the quills. As the quills and fur melt in the flames, they are pounded or scraped off with a long stick. Every bit of fur is removed to be certain no quills are left, until all that remains is a black, hairless body. After this is done, the porcupine is buried in the snow to cool.

Singeing is not just a safety measure; it is also a way to flavor the meat. The charred skin is not removed before the animal is boiled, because the Kutchin enjoy the taste it gives. They point out that Eskimos skin porcupines instead of singeing them, obviously not knowing how to prepare them correctly. The meat of this animal is often incredibly fat and greasy, and it tastes something like strong pork.

The Tranjik Kutchin have very definite taste preferences. For example, some relish porcupine meat, others eat it as a matter of course, and a few refuse to eat it at all. The same is true of beaver, to an even greater degree. Some people simply refuse to eat it, and others do not care for young beaver, old beaver, or beaver fat. One old man said he never cared much for black bear meat, except young ones or nice fat adults.

The Kutchin had a few taboo animals in the past, probably including dog, wolf, fox, wolverine, raven, and eagle (McKennan 1965, p. 84). One old man said, "Lots of people don't like certain food. I don't know why. Wolf, wolverine, and raven are hard to swallow, even if you try it." Today's adults do not appear to have a "taboo" concept regarding animals such as these, but feel toward them much as a member of our culture would feel about eating caterpillars. One is led to wonder if the word "taboo" or "prohibition" in anthropological literature might often incorrectly imply a sanctioned restriction on eating certain animals when the people are in fact simply repulsed by them.

The Kutchin's food preferences are markedly different from those of the North Alaskan Eskimos, who hardly seem to have a concept of disliking animal foods. There are certain culturally uniform preferences, usually stated in terms of the best kinds of meat. Thus the Wainwright Eskimos say, "You never get tired of caribou." But I do not recall hearing any adult Eskimo express a personal dislike for a native food.

Snowshoe Hare

Population

Snowshoe hares (*Lepus americanus*) are found throughout the boreal forest of North America and are well adapted to their subarctic habitat. Their feet are unusually large and well furred, with webbing between the toes which helps support them on the deep powdery snow. Their fur changes from brown in summer to white in winter, providing year-round camouflage.

The population of snowshoe hares is remarkably variable, fluctuating between incredible abundance and virtual extinction. These changes in numbers tend to be cyclic, with a period of seven to twelve years between highs. Estimates of the number of hares per square mile in peak years run from one thousand to thirty thousand in favorable sites, whereas in low years there are so few that it is hard to estimate their numbers. Indicators of their scarcity are expressed in terms like "one track seen in five days of snowshoeing," or "only two snowshoe hares killed all winter despite constant hunting by the Indians" (Keith 1963, pp. 62, 75, 140).

This variability in population epitomizes a phenomenon which is endemic in the boreal forest environment, where almost every food resource is subject to regular or irregular fluctuations in abundance. Thus the population of hares and its significance in the Kutchin economy are closely interconnected with the numbers of other animal species. The period of this study, for example, came at a low point for fish in the Black River country, but a fairly high point for hares; so the people turned to hares as a major source of dog food and as an important food in their homes. Furthermore, there is a tendency for the fluctuations of predatory animals such as red fox and lynx, which are important fur species, to be synchronized with those of snowshoe hares (Keith 1963, pp. 65–67).

Hunting

The principal methods of taking snowshoe hares are hunting and snaring. Hunting is more seasonal because it cannot be done effectively in winter, and although it goes on during the summer months, hares are so well camouflaged that it is difficult to see them in the thick foliage. By late August, however, the grass begins to die down and leaves fall, making the hares' concealment less perfect. Furthermore, rabbits start turning white by early September and are easily spotted against their drab surroundings. And if the snow falls early, while the rabbits are still brown, they stand out equally well against the white background.

Fall hunters look for rabbits mostly in large stands of willow along the rivers, lakes, and meadows. They can scare them up by walking through the willows during the day, but prefer to wait until

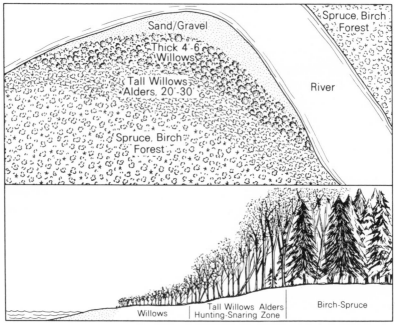

Top and cross-sectional views of a willow-covered bar on a river bend. Such areas are ideal habitat for snowshoe hares and for moose.

late afternoon when they come out to feed along the open edges of the brush. Sometimes two hunters work together, one back in the willows and the other along the edge, driving rabbits toward each other. Since the animals are often heard before they are seen, it is best to hunt in calm weather. A good hunter walks very quietly and pauses often, listening and watching for his game.

When an Indian sees a rabbit hopping off into the thicket ahead, he immediately makes a series of low, short whistles, which often causes it to stop in its tracks so he can take aim with his .22 rifle or light shotgun. If his shot misses, he whistles again as the hare moves away, sometimes making it stop again and again. Rabbits are shot anywhere in the body because they are so fragile that even a slight wound will stop them. Hunters usually have a small homemade pack bag that hangs on their back for carrying their catch.

Rabbit hunting comes to an abrupt halt as soon as the animals have turned completely white and the ground is snow covered, for then they are almost perfectly concealed. It is a lucky hunter who shoots two or three rabbits between October and February. One method that can be used successfully at this time, though it is rarely done today, is to cut down a number of spruce, birch, or willow branches and pile them in a row or stack. Hares are attracted to this fresh feed. The hunter goes to that place in the evening and waits for their appearance.

By late March and early April snowshoe hares begin coming out from their concealing hollows to sit in the sun's warm rays. Now men, women, and children start hunting them in earnest, especially in the evening on clear days when the sun is low and bright. River and lake banks that face the setting sun are the best places for this kind of hunting, because the rabbits are easily seen and are basking so contentedly that a hunter can approach them without much difficulty. By the end of April they are turning gray or patchy brown, and so they show up clearly against the snow; and if the snow disappears before they turn brown they also stand out clearly in their dark surroundings. By the middle of May they are safely camouflaged in the summer forest.

Snowshoe hares are also hunted by conducting drives, a technique that can be used at any season but is usually reserved for winter. In places where willow stands are set apart from other vegetation, particularly on islands or narrow points along a river, a group of people move down the length of the stand, keeping in an even line, driving the rabbits ahead of them. Each person zigzags in order to cover all the space between himself and the hunters next to him, otherwise the animals will just sit still and let them walk by or will run back through the drive line.

Anyone who gets within range of a hare shoots it, and the ones that run along ahead of the drivers emerge at the end of the stand where waiting hunters kill them. This is an old technique, dating from the time when hunters used blunt arrows that killed hares by concussion. This kind of traditional hunting was also combined with snaring. Before a drive began all the hare trails at the far end of the stand were set with snares. Women tended these snares as the drive proceeded, killing rabbits that were caught. Drives are seldom, if ever, conducted today.

Snaring

The Tranjik Kutchin take far more snowshoe hares by snaring than by hunting. Snare lines are maintained around the village more or less through the entire year, but the amount of activity varies considerably according to season. During the summer a few people will put out snare lines to add some variety to their diet or to catch hares for dog food. Snaring activity increases in late summer and early fall, when people want to build up a surplus of meat for the cold months ahead. Freeze-up and the early snowfalls give access to snaring areas that were difficult to reach before. But after a month or two, as the cold grows more intense, fewer people keep snare lines out. Most people set snares from time to time through the winter, and a few keep lines going constantly.

Snaring rabbits is a job shared by men, women, and older children, but women are the most active. Going out to the snare line is a pleasant diversion, a chance to escape a houseful of children, and often an opportunity to take a walk with another woman. Sometimes two women put their lines out together, alternating sets. Young boys may accompany their mothers, and by the time they are ten to fourteen years old are able to run little lines of their own. And old people find snaring a means by which they can be self-sufficient. Active hunters also set out rabbit snares, but generally do so away from the village, where they can make better catches than those who stay within a mile or so.

In most years the powdery snow accumulates deeply enough so that people need snowshoes to set and check their lines. If the snow reaches 15 to 18 inches, it is very hard to wade even a short distance through it with only boots on, and, in fact, snowshoes are desirable even when there are only 8 to 12 inches of snow. But they are only needed to break open the trail, and once it is hard and packed the snowshoes can be left at home until it snows again.

The Black River people, like all Kutchin and many other northern Athapaskans, make two types of snowshoes. The first, called hunting snowshoes, are 4½ to 5½ feet long, 8 to 10 inches wide, and rounded in the front. They are used for walking over fresh powder snow while hunting or trapping. The second type, trail snowshoes, are approximately 3 feet long and 8 to 9 inches wide, with a pointed and sharply upturned front end. Since these smaller snowshoes allow the wearer to sink more deeply into the snow, they are used either to break a trail for a dog team or to walk on a previously broken trail. "Hunting shoes" would not work for breaking trails because they do not sink deeply enough to make a useful track. "Trail shoes" are somewhat heavier and sturdier than the hunting type and can therefore withstand longer and harder use.

The Chalkyitsik Kutchin use snowshoes less today than in the past. Hunting snowshoes have become uncommon, though almost every man owns one or two pairs of trail snowshoes. The introduction of snowmobiles has lessened the need for snowshoes because men seldom have to break a trail; but on the other hand they are sometimes necessary for walking home when the machine breaks down. Snowshoes are still used rather extensively by women and others who set rabbit snares or conduct various activities on foot.

Returning to the subject of snaring, certain areas around Chalkyitsik are especially good for snare lines, though when rabbits are common they can be caught almost anywhere. The best places are the large stands of willow and other brush that grow on the gently sloping sandbars along the inside of bends in the Black River. People often cut narrow paths into the willows, where hares are most abundant, setting snares along the many hare trails. The paths are kept as narrow as possible, to minimize the open space that might allow ravens to spot snared rabbits. Snare lines are also set along all the major trails around Chalkyitsik, and many footpaths radiating off from the main trails are used almost exclusively for snaring hares.

Almost any place where hares are common can be made into a good snaring location by chopping down a long row or "fence" of willows and other kinds of brush. The branches are laid in a line, and small passageways are made through the fence so hares will hop through from one side to the other as they feed on the fresh branches. After a couple of days, snares are set in these openings to catch the hares as they try to go through.

The first step in setting snares is to locate the animals' trails. Hares move around a lot between good feeding places, usually following well-defined trails, and during the summer it is fairly easy to detect these trails by watching for narrow pathways 5 to 7 inches wide, where the ground litter is matted down and the grass is parted.

When the leaves start dropping in the fall they become somewhat more difficult to see because leaves often cover them, but these are quickly trampled down, making the trails visible again.

Indians find rabbit trails by walking along a footpath or sled trail and watching the brushy margins at each side. Wherever a rabbit trail crosses the path there is a small opening on each side where the surface is somewhat trampled. This is difficult to describe, but surprisingly easy for anyone with an attentive eye to see. The Indian looks for rabbit trails that appear worn enough to be clearly defined. He also wants to find places where trails pass through natural constrictions, such as a pair of bushes a few inches apart or an opening between piles of brushy debris. If the trail is open on both sides, it is too easy for the animal to hop around the snare, which obtrudes noticeably into the natural setting.

During the winter months a good covering of snow provides a perfect tableau of every move the hares make; each trail is clearly visible, and the amount of trampling is an infallible indicator of its popularity as an avenue of travel. A good trail consists of a little trough running through the snow, sometimes a couple of inches lower than the surrounding surface. It is well packed, so that individual footprints do not show. A poor trail has been traversed only a few times and is not packed into a trough. Good trails are used all year long.

The Chalkyitsik Kutchin today use a simple kind of rabbit snare, identical in principle to the large moose and bear snares described earlier. The snare itself is always made from number 2 picture wire, a strong braided wire just stiff enough to hold its shape but flexibile enough to tighten easily when an animal enters it. Everything else needed to make a set can be found in the woods, and no tools at all are necessary.

Each snare wire is about 20 inches long and has a ¼-inch diameter loop at one end made by simply twisting the wire around itself to make the sliding noose that eventually forms the snare. When an Indian finds a good hare trail, he looks for a straight, dry branch about 4 to 6 feet long and little thicker than his index finger. This branch will be the toggle.

He puts this branch horizontally across the hares' trail, about 8 inches above the ground, sticking it into the brush on both sides

A snare set for snowshoe hares, with a long stick used as a toggle. Twigs are pushed into the snow alongside the snare to prevent hares from hopping around it.

so it is fairly solid. Then he wraps the free end of the snare wire very tightly once or twice around the toggle, twisting it so it will hold firm. This done, he makes a round noose about 4 inches in diameter, 2½ to 3½ inches above the ground, with ½ to 1 inch of wire between the toggle and the loop. He centers the snare in the middle of the trail and hangs it straight down.

There are usually a few inches of open space on each side of the noose, and if they are left the hare will hop around the set. So now the Indian breaks off some slender branches 12 to 20 inches long and pokes them into the ground or snow on both sides of the snare, 1 to 1½ inches apart, forming a barricade with an opening where the snare hangs. Some people also put a single short twig under the middle of the loop to discourage the animal from going under it.

Little effort need be made to avoid getting human scent on snare sets or to prevent footprints and other disturbance in the snow. The Kutchin often put their sets together rather hastily and haphazardly, probably feeling that a greater number of simple sets is better than a few elaborate ones. They might miss a few hares, but their overall success is maximized. When setting snares on foot in good habitat the Kutchin make a set at almost every hare trail, sometimes placing snares only 5 to 30 yards apart. But if they travel by snowmobile or dog team they tend to scatter their sets more, using only the best trails.

A snowshoe hare usually dies quickly when it gets into a snare. As soon as it feels the loop catch around its neck, the rabbit starts leaping and jerking frantically in an effort to escape, insuring that unconsciousness and death come quickly. Thus, chances are that the Indian will find his catch dead, and in winter frozen solid as well.

Not every hare struggles hard enough against the snare to kill itself, and if it is not intensely cold the animal remains alive. In this case the Indian grabs it by the shoulders or hind feet while the snare still holds it neck. Then with his free hand he presses the rib cage between his thumb and fingers, locating the hard, thumping heart. He squeezes the heart for ten to thirty seconds, until it stops beating; or he pinches the heart, simultaneously pulling back, tearing it loose, causing the hare to die quickly and without a struggle.

Needless to say, many snares are empty when the line is checked, for a number of things other than skill in setting affect snaring success. A fresh snowfall, or in open places a heavy blow and resultant drifting, can ruin sets by elevating the snow level in the trail or burying the snare. In spring the process is reversed, and melting snow leaves snares high above the trails. Temperature also affects snaring success, for when it drops to −40° and colder snowshoe hares do not move around much. They huddle in little snow hollows, such as small snow caves under deadfalls, and stay there until it warms up.

A snare line in good habitat may produce hares over a period of weeks or, to a much lesser extent, months. There is no definite rule on when a line will be moved elsewhere, but generally it is left until very few hares are taken, perhaps none for days at a time.

Much depends on the size of the surrounding habitat. A small willow stand, for example, cannot be expected to produce for long. Hares may move in or out of an area en masse, causing drastic changes in snaring success. Sometimes an area will have many rabbits for weeks, then they move out and hardly a track can be found. These movements are especially marked in the less favored habitats, whereas dense stands of underbrush always seem to have plenty of hares.

Loss to scavengers is another major factor influencing snare line productivity. Ravens often spot a snared rabbit and in a few hours' time reduce it to bones. Once these birds locate a snare line they will stay around and clean it out, and so there is nothing to do but move the line. The Kutchin usually try to place their snares in thick brush where they are difficult to see from above, and check their lines early in the morning before the ravens find them. Hawks, gray jays, and occasionally weasels damage snared rabbits; and

A spring-pole snare in a snowshoe hare trail. This is a traditional set, no longer in use today.

other less frequent raiders of rabbit snares include marten, red fox, loose dogs, and sometimes wolves.

In former times the Indians prevented scavenger losses by making lifting pole snares. These devices would lift a snared animal and hang it well above the ground, making an immediate kill and putting it out of reach for most scavengers. There were two types, spring pole snares and tossing pole snares. Neither is used today because the people feel it is unnecessary to bother with such devices. All of the adults have seen them in use, however.

The traditional snare noose was made from braided sinew and, although it is a strong enough material, animals could chew it to escape from a fixed snare. Lifting pole snares were necessary to prevent such losses by hanging and killing the animals quickly; but once wire became available these elaborate devices were unnecessary. Braided picture wire could not be chewed and rarely broke from twisting; so people began using fixed toggle snares like those described above.

The tossing pole set consists of a snare fastened to the end of a 6- to 8-foot pole, which rests on a fulcrum such as a forked stick. The pole is set well off balance and is rigged so its light end is fastened about a foot above the ground. The attached snare hangs in the middle of a rabbit trail, with barrier twigs alongside to keep the animals from going around it. The pole is held down by a trigger mechanism, and when it is sprung the heavy end drops to the ground, lifting the snare end with the rabbit attached.

There are two trigger mechanisms. One simply involves bracing the heavy end of the tossing pole with a vertical stick. A snared rabbit moves the tossing pole enough to dislodge it, the heavy end falls, and the animal is lifted (Osgood 1937, p. 92). The second is a more complex mechanism which is highly effective. The tossing pole is set up as described above, but the snare is attached to a small trigger stick, which is also tied to the tossing pole by a short piece of line. To set the snare, the tossing pole is pulled down so that the line can be looped under a fixed horizontal toggle that spans the hare trail. Then one end of the trigger stick is hooked inside the line to secure it, and the attached snare is adjusted to hang in the trail. When a rabbit is caught, it jerks the trigger stick, releasing the line from around the toggle; the pole then snaps upward, lifting the animal (see illustration; also Osgood 1940, p. 239).

Spring pole snares use the second type of trigger mechanism, but are made with a bent live sapling instead of a tossing pole. This device is handy in the summer, when it is easy to bend a willow growing near a rabbit trail, but it cannot be used in the winter, because frozen wood lacks the necessary spring.

Snowshoe hares are also caught with steel traps. The method is extremely simple. A small (no. 1) trap is set in the middle of a hare trail, its chain fastened to a stick toggle 5 or 6 feet long, placed alongside the trail. If the trail is wide, vertical sticks can be set up alongside the trap to keep the hare from going around it. When a rabbit gets caught in a trap, it will twist and break its leg but will not chew the leg and escape. The Kutchin make no effort to conceal the trap, considering it unnecessary. Rabbit trapping is rare, probably because traps are too valuable to use for this.

Uses of Hares

When the Indian brings in a number of snowshoe hares, he is likely to skin and butcher them immediately. Skinning can be done entirely by hand. First, a little tear is made at each "ankle," and the skin is peeled down the legs, tearing it along the inside of each leg to a point near the anus. Then the skin is simply peeled off like removing a sock by turning it inside out. The forelegs are skinned down to the "wrist," where the skin is torn or cut. The head may be skinned carefully, but usually the Indian merely cuts or tears the hide free at the neck.

If they are not discarded, rabbit skins are usually dried, either by hanging them outside or by stuffing them with paper and placing them in a warm spot inside the house. Dried skins are sometimes used "as is," without further processing. They make fine insulative socks for winter use. A person simply pulls an inside-out skin onto each foot before putting on his boots. These socks last for a few days, then become torn and are discarded. Hare skins are often extremely thin and fragile, and so it is best to pick the thickest ones for socks and work them a little by hand to take out the stiffness before wearing them. Skins can also be cut open into a flat

piece and used for insoles, for lining inside mittens, or as a kind
of scarf to protect the neck in cold weather.

Hares were an important source of meat for the Chalkyitsik
people and their dog teams during the time of this study. Some
families used them for a good percentage of their meals during certain periods, such as midwinter, when other meats were hard to
obtain. A few families probably consumed more hare meat during
1969–70 than any other food, largely because other game species
such as fish, moose, and bear were scarce at that time. This illustrates the role that snowshoe hare and other small game species
have played in the Tranjik Kutchin economy since the precontact
era. In good times they are a supplement, in hard times a lifesaver.

All of the older Kutchin can remember times of severe food shortage, when "If you get game, you eat. If you get nothing, you
go hungry." If people had only rabbits at such times they would
probably starve to death, because these animals are too lean. The
same might be true if they could get only thin moose. People cannot
live on lean meat alone, but if they have enough fat they can survive
indefinitely. This is why old people say that the best find during
starvation periods is a bear in its den—"plenty of fat there." Fish
is also an adequate diet, except the lean northern pike.

A recurrent time of scarcity is the spring, especially when there
is an early thaw followed by cold weather which causes the snow
to develop a hard crust. This makes it very difficult to stalk moose
because of the noise, and makes rabbits hard to snare because they
run on the hard snow with little regard for trails. If the river has
open places, they may freeze over again, forcing the waterfowl to
head south. And if the muskrat houses have disintegrated, their
water hole entry freezes and there is no way to catch them. If
the snow has melted, the people also have no means of traveling
around after game. The Kutchin economy can be crippled for several
weeks, and if there are no food reserves the people may starve.

Despite these potential difficulties the living Kutchin seem unable
to recall any actual deaths from starvation in their own time,
although they have all known hunger and have even seen most or
all of the dogs starve to death. It is certain, however, that death
by starvation was not unheard of during the aboriginal past. Starvation cannibalism is recorded for the Chandalar, Porcupine River,

and Peel River Kutchin, as well as the Tanana, Chipewyan, Ingalik, Tanaina, Slave, Yellowknife, Dogrib, and Hare (McKennan 1959, pp. 38–39; Morice, n.d., pp. 133–34).

Squirrels

Red Squirrel

The red squirrel (*Tamiasciurus hudsonicus*) is one of the most characteristic and personable animals of the boreal forest. It is called *dlak* in Kutchin, a name which imitates the sound of its ubiquitous chirping call. These little creatures are common during all seasons except winter, when they spend most of their time in burrows under the ground or tunnels beneath the snow. Red squirrels are very common in spruce forests, and since they are relatively fearless animals, squirrel hunting would be a sure way to get meat. The Kutchin rarely hunt them, however, because they are said to taste bad and because the skins are worth only twenty-five cents.

Red squirrels are often caught in snares, because they like to follow hare trails. They also have their own, somewhat narrower, network of trails; so if someone wants to catch squirrels he can set small fixed-toggle snares in these trails. They can also be caught with steel traps set either at the openings of their burrows or against the base of a tree.

The Kutchin and other northern Athapaskans must have had uses for squirrels during aboriginal times. They were certainly eaten, but probably were not highly desired. The modern Kutchin usually discard even the ones caught accidentally in their rabbit snares.

Arctic Ground Squirrel

One of the least common food animals utilized by the Chalkyitsik Kutchin is the arctic ground squirrel (*Citellus parryi*). This animal lives in dry, open localities such as hillsides and river banks, and it is active only during the spring and summer months. Since ground squirrels are not common in the country around Chalkyitsik, the only way to catch them in quantity is to know the best locations. Small colonies are scattered here and there, but individual burrows may be encountered anywhere in fairly open places.

Ground squirrels can be hunted with .22 rifles, but since there are no large colonies and they tend to be quite wary it is difficult to hunt them productively. Occasionally a rabbit or grouse hunter will come across one and get close enough to shoot it. The first rule for hunting these animals is to aim for the head only. A hit almost anywhere else will leave it with enough strength to get back into its burrow and die out of reach.

Few of the Chalkyitsik Kutchin go hunting specifically for ground squirrels, but they are frequently trapped, often by old people, who love to eat these fat little animals. A steel trap, number 1 size, sometimes rubbed in dirt first to minimize the human scent, is placed directly in the mouth of a burrow. Its chain is toggled to a 3- or 4-foot stick or to a stake put in the gound next to the hole. Dirt may be sprinkled on the trap pan and spring to further cover any scent and make the exposed trap less obtrusive, but this is not really necessary. When a squirrel tries to enter or leave the burrow it can hardly miss the trap.

Snares are also set for ground squirrels. Spring pole or tossing pole snares can be placed either right at the animal's hole or along its trail. The modern fixed toggle snares can also be used. The snare loop is made about 2 inches in diameter and 1 inch off the ground, and the setting techniques are essentially identical to those described for hares, but on a somewhat smaller scale.

III TRAPPING

10 The Trappers

Introduction

Fur brought the white man into Kutchin country, fur kept him there, and fur has been the nexus between the Indian and the world outside for most of the past 120 years. When Alexander Murray established Fort Yukon for the Hudson's Bay Company in 1847, his sole motivation was to initiate trade for valuable furs. And so it began that the white man came to the North not to steal land, not to wage war, but to do business. Since the Indians lived on land that was never to prove attractive to large numbers of whites, the relationship between these two peoples remained largely mercantile until very recent times.

Murray was quick to notice that the country surrounding Fort Yukon supported extraordinary numbers of fur-bearing animals. At one point he refers to its "super-abundance of beaver and martens" (Murray 1910, p. 54). But there were also lynx, mink, muskrat, wolf, fox, and wolverine in equally notable quantities, as we will see shortly. The Kutchin had always taken some fur animals, using their highly effective deadfalls and snares, but for the most part these animals were peripheral to the native economy. Now the white man wanted fur and would pay handsomely for it with highly desired trade goods. That was enough for the Kutchin, who began to devote more and more effort to catching furbearers. It is hard to say when trapping became a dominant force in their lives, but by the turn of the century they were probably modifying their entire life-style to fit into a trapping regime.

During the early period of fur trade, the people lived most of the year in family groups, scattered across the land wherever there were food resources to exploit. Some energy was devoted to trapping, enough to get a few supplies, perhaps a rifle or ammunition. As time passed the Kutchin became increasingly dependent on trade goods, which necessitated an ever-greater trapping effort. Steel traps began to replace snares and deadfalls for catching furs as rifles displaced bows, spears, and snares for big game.

Finally, I cannot say when, the people began to establish permanent one- or two-family settlements along the river, dividing the surrounding country into individual trapping territories. Perhaps white men had something to do with the territorial idea. By the early twentieth century a fair number of white men had come into this region, perhaps an overflow from the Gold Rush, and they began to trap. The Indians welcomed them, usually becoming relatives by marriage rather quickly, and a process of mutual assimilation began to take place. The white man learned native outdoor skills and reciprocated by introducing a whole constellation of ideas, techniques, and values. So Kutchin and white man lived as neighbors, sharing the same lifeways or depending on each other in a trapper-trader relationship.

Trapping dominated Kutchin country for the entire first half of the twentieth century. The routine of life centered upon winters spent in small family groups out on the scattered traplines and summers of trading and fishing at large encampments and centers like Fort Yukon or Rampart House. Dependence on goods from the Outside steadily increased, and the trapping economy enjoyed a great florescence. Meanwhile, however, a new era of change loomed ahead.

In the decade following World War II, a number of things happened that began attracting the Black River people to larger settlements and away from the scattered, lonely trapline cabins. The value of furs declined, summer jobs and welfare money became available, and schools were built for the children. The old trapping life, which had become as much the pattern of Kutchin culture as the nomadic hunting and fishing existence which preceded it, began to disappear. This process is still going on today, when the people live in villages from which the trappers make brief excursions to the trapline. Trapping skills, which grew up during the timeless aboriginal past and were changed and elaborated after white men arrived, are still perpetuated by the old-timers and adults. But trapping as a way of life, as *the* way of life, has practically disappeared since villages, jobs, and schools came into the Black River country.

The next few chapters will, I hope, give an idea not only of what trapping is but of what it means to the people as a mode of existence. The fur trade had an immense impact on the Kutchin, in far more ways than I can hope to understand or discuss here. Perhaps most important, the vigorous fur economy which existed here during over a century of growing contact with the Outside was an essential determinant of the peaceful intermingling of European and Kutchin culture. The white man came here and stayed for the sole purpose of conducting business with people whose claim to the land was never seriously challenged. The Indians welcomed these newcomers even to the point of allowing them to establish their own traplines and live as competitors on their land, feeling that they had much to gain by their presence. So a pleasant symbiosis was established, a dramatic contrast to the violent collision of Indian and white man that occurred almost everywhere else in North America.

The chapters that follow survey the long and involved subject of trapping, first with a discussion of the modern trappers and their seasonal activities, skills, and productivity. Then comes a detailed consideration of the logistics of trapping—the complex of activities related to winter travel. This information will lay the groundwork for understanding the discussions of trapping techniques which follow.

Chapters 12–17 deal with the methods used by the Tranjik Kutchin for trapping fur animals. The major species are dealt with in separate chapters, and several minor ones are lumped together in a single chapter. But although each species is given a separate discussion, it will become apparent that the same trapping methods apply generally to most kinds of fur animals. Thus there are a number of basic principles a trapper follows in making his sets, with variations to adjust to the size and behavioral peculiarities of each species.

The construction of trap and snare sets is not elaborate or complex and may be learned without a great deal of training. This does not mean that the trapper's art is a simple one, however, because there is more to catching fur animals than merely setting traps and snares. The Indian must be intimately familiar with the habitat, movements, general behavior, and indicators of the game he is after. Trapping, like hunting or any other vocation, requires a lifetime of accumulating knowledge and experience to develop true mastery. Although a man is able to learn the basic principles of trapping in a year or so, it takes much longer before he becomes an expert.

The Trappers

Modern Trapping Activity

Despite a gradual diminution in the importance of trapping over the past twenty years, it remains a major economic activity of the Tranjik Kutchin. They still consider winter and early spring the trapping season, and they refer to themselves first and foremost as trappers. Fur is a main source of income for a fair number of Chalkyitsik men. But at the same time, virtually all of the Kutchin explicitly state that they would rather earn a living by wage employment than by trapping. And with easy access to jobs and welfare, many now devote only a limited effort to obtaining fur. Those who can get enough money by other means trap only to earn supplemental income, varying their activity according to need.

During the summer of 1969 almost all the men in Chalkyitsik were steadily employed fighting forest fires. Their earnings were great enough (one thousand to three thousand dollars per man, plus equal amounts for older boys) so that many took little interest in trapping during the following winter. This was true despite an abundance of fur animals and the consequent success of those who trapped. Out of twenty-five potential trappers, only six devoted a major effort to trapping activity. These men had long traplines far from the village, ran them regularly throughout the winter, and earned good incomes from their work. Another four men carried out limited activity, either trapping close to the village or spending only part of the season in these pursuits. Nine more did very limited trapping, going out on the line only a few times during the season, often just to help another man temporarily. And six men who could have gone out did no trapping at all.

Attenuated trapping activity and a concomitant decrease in the size and complexity of traplines show a clear trend away from a fur-based economy. It is also worth noting that all of today's trappers are adults, and very few men under twenty-five or thirty years of age show any interest at all in bush life. In this fact alone, prospects for the future are clear.

The Partnership

Although partner relationships are an institution of long standing among the Tranjik Kutchin, they are perhaps more common today than ever before. Virtually all trappers who stay out on the line overnight or travel fairly long distances by snowmobile have partners. The more localized trappers, on the other hand, often go out alone.

The partnership arrangement is generally viewed as a matter of convenience for two men who can work well together and who are approximately equal in their ambition and skill. But if anything characterizes the partnership it is fragility. These arrangements seldom last more than a year or two, because the men cannot get along well enough for a longer period or because for some reason another partnership seems more convenient. Most often partners seem to grow tired of each other, then a few years later they team up again for a year, and so on.

In former times, when fathers and sons often trapped together, partnerships could provide the means of instruction for apprentice trappers. Nowadays partners go trapping together for several reasons. For one thing, they want companionship during the long idle nights of the dark winter season. Partners also provide a measure of security, so that if a man is injured or becomes sick someone is there to take emergency measures. With snowmobiles it is almost imperative that each man have a partner, because of the danger of a breakdown or an injury-producing accident.

Partners share food, gear, and cabins, but their traplines are kept separate. Thus one man might bring in large catches and the other very small ones, but the take is not shared. Even if they set traps along the same trail, each man keeps his separate and gets only

Trapping partners taking a lunch break on the trail. They sit on a bed of spruce boughs near the fire (*foreground*). Cardboard boxes contain their "grub."

the animals that end up in his sets. One exception to this pattern occurs when a man is "hired" by another to go out and run his trapline. In this case the two men divide the catch, usually on a fifty-fifty basis.

The Season

Preparations and Equipment

In earlier times, when trappers stayed out on the line throughout the winter, preparations for trapping began early in the fall. First it was necessary to load families and their provisions into boats for the journey upriver to the main trapline cabins. This was usually done early enough, perhaps in July or early August, so that a good supply of fish could be caught and dried. At the same time there were other preparations to be made for the long cold season ahead. Cabins had to be repaired, equipment such as toboggans built or

A trapper's outfit, including snowmobile and toboggan, tent, rifles (in cases), snowshoes, ax, traps (piled behind ax), and snares. The structure on the left is a cache.

readied for the trail, new clothing made, firewood cut, and the trails cleared of overgrowth.

Nowadays this routine has changed drastically, since trappers live year-round in the village. Those who trap on the Black River try to visit their cabins during the fall to make minor repairs and see that things are in order. Some trappers carry equipment to their cabins by boat in the fall, but they usually go there only to fix up the cabins. If it snows early a visit can be made by dog team or snowmobile to deliver equipment and supplies.

Trappers need quite an assemblage of equipment in order to carry on their work and to live comfortably in the bush. Some of their equipment is carried with them on the trail, and some is stored in the line cabin. Of course the modern trapper does not need a completely furnished cabin, since his family stays in the village.

The following list includes all the essential equipment and supplies used by modern trappers:

Dog team or snowmobile
Toboggan or sled, or both
Dog harnesses, lines, and chains
Tent
Hunting canoe (for spring muskrat hunting)
Winter clothing
Heavy rifle, .22 rifle, shotgun
Snowshoes
Chain saw or Swede saw
Canvas tarps (two or three, various uses)
Sleeping bag
Camp stove
Cooking and eating utensils
Lanterns (gasoline and kerosene types)
Tool kit (hammer, pliers, files, nails, screws, etc.)
Ax
Ice chisel and shovel (for beaver trapping)
Radio (not essential, but often carried)
Traps and snares (number variable)
Hide stretchers
Skinning knives and scrapers
Wire (for miscellaneous uses)
Rope (various sizes, many uses)
Trap baits and scents
Ammunition
Gasoline and kerosene (for stove, lanterns, snowmobile, chain
    saw)
Oil (for snowmobile, chain saw)
Dog food (meat, fish, commercial)
Food supplies (tea, flour, sugar, etc.)

The most essential items a trapper owns are his traps and snares, which he usually refers to as his "equipment." The Kutchin stress that if a man wants to catch lots of fur, he has to have plenty of equipment. In other words, the more traps a man sets, the better his catch will be. The best trappers in Chalkyitsik today set out 150 to 200 traps and perhaps 30 snares during the winter season; and they use 150 or more snares for beaver during the spring. Traps and snares come in a number of sizes, each designed to catch certain species. Since the Indians take a variety of fur species, they must provide themselves with different kinds of equipment.

It is important to keep traps and snares free of foreign scents, and so during the summer months they are stored outside the house, away from the telltale odors of smoke, gasoline, dogs, and humans. Usually they are put in an outdoor cache, hung on a wall to prevent their touching anything. One man said that he puts a spruce bough inside his trap sack to keep foreign scents away. Traps and snares may also be rubbed with spruce boughs, or boiled with them, to remove all scents.

Trapping Season

The Black River Kutchin honor trapping seasons established annually by the Alaska Department of Fish and Game, and indulge in only minor hedging around the closing dates for some species. When fur animals are encountered during the off-season they are not molested in any way, with the occasional exception of the edible beaver and muskrat.

There are several reasons why the legal season is respected. First, the Tranjik Kutchin do not kill animals needlessly. Since the fur is not prime at other times and the meat of most furbearers is not desired as food, there is no cause to kill them except in season. Second, they have accepted the conservation ethic (I do not know if it predates contact), realizing that animals are best saved for times when they are most useful. And third, they had some trouble with game wardens in the past. A few arrests were made and minor fines were levied, but this was enough to inspire a fear of the law.

The legal trapping season for most species opens on the first of November. There is generally enough snow for good travel by this time, and some men begin setting traps in the vicinity of Chalkyitsik immediately, limiting their activities to the nearby area. Trappers make a concerted effort to move out to the main traplines by November 15. They often say that if a man does not set out by that date there is little use in going trapping at all, because it is important to get started before deep cold sets in and curtails the activity of men and animals alike. Heavy trapping continues from mid-November into December, as long as the weather holds out, then comes a midwinter slowdown.

February and March are said to be very good months for trapping because the animals are active again after the coldest months have passed. Around March, however, most trappers show a decided waning of interest. They begin looking forward to pulling out their traps, although a few keep on through the spring beaver and muskrat seasons. For most of the modern Kutchin, the season for active trapping runs from mid-November until sometime in March. If muskrats are abundant there is a resurgence in April and May, when trapping for these animals is best.

Traplines

As they are defined in practice by the Tranjik Kutchin, traplines are areas in which individuals or families have exclusive rights to all furbearers. These rights explicitly do not include any resources other than fur animals, and other kinds of game are hunted without respect to territoriality. The boundaries of individual traplines generally do not consist of imaginary lines drawn around a given tract of country, but instead are rather hazily defined zones which come to be regarded as the limits of a particular man's territory. It would be very difficult to put traplines on a map, because they are defined primarily in terms of trails along which a man sets his traps and snares and lakes, sloughs, and creeks to which he has exclusive trapping rights. Thus a trapline is often a circuitous complex of trails, plus a certain unspecified amount of surrounding territory, and a number of bodies of water along these trails. Traplines belonging to different individuals often cross each other and interdigitate in very complicated ways. People seem to know "intuitively" how far apart they should keep their trapline trails in order to give one another a good-sized territory. But there appear to be no clear boundaries beyond these areas surrounding each man's trails and the lakes which he is considered to own.

Traplines are in a constant state of flux, now that there is much unutilized land available here. If a man wishes to move into an unused area, all he needs to do is make a trail through it, or clear out an old one that has become overgrown with brush. If he uses that trail for several years the line is recognized as his, but if he leaves it unused for an equal time anybody who wants it may take it over. In a few cases where the same family has made and used

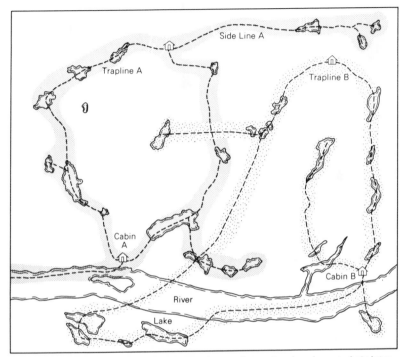

A schematic representation of two neighboring traplines, showing characteristic inter-digitation. Stippling and shading indicate the breadth of "owned" territory. Note that traplines often run from lake to lake.

a large number of trails throughout a given region for many years, that region appears to be considered the property of the family occupying it. Thus an outsider would not make a trail into the region without obtaining permission from the owners. Most traplines, however, are apparently defined only as a number of trails and lakes.

So the country around Chalkyitsik is interlaced by a large number of trails, radiating out from the village and fingering into hills, valleys, lakes, creeks, and rivers. The trails are far more numerous than any one man can remember, exist in widely different states of repair and detectability, and are used by varying numbers of men each year. Trails can be classified into three types:

1. *Main trails.* This includes the major trails, used by a large number of individuals each winter for travel to trapline cabins or

hunting areas. Anyone can set traps along main trails, wherever he wishes, even a few feet away from another man's set. Snares cannot be set in the middle of these trails, as is done on the more private ones.

2. *Trapping trails.* These are generally used by only one man, who sets his traps along them and claims exclusive rights to the fur resources occurring here. Other persons may use these trails on a limited basis, should they occasionally travel through the area. They will probably be inconvenienced by snares in the trails, however.

3. *Side lines.* Each trapper makes short trails a few miles long that branch off from his trapping trails. These generally run through good trapping areas which are off his general direction of travel. Some take only an hour or so to run, others require a whole day (by dog team or on foot). Usually they are narrow and crooked, and many trail snares are set in them.

In addition to obtaining traplines by clearing or reopening trails, Indians may acquire them through bequest or inheritance. Several lines now in use around Chalkyitsik were obtained in this way, in every case by a man from his father. A third way to acquire traplines is by purchase, a method which has been utilized occasionally over the years. In the late 1940s Shimkin (1955, p. 228) found that twenty-one out of thirty-eight Fort Yukon area trappers had acquired lines by clearing trails and putting up cabins along them. Another twelve were owned through bequest or inheritance, nearly all from patrilineal relatives. And five lines had been purchased from nonrelatives.

This does not mean that a man who uses a trapline is certain to be its owner. In the first place, many of the trappers operating out of Chalkyitsik today either do not live there all year round or have not been there long enough to establish their own lines. These men trap as partners of men who own traplines. In this case the two men generally utilize different trails, make their own sets, and keep whatever they catch. Traplines can also be rented, either for cash or for a percentage of the take. Sometimes a man will allow someone else, such as a brother or close friend, to use part or all of a line. This is commonly done with a beaver house or muskrat lake that the owner does not plan to use himself.

The Kutchin are careful not to violate another man's territory by setting traps in it, or to "bother" someone else's sets. The possibility of stealing fur from one another is apparently so remote that it is never even discussed. With few exceptions trapline trails, side lines, muskrat lakes, and beaver houses are left strictly alone for the use of their acknowledged owners. People even avoid traveling on another person's trail as much as they can. Since each person owns a number of trails and lakes, sometimes in widely separated areas, it is hard for everyone to know just which ones are owned at a given time. If a man discovers a trail or lake that he did not know of previously, he will probably ask neighboring trappers about it before using it. If he sets there without inquiring first, he may find himself "kicked out" by someone who claims it.

In the years when trappers stayed out in their main cabins all winter, their traplines were extensive and complex. They usually formed large circuits with a number of cabins spaced about a day's travel apart. Side lines that ran out from some of these cabins required an extra day, or part of a day, to check during each run of the circuit. The time required to make a complete round of the line varied from one to two weeks. It is difficult to estimate the length of such lines, but they perhaps ran between 100 and 250 miles. Until the 1940s and 1950s there were such active traplines all over the Black River country, far beyond areas that are ever seen by the Chalkyitsik people today.

In the late 1940s about a quarter of the Fort Yukon region (including the Black River) was unclaimed and some 15 percent comprised inactive traplines (Shimkin 1955, p. 314). Today the amount of unused territory is far greater than it was twenty years ago. The country is definitely exploited far below its capacity because there are relatively few trappers, many of whom make only a desultory trapping effort. The few lines which are consistently subject to heavy exploitation are probably restocked from the surrounding regions. The only area trapped to the point where fur is always hard to find is that immediately surrounding the village.

Three distinct types of traplines are used by the modern Chalkyitsik Indians:

1. *Village Lines.* These are short traplines, only a few miles in length, which are usually checked on foot from Chalkyitsik. Old

men who are no longer able to make extended trips frequently set out these short lines.

2. *Single Circuit.* This is a common modern trapline which is run with a dog team or snowmobile. It is in the form of a long circuit which starts and ends at the village, generally without side lines or with very short ones. This type of line may be very long, up to 100 miles if a snowmobile is used, so that one or two cabin stops are required along the way. Often, however, it is short enough to be run in a single day.

3. *Circuit–Side Line Complex.* This is the largest type of modern trapline, requiring the most time to run and closely reflecting the traditional pattern. It usually consists of a main trail which leads to the principal trapline cabin, then a long circuit trail that runs out from the cabin and returns to it, and one or more side lines that branch out either from the circuit or from the cabin itself. Generally there are cabins along the circuit, which takes from one to four days to run. Traps are set along the main trail (where anybody can set), the circuit trail, and the side lines. Side lines, incidentally, are usually a single "straight" trail run both ways rather than a circuit. Some trappers use a snowmobile for their level trails and a dog team for circuits or side lines in hilly country.

A single person may operate more than one trapline during a given season. For example, one man had four widely separated lines in 1969–70. In all, sixteen traplines were operated by Chalkyitsik Kutchin during the winter of 1969–70. Of these three were local village lines, seven were single circuits requiring one or two days to run, and six were the large circuit–side line complexes. These sixteen lines were owned by twelve different persons but were trapped by a total of nineteen men, because a number of partnerships were formed between trapline owners and nonowners.

It is difficult to delineate the total area exploited by Chalkyitsik trappers because the number and size of lines which are used vary tremendously from year to year. The major trapping areas extend east into the Black River and Salmon River country, south along the Grass, Sucker, and Little Black rivers, west along the Black and Porcupine rivers, and north and east in the Porcupine River country.

There is a tendency for the various traplines to be somewhat specialized for particular fur species. Men who trap in hilly country make good catches of marten, wolf, and wolverine, for example, whereas the flats are best for lynx, mink, muskrat, and beaver. A man whose trapline encompasses a variety of habitats may decide to specialize in certain species. If lynx prices are high, he might concentrate his effort in the flats and stay out of the hilly marten country. Each trapline has a number of trails which are intended specifically for the exploitation of particular species, such as a "mink line," "marten line," and so on.

Trappers follow a wide variety of setting and checking routines, depending on the length of their lines, distance from the village, means of transportation (dog team or snowmobile), weather conditions, and desire to return home. Most men stay out only one to three days, but a few will remain away for a week to ten days. Regardless of how long they are on the trapline, all the men agree that they like to return to the comforts of home as quickly as possible. The Kutchin carry out all trapping and hunting activities at what seems to be a very fast pace, and feel that a good outdoorsman is always one who can work rapidly. In trapping, the more sets a man can make in a day, the more efficient he will be at catching animals. Occasionally, haste is carried to such an extreme that it results in carelessness.

The first trip to the line, when sets are made, usually takes about twice as long as the later visits to check them. Traps should be checked every four to ten days, and a good trapper tries not to leave them any longer. On each trip he checks all of his lines once, removing game and resetting the traps, then returns home to "let them work again." If lines are checked too frequently not enough fur will be taken to make the effort worth while. The longer he waits, the more fur the trapper will find in his sets. But if he waits too long he will lose some of his catch, and the traps with game in them will not be available for other animals that come along.

Trappers are attentive to other factors in scheduling their runs, particularly the weather. When it is relatively warm they expect good catches because the animals are moving around. But during cold snaps, when the temperature falls to $-30°$ to $-50°$, the animals are not moving enough to make for good trapping. When a man sees an abundance of fresh fur sign as he checks his traps he will

probably wait only a short time before returning, because he is
sure there will be animals in his sets within a few days, and he
wants to retrieve them quickly.

Cabins and Shelters

Adequate shelter is essential for trapping and other cold-season
activities. Whenever he travels far from the village, the Indian must
keep in mind the availability of shelter, especially when he uses
a snowmobile, which can break down and strand him far from home.
Thus he should know the location of every cabin in the area he
travels, and he must be able to construct an adequate shelter on
the spot should these cabins be out of reach.

Temporary Camps

The Chalkyitsik Kutchin much prefer to use a cabin or tent during
the cold season, but are occasionally forced to camp without shelter
because of an emergency or because they have decided to save
weight by leaving their tent behind. Men who drive snowmobiles
usually carry a sleeping bag and some food on any long trip in
case of emergency, but they camp out much less frequently than
in the days when they relied exclusively on dogs. As long as the
machine is running they can travel a considerable distance to reach
a cabin.

An open-air camp is made by scraping away the snow to create
a space large enough for a sleeping bag. Then a windbreak of spruce
boughs or young spruce is made around three sides of the sleeping
place. If there is any wind, the open side is to leeward. A fire
is built on the open side, on cleared ground, parallel to the man's
sleeping position. He piles heavy logs, such as slow-burning poplar,
on the fire before retiring, and rekindles the blaze as frequently
as is necessary to keep warm. If it is especially cold another spruce
wall is built behind the fire to keep the heat inside the enclosure.
When it is snowing, a slanting frame may be erected and a piece
of canvas placed over the top. Under his sleeping place the Indian
puts a thick layer of dried grass (if available) with a good bed of
spruce bough tips on top.

The old-timers always carried a caribou hide to use as a mattress on top of their layers of bedding. Today caribou skin is hard to get, and so the Kutchin substitute a piece of canvas or cloth. Before the white man came the Kutchin used sleeping robes, heavy blankets made from caribou, hare, or muskrat skins, but the modern Kutchin prefer commercially made sleeping bags. Two down-filled bags are often used, one inside the other, for maximum warmth. But when it is 30° to 50° below zero a good fire burning nearby is essential for comfort. One trick a winter traveler might use in extremely cold weather is to camp on high ground. The Chalkyitsik people never mentioned this as a specific technique, but they are well aware that during cold snaps the temperature on a hill may be ten to twenty degrees warmer than that in a low valley.

The modern Chalkyitsik Kutchin prefer wall tents for temporary winter camps; they use small (about 7 × 7 feet) commercially made canvas types. Using one of his snowshoes for a shovel, the Indian clears the ground of snow where he is going to erect his tent. Later on, this cleared space is covered by a layer of spruce boughs, which will help to insulate the sleeping area. The walls of the tent have flaps that are held down by piling snow on them around the outside, since tent stakes cannot be used in frozen ground. In the not-too-distant past the Black River people lived in large wall tents for much of the year, even through the cold winter months. These tents were usually surrounded by a low wall of logs to make them more weatherproof. Tents such as these, and their smaller counterparts, are held up by a pair of crossed poles at each end of the ridge. Any tent can be heated with a small wood-burning stove, even in extremely cold weather, but as soon as the fire dies away the cold penetrates.

The Tranjik Kutchin and other northern Athapaskans live in powder-snow country and therefore cannot make snow-block houses like the famous Eskimo igloo. But they used, in former times at least, a kind of snow shelter that was ingenious in its own right. The older adults living at Chalkyitsik have seen these snow houses and presumably could make them if a situation called for it, but it is doubtful that snow shelters have been made here in recent times.

To make one of these shelters the Indian first uses a snowshoe "shovel" to pile up a large heap of snow. Whenever snow is disturbed, especially in cold temperatures, it hardens quickly. Thus within thirty minutes to an hour the snow pile is hard enough so that it can be hollowed out inside. After the space inside is made large enough, a fire is built on the floor, and when the walls begin to melt the fire is extinguished so that the surface of the walls freezes to a hard glaze. A small ventilation hole is made somewhere in the roof, and the house is ready for use.

The Indian then spreads out his sleeping bag and closes the door by hanging his parka from wooden pegs stuck in the wall. One man who had used these shelters said they were so effective that when he was inside he was unable to hear the wind blowing. Snow houses like this can presumably be made large enough for several people, as their dimensions are limited only by the size of the snow pile.

Log Houses

The traditional Kutchin used a variety of shelters. Some of these were built of logs and poles and were a kind of native precursor to the log cabins introduced after contact with white men. Single and double lean-tos have been described for the Kutchin, as well as semipermanent rectangular log houses (see Osgood 1936*b*, pp. 53–54; McKennan 1965, p. 43).

Every house in Chalkyitsik today, and every dwelling in the surrounding country, is a log cabin. The Tranjik Kutchin are expert in the construction of cabins, from the tiny one-room line cabin to the large multiroom village home. These cabins are essentially identical to log houses that can be found almost anywhere in North America, except that most of them have dirt-covered roofs. There is considerable variation in the size and elaborateness of Kutchin cabins. Some of the village houses have two or three separate rooms, measure up to 40 feet long, and are fairly well furnished. Other village homes are smaller, sparsely furnished one-room affairs, measuring only 15 to 25 feet square.

Trapline cabins vary even more. There are large cabins which housed families during the heyday of trapping and are now used as main trapline cabins by men who still operate the old lines. The

Trappers with their snowmobiles, gathered at a small line cabin.

"out-cabins," those scattered along various traplines and built for stopover shelter, tend to be rather small and simple in construction. Some measure a scant 10 feet square, and are just high enough to stand up inside. Some are fairly new and in good repair, but more often they are very old and in sad condition.

Obviously, the comfort and convenience of trapline cabins varies tremendously. The main cabins are often well built and almost as well furnished as the village homes. They may contain crude wooden beds and a variety of cooking utensils, tools, and miscellaneous items. Some cabins are practically bare, however, containing almost nothing beyond a stove and a couple of boxes to sit on. At home or in the line cabin, the Kutchin like to be comfortably warm. Houses are rarely cold and only occasionally become too hot. A temperature of 70° to 85° is preferred. Trapline cabins vary greatly in warmth depending on their condition, out-cabins tending to have many cracks and openings which admit cold. Getting up on a frigid morning in one of these little houses is quite an experience.

Trapping Productivity

The Black River Kutchin have always been unusually successful trappers. Their country is extremely rich in fur animals, and the people have traditionally put a major effort into trapping. But even under the best conditions trapping is an unstable way to make a living. The number of furbearers varies considerably, and fur prices are notoriously unstable; so a trapper never knows from one year to the next if his efforts will pay off.

Like most other animals in the boreal forest environment, furbearers are subject to marked changes in population, which may be long-term and widespread or highly localized and ephemeral. If there is anything a trapper cannot bet on, it is the size of his catch. He never knows from one year to the next, or from one day to the next, if he will strike it rich or come home empty-handed. Any trapline is capable of outstanding productivity or nearly complete failure, and the same line may be a great producer one month and a total disappointment the next. Small wonder the Kutchin stress the importance of luck in determining a trapper's success.

The prices paid for furs are also subject to marked, if less precipitous, fluctuations. Increases or decreases in the value of fur usually occur over a period of years, and so a trapper has some idea about the way prices are likely to go before the season begins, on the basis of trends in recent years. Dramatic price declines have been known to occur, however.

There have been a number of peaks and lows in fur prices over the past century. In the early days a pelt was worth very little by modern standards. At Fort Resolution in 1864, for example, a red fox, marten, wolf, or beaver would bring fifty cents. Mink were worth a dollar, wolverine a dollar and a half, and muskrat only eighteen cents (Morice, n.d., p. 231). Fur prices increased greatly around World War I, fell off in 1922, recovered until 1929, and then declined. The 1920s were the real heyday for trapping. Beaver and lynx brought Black River trappers up to one hundred dollars apiece; fox and marten were worth about fifty dollars. During this period the Tranjik Kutchin earned more than ever before or since, and some became quite wealthy.

During the depression of the 1930s prices declined, but they experienced another boom during World War II, then dropped again in the 1950s. In recent years fur has slowly increased in value until the Chalkyitsik Kutchin feel that trapping is once again paying off. During the period of this study, trappers were getting from ten to twenty-five dollars for marten, ten to thirty dollars for mink, twenty to sixty dollars for lynx, fifteen to thirty-five dollars for beaver, ten to twenty-five dollars for fox, and about one dollar for muskrat. There was no evidence at this time that fur prices were being influenced by the "ecology movement" and its associated opposition to trapping and the use of animal pelts.

The following statistics on trapline earnings for 1969–70 are estimates based on trappers' statements about catches, prices paid for these catches, and estimates of total fur take multiplied by average prices paid at the time. The highest earnings, by a man who remained out on the trapline for much of the winter, ran to about three thousand dollars. Another man, who shared some of his take with partners, probably brought in between fifteen hundred and two thousand dollars worth of pelts. A man who trapped mostly alone earned about one thousand dollars, and two others who ran their lines together grossed around six hundred dollars apiece. There were probably several more trappers who made around five hundred dollars, then a group below them who made anywhere from five hundred down to twenty-five or fifty dollars.

It is extremely difficult to estimate the net income of Chalkyitsik trappers. A large cash outlay is necessary for trapping, but the equipment serves many other purposes and is usually paid for with wage labor or welfare money. Trapping is an important assist toward meeting winter living expenses, replacing old equipment, and purchasing some luxury goods. The active trappers are, in short, making enough money to pay their expenses and earn something besides. Trapping is a winter job for them in a place where other wage-earning employment is nearly impossible to come by.

Modern trapping incomes are only a fraction of what has been earned in the past. To some extent this results from changes in fur prices. More important, however, the effort put into trapping was far greater years ago than it is today. If there had been any trapping operations in this region during 1969–70 that equaled the effort expended by trappers thirty years ago, they might well have earned somewhere between five thousand and eight thousand dollars.

An old man who was formerly one of the best trappers in the whole region trading into Fort Yukon quoted his best catches for several fur species. In different years he had taken 180 lynx, 175 mink, 120 marten, 315 fox, and 2,200 muskrats. This one man caught as many of each species as some entire villages in other regions are able to produce. In his best year of trapping he made fifteen thousand dollars. This was probably around World War I, when fur prices were very high. And he was not the only man who made this much money at some time in his career.

Other old men, less exceptional in their abilities, quote their top earnings in the seven thousand to ten thousand dollar range. Younger men achieved their highest incomes during the 1940s, when a good trapper made about five thousand dollars, perhaps up to seven thousand dollars in some cases. Needless to say, it has not always been so good, but I have no data which could be used to figure average annual incomes for Chalkyitsik trappers.

Comparative statistics on fur takes and trapping incomes from other regions clearly indicate that the Tranjik Kutchin exploit an extremely rich area. In the Huslia-Hughes region of the Koyukuk River, the older men quote their maximum trapping incomes as around three thousand dollars. The best old trapper in Huslia once made something around four thousand dollars. In 1943, when fur prices were relatively high, trappers at Fort Nelson, British Columbia, earned three thousand to four thousand dollars. At Nelson Forks, not far away, earnings were fifteen hundred to three thousand dollars in the same year (Honigmann 1946, p. 103).

These statistics are scattered, but they indicate that the Tranjik Kutchin have been productive trappers in the past. The Black River and Porcupine River country is ideal habitat for furbearers because it is diversified. There are extensive marshy flats with a multitude of lakes and sloughs, excellent for muskrat, beaver, and mink. The neighboring hills are fine marten country, with fair numbers of wolves and wolverines. When snowshoe hares are common, lynx are found everywhere. Fox are also abundant at times, especially along the river courses. The country has a wide variety of habitats and perhaps this has something to do with its wealth in furs.

Beyond this, the success of the Tranjik Kutchin must relate to an attitude toward trapping as a way of life. The old-timers speak of trapping as if it were their highest aim in life, their greatest interest and concern. These older Kutchin consider themselves trappers first and foremost. Because of this attitude toward trapping, the Kutchin perhaps worked at it more ambitiously than some other northern Athapaskan peoples. Thus the rich land was vigorously exploited, with high trapping yields as the result.

11 Winter Travel: The Logistics of Trapping

Introduction

Techniques of winter travel are of particular interest today, because in the past few years efficient mechanized snow vehicles have been introduced in the North and have quite suddenly replaced dog teams as a major form of transportation. This chapter begins with a description of dog teams and their use, followed by a comparison of dog team and snowmobile performance. But there is much more to getting around in this environment than knowing how to drive a dog team or snow machine. The traveler must also know how to find his way unerringly, cope with a wide variety of snow and ice conditions, and be able to predict the weather and adjust to its changes.

Knowing how to get around efficiently and successfully in the winter subarctic environment is not just a matter of convenience; it is a matter of life and death. An incorrect decision on the river ice, for example, can send a man suddenly and precipitously to his death. Travel expertise is therefore no less essential to the Kutchin than skill in hunting and trapping.

Dog Teams

The Indian Dog

The Kutchin used dogs long before white men arrived in their country, but not for pulling sleds or toboggans. Their dogs were used primarily in hunting until they were put in harness following the example of European fur traders. It is not surprising, therefore, that the Indian dog is not generally considered as good a draught animal as the famous Eskimo "husky." True Indian dogs are seldom discussed in the literature and when they are mentioned it is usually in an uncomplimentary fashion.

Jones (1866, p. 324) describes dogs of the Yukon Flats Kutchin as "miserable creatures, no larger than foxes." The aboriginal breed was undoubtedly improved by intermixture with dogs brought from other areas, particularly those of Eskimo origin. According to Mason (1924, pp. 52–53), the Kutchin dogs are

a mixture of every known breed in existence, with husky predominating. They vary greatly in appearance, but as a rule they are larger in the leg than the huskies, not quite so well furred, and a good deal lighter in build. . . . [The Indians] generally do not treat their dogs as well as do the Esquimaux. . . . All summer long the starving brutes scavenge round the trading posts, their release from that only coming with winter, which brings them hard work, frequent beatings, and a very insufficient ration of food.

Today, the Tranjik Kutchin dogs are extremely heterogeneous and are subject to varying amounts of care. They come in a great variety of sizes, colors, and shapes, but a few generalizations can be made about them. They look basically like "huskies," in the sense that most have pricked-up ears and carry their tails curled and high, and they often have huskylike facial markings. Their build is relatively small and slight for pulling; they average perhaps fifty to sixty pounds, with a range of forty to eighty pounds. They are long-legged and narrow in the chest, and they seem to be swift rather than strong. Compared with Eskimo sled dogs, they are rather small and motley-looking animals.

The Kutchin make no apparent effort to improve their dogs by selective breeding. There is some selectivity in the killing of dogs, but this is by no means always true. Puppies are kept alive if there is food for them and killed if there is not. A dog will be killed if it has obvious detrimental qualities such as physical deformity or if it refuses to pull, but many disadvantageous characteristics such as small size, weakness, extreme aggression, or great fear of humans are not culled out.

Housing and Care

The Chalkyitsik Kutchin prefer to keep their dogs tied in a brushy place, well protected from the wind and out of the way. If there is no brush near a man's cabin he usually makes windbreaks or small houses for them, because when dogs are kept out in the open where cold and wind strike them directly they require more food to maintain body heat. During the winter the Kutchin provide a thick bed of grass for each dog to lie on. Every effort is made to keep the animals tied, but there usually seems to be a loose dog somewhere in the village, scavenging for food and raising a commotion among the other dogs. If a particular dog is loose much of the time, both the animal and its owner are likely to find considerable hostility directed toward them.

Feeding is the most important aspect of dog care, because a dog's condition is directly contingent on what it is fed, how much, and how often. During the summer dogs are usually fed every other day, but once cool fall weather arrives they are fed daily. This is done both to maintain them in the colder temperatures and to fatten them for winter. Both Eskimo and Indian dogs seem to have low food requirements, especially when they get no exercise and are sheltered.

The most popular dog food at Chalkyitsik is a boiled mixture of commercial dry dog food or cornmeal, plus fish or meat and any fat that is available. The food is prepared in a large metal pot over an open fire. Of course, meat or fish can be fed straight, but the Kutchin usually do not have enough to use without the addition of commercial mixtures. One-half a salmon each day, for example, is enough food for a dog. One hare per day is ample during fall and spring, but in cold weather two or three are needed for each dog. Beaver and muskrat are considered particularly good dog foods, but other fur animals are less highly regarded.

The Kutchin often find themselves with dogs that they do not want, and they feel no hesitation about killing such animals. The idea of using the meat or skin, however, is utterly repugnant to them. When the people run short of feed and their dogs start losing weight, they may shoot their oldest or least valuable animals. This is especially true today, when snowmobiles are replacing dogs and people feel little need to keep their teams. The Indians may be quite spontaneous in their decision to kill an animal, as, for example, the man who shot a dog because it was not pulling well when he set out for his trapline.

Most of the dogs that live to adulthood are killed before they grow old. Pulling dogs in Chalkyitsik are surprisingly young, averaging two to five years, with few over seven years old. This is a much younger average than the Eskimo dogs at Wainwright, Alaska, for example. The Kutchin seem to feel that by the fifth to seventh year dogs are past their prime, at least in terms of speed. Old dogs are noted for strength and stamina, but the people apparently value speed above those qualities.

Uses and Training

Before the white man entered Kutchin country the people kept a few dogs to run down game animals and hold them at bay until the hunters arrived on the scene. They may also have been used for packing during aboriginal times, but if they were as small as the early writers imply it is difficult to imagine their being able to carry much of a load. Most likely, dog packing came after early contact, when the Kutchin had larger breeds of dogs. It apparently became a common practice for summer travel, and it still continues on a limited scale. Old-timers occasionally use pack dogs when they hunt on foot near the village.

The aboriginal Kutchin used hand-pulled sleds, which were about 8 to 10 feet long and upturned at both ends. The oldest of the Black River people have never seen these sleds, but know of them from stories told by persons long dead. The double-ended sled was a very simple type which does not appear very well adapted to this environment. It is small wonder that it disappeared rapidly after the introduction of toboggans, brought in by the Hudson's Bay Company men.

The modern toboggan, described later in this chapter, is ideal for these interior forests. It rides on top of the deep, fluffy snow, so that a minimum of effort is required to pull it, and it is provided with tough mooseskin sides which permit easy accommodation of large loads. Upstanders at the rear make it easy to guide, and a standing place behind them allows a man to step on and off when he alternately rides and runs.

Modern dog teams usually pull toboggans, but for certain purposes a hardwood sled is used. The old Yukon sled, introduced here before the turn of the century, has been replaced by a lighter, more fragile type. Sleds are handy on the shallow snow of fall and spring, and their lightness makes them ideal for racing on a hard-packed trail. There are now few sleds in Chalkyitsik except those used for racing.

Until the last few years every active adult male in Chalkyitsik owned a dog team. Since this was the only means of winter transportation, the team was put to a wide variety of uses. Most important of these were winter and early spring hunting, travel associated with trapping, transportation between settlements, hauling firewood, and racing. Since the advent of the snowmobile some men have given up dogs entirely, and others use them only for recreation and racing; but a number of Indians who do not own a machine still use dogs for all purposes. Those without snowmobiles, however, often travel with snowmobile owners, leaving their dogs behind.

Some men who own snowmobiles still maintain dog teams for a number of reasons: Certain people keep them solely for racing; a few take both dogs and snowmobiles out on the trapline, using the dogs for marten trapping in the hills; and others keep a number of dogs around just in case their machine breaks down and they cannot afford a new one. Alaskan natives are not yet prepared to take snowmobiles for granted. "How do we know, maybe next year or two years from now no more jobs, no more gasoline, or maybe they stop making those machines. Better keep a couple dogs around anyway."

Most Kutchin do not train their dogs particularly well, at least by comparison with the North Alaskan Eskimos. This condition may be somewhat exaggerated today, as dogs are used less frequently and the best dog mushers have given them up in favor of machines. Even in the finest racing teams, however, the dogs are reluctant to obey commands. Lead dogs often refuse to respond to their driver, forcing him to shout and crack the whip for several minutes before they turn in the proper direction. If the team is small or the load heavy enough so that he can run faster than the dogs, the driver may occasionally lead them himself, or at least run up and drag the leader in the right direction. Poorly trained leaders are less detrimental here than in Eskimo country, because in the soft snow of the forest dog teams nearly always follow preexisting trails. On the tundra and sea ice where there often are no trails, Eskimo lead dogs must be very responsive to their masters' commands in order to maintain proper direction. This may help to explain why Eskimo dogs are better trained; but in general, Eskimo drivers are much more exacting and demanding with their animals, and their teams seem generally better disciplined than those of the Indians. It is interesting in this regard to note the following comment regarding another Athapaskan group, the Kaska:

> The Indians attempt to teach dogs to obey a few simple commands, but confess their lack of success in this effort. Old Man admitted that white men trained dogs far more successfully. [Honigmann 1949, p. 273]

Size of Dog Teams

The number of dogs maintained and used by the Black River Kutchin has changed considerably since the end of the past century. The oldest people say that in their youth the Indians had very few dogs; a man might own up to three dogs and some men had none at all. When times got hard the dogs would starve to death, and then it was difficult for people to get dogs again. It seems, therefore, that limitations in the supply of dog food were the primary factor determining the number of dogs owned (cf. Osgood 1936*b*, p. 64).

As time passed the economic situation changed. Imported technology (such as firearms, nylon fishnets, and fish wheels) increased the Indians' exploitative efficiency, while purchased foods released more native produce for use by the dogs, and the number of dogs increased. People began using teams of four or five animals; and then in the heyday of trapping they used teams of up to seven. One man reported having two teams of seven each, which he would rotate for his two traplines, running a four-day line with one team, then taking a fresh team for the second circuit.

The Tranjik Kutchin agree that within the past thirty years 7 dogs has been considered a large team. In 1940 the average number of work dogs per household at Fort Yukon was 4.9, but a rabies epidemic reduced that figure to 2.2 in 1948–49. These statistics may be somewhat deceptive because they do not indicate the average number of dogs per team. In Chalkyitsik there were 5.5 dogs per household in 1970, but this figure includes a number of households which owned too few dogs for a team. The average number of dogs per team was about 7.3, probably a higher figure than at any period before the past decade.

Dog teams in Chalkyitsik today run from 4 to 12 dogs, though some men have seen larger teams. Men who have put up to 15 or 16 dogs in one team feel that this is much too difficult to handle on the twisting trails which characterize this country. When the dogs have to be hitched singly (rather than in pairs as is done in open country), the string of dogs becomes too long for the crooked trails.

There are 140 to 150 dogs in Chalkyitsik, about 120 of which are adult working animals. Many of these dogs, however, are in a sort of "retirement," either because their owners rarely go out hunting, trapping, or hauling wood, or because they have been replaced by snowmobiles. Thus the large number of dogs, which exceeds the number of people by about 50, does not reflect the degree of dependence on dog teams here. In 1969–70 there were four men who depended entirely on dogs for transportation; four others depended on them in part but also used snowmobiles; and five men owned teams but seldom used them.

The greatest dog mushing activity takes place around spring racing time, for a period of two or three weeks. During this period men, women, and children drive and train dogs, their prime motives being the money and prestige that can be had if they finish well in the competition. But except for this brief flurry, the dog team is in its death throes here. Once a man owns a snowmobile he seldom bothers with dogs, except for a token effort to shape them up for races. After a year or two with a machine, men tend to decrease the number of dogs they keep, eventually getting rid of all but one or two. Despite this trend, dog teams are utilized more in Chalkyitsik than in most interior Alaskan villages.

The Snowmobile

Enter the Iron Dog

Snowmobiles have taken hold in Alaska over the past eight or ten years, beginning with the cities and larger settlements and filtering into the smaller, more isolated villages. In the last five years there has been a tremendous acceptance of these machines throughout the state, and a corresponding precipitous decline in the importance of dog teams. This minor technological revolution has now reached into all of the native villages, regardless of how isolated they are.

In Huslia, for example, some families own two or three snowmobiles, and the use of dog teams is almost nonexistent. The process is less advanced in Chalkyitsik because snow vehicles first arrived here only three years ago and the people still own relatively few of them. In 1968 there were three or four; this figure increased to six in the fall of 1969 and to ten by the following spring. Thus about half of the active adult males owned snowmobiles by the spring of 1970. The Chalkyitsik people have developed a very heavy dependence on mechanized travel in this short span of years. Owners largely shun the use of dog teams, and nonowners often arrange partnerships with owners so they too can leave their dogs at home. Nearly all men who do not have machines express strong desires, or definite plans, to obtain them; and there are no dissatisfied owners.

Snowmobiles are used primarily for transportation in hunting and trapping and for hauling wood and water. In addition to these basic uses, they serve a multitude of lesser functions. They are used for visiting neighbors, for hauling junk to the dumping place, for endless joyriding, for carrying children to school, for going to meet the airplane, for racing, and for travel between villages.

A toboggan is pulled behind the snowmobile for hunting and trapping. It is built on the same design as that used with dogs, but is somewhat larger. The Kutchin usually make their toboggans of locally obtained birch but occasionally use hickory or oak shipped in from Outside. Snowmobile toboggans are 10 to 14 feet long and 20 to 24 inches wide, whereas those pulled by dog teams are 8 to 10 feet long and 16 to 18 inches wide. They are sharply upturned in front and have wooden handlebars about 3 feet high near the back. Toboggans are always provided with sides about a foot high, made from heavy moosehide stretched between the front end and the handlebars. The sides keep the load in and the snow out, and they must be very tough to withstand the beating they take. A tow rope 6 to 12 inches long connects the toboggan to the snowmobile.

Snowmobiles and Dog Teams: A Comparison

Everyone who has had experience with both dogs and machines indulges in comparing their merits and performance, and speculates on their economic and social impact. Many of the Kutchin feel that machines are the best thing that has ever happened here; but as much as some people swear by them, others curse their very existence. What follows is a comparative summary of dog teams and snowmobiles, with a few notes regarding the impact of this technological change on Kutchin life.

1. *Speed.* One of the most important advantages snowmobiles have over dog teams is their speed. They are considerably faster than dogs, with less variation in speed owing to snow conditions or size of load. The Kutchin point out that a good dog team can often travel along the rough and winding bush trails at a better pace than a snowmobile; but on open meadows, lakes, and rivers machines are much faster. They can be slowed considerably by deep snow, very large loads, and rough terrain, but only in the last case will their speed fall below that of a dog team.

A good day's trip by dog team, setting traps or hunting along the way, is 25 to 35 miles. A man I traveled with sometimes ran his entire trapline with a snowmobile, well over 100 miles of winding trails, in a single twelve-hour day. The implications of this greater speed are clear. The hunters and trappers spend far less time covering the same territory, which frees them for other activities or for relaxing at home. Men are less reluctant to undertake a hunting trip which they might otherwise decide against and therefore tend to be more productive.

2. *Power.* It should be evident from the comments above that snow vehicles are more powerful than dog teams. They can haul much heavier loads, at greater speeds, and they do not tire. I have seen a snowmobile hauling an entire moose through 18 inches of unbroken snow at speeds faster than a man could run. Dogs could

hardly pull an empty toboggan through such snow without a man's walking ahead on snowshoes to break a trail. Dogs are unquestionably superior, however, for travel in hilly terrain. Snowmobiles do not have a good traction on slopes of any kind, especially when they are pulling a load.

3. *Reliability.* Reliability is a great point of superiority for dog teams—they do not break down or run out of fuel. When a man hitches up his dogs he knows he is certain to reach his destination. It may take time, but he will get there. There is no such guarantee with a machine, which may or may not start, and may or may not keep running until it arrives. All factors considered, snowmobiles are fairly dependable, but in this country anything less than 100 percent reliability is dangerous. Men from Chalkyitsik have been forced to walk 20 miles or more in temperatures as low as −65° when their machines ran out of gas or suffered a breakdown which they could not repair on the spot.

Snowmobiles often will not start when it is colder than 30° below zero, unless they are warmed up inside a heated shelter. And once a machine has been running it is best to start the engine every hour when not in actual use to keep it warm. A man out on the trail must keep this clearly in mind, lest he find himself stranded somewhere with a frozen machine. Dogs may not like to pull in this kind of weather, but they will always do it when called upon.

4. *Comfort.* Dog teams may take longer to reach their destination, but the rider is likely to be far more comfortable on the way. Snowmobilers often become exhausted and sweaty, even at −30°, from the exertion of steering and hanging on as they travel rapidly through winding trails. But on the open meadows and frozen lakes little effort is required to hang on, and the rush of supercooled air chills exposed flesh and sends cold through the heaviest clothing. When the temperature is low there is a very real danger of frostbite for snowmobile riders. When a dog musher gets cold he can easily step off and run behind the toboggan to warm himself, but at snowmobile speeds this is impossible. Snowmobile travel is also incredibly uncomfortable because of constant jarring and bumping caused by rough, winding trails or by hard drifts in open areas.

5. *Danger.* There is no question that it is much safer to travel by dog team than by snowmobile. Besides the danger of a breakdown and subsequent exposure, which a dog musher does not face,

there is the more serious risk of colliding with a tree or upsetting on a curve or bank. If a man is hurt and his machine no longer works, he may freeze to death before help arrives. Chalkyitsik men usually travel with a partner, which is a distinct safety factor. A single traveler usually tells someone when he should return, and if he is not back by that time the people will go searching for him.

Snowmobiles are also more dangerous than dog teams for travel on lake and river ice. Sometimes water flows out over the ice surface and remains unfrozen beneath the insulative snow. If a snowmobile runs into an overflow in very cold weather it will freeze in almost immediately, stranding the driver, who must walk through water to get away from it. Dog teams will not freeze into an overflow, and in fact they will usually turn away or stop as soon as they feel moisture under their feet. Perhaps more important, dog teams are much less likely to break through thin ice, because they are lighter and spread out over a larger area. The weight of a snowmobile is concentrated in one small area, and if it breaks through thin ice it will sink to the bottom immediately. Since the driver sits on top of the machine, he stands a good chance of going down with it.

One final note on safety. A man in dire circumstances can always eat his dogs; but a man with a snowmobile lacks this option.

6. *Convenience.* Snowmobiles are much handier than dog teams for short trips; they require no harnessing and unharnessing; they do not have to be tied when a man walks away from them to cut wood, hunt, or set traps; they will never run away or fight. A major inconvenience of dogs is that they require regular feeding, a particular bother during the summer when dogs are of no use and their owner may wish to leave the village for wage labor. The Kutchin cite this problem as a major factor in their preference for machines.

The use of dog teams is also affected by light conditions. Snowmobiles can travel day or night, moonlight or pitch darkness because they are provided with a bright headlight, a great advantage during the short days of winter. Dog mushers, on the other hand, rarely travel at night and must plan to reach a cabin by evening. They could travel by moonlight if necessary, but they are strongly averse to doing so.

7. *Economic Factors.* The relative cost of snowmobiles and dog teams is of more concern to the Outsider than to the Kutchin. The

machines cost villagers nine hundred to twelve hundred dollars or more, plus four hundred to six hundred dollars per year for fuel and maintenance. They depreciate rapidly because of very hard use, and so the Kutchin usually replace their vehicles after only one or two years. This means the cost of a new machine must be added about every two years, less trade-in or sale price for the old one. As a rough estimate, snowmobile owners average about a thousand dollars a year in total operating costs (G. R. Bane, personal communication).

The cost of dogs is usually nothing, since they reproduce themselves; but if purchased they cost ten to twenty-five dollars in Chalkyitsik. Their working life averages three to seven years. Food is by far the greatest expense for a dog team, but it is highly variable. This cost can range from nothing, if fish and game are used exclusively, up to five or six hundred dollars a year on a diet of strictly commercial food. Since the Indians always use some local fish and meat, they probably spend no more than three hundred dollars a year on dog food. Some spend considerably less, some might pay more, depending on their success in hunting and fishing.

Obviously, then, dogs are far cheaper than snowmobiles. But they have a lower "earning power" as well, because they reduce a hunter-trapper's mobility. There is no way to put figures on the difference, but it is worth noting that two of the most successful trappers in Chalkyitsik relied exclusively on dogs, and two others used both dogs and machines. A man can certainly hunt and trap successfully with dogs, but he must spend far more time at it than the snowmobile owner.

8. *Summary.* All the economic considerations outlined above should be viewed only as a backdrop which is not particularly relevant in the minds of the Chalkyitsik Kutchin. To them it is the noneconomic factors that are significant. Most important, machines are considerably faster and more powerful than dogs, and this is the major reason no man prefers dogs today.

The acceptance of snowmobiles puts a considerable financial burden on the Indians, who must find means of purchasing new machines and paying the operating costs. This pressures them to find employment for a part of the year and increases their desire for unearned welfare income. It may also stimulate the Kutchin to put more effort into trapping to help finance their vehicles.

Snowmobiles have greatly increased the Indian's mobility, enabling him to maintain or even expand his exploitative range while spending less time away from the settlement. This stabilizes or reverses a strong trend toward diminution of the territory utilized by villagers in many parts of Alaska, including Chalkyitsik. When snowmobiles replace dogs the Indians are also freed from having to catch the fish or other game required to maintain a team. This change has its social repercussions.

Formerly the men did little fishing for dog food, leaving this job to the women and children. Men often left the village during the summer to hunt, and they do so today to find wage labor. The rest of the family is (and was) left in the fish camp or settlement to put up a winter's supply of dried fish and small game. Today fishing has become far less important because there are so few dogs, and the women and children no longer need to make this economic contribution (G. R. Bane, personal communication).

Pathfinding

Trails and Trail Marks

The country exploited by the Tranjik Kutchin is mostly covered with thick brush and forest so that trails must be cut and maintained, in contrast to the Koyukuk River region where the undergrowth is so sparse that maintained trails are unnecessary.

The Chalkyitsik Kutchin have an elaborate network of foot and sled trails interlacing the region they exploit. The foot trails, used primarily for summer travel and for local trapping on snowshoes in winter, are narrow paths that wind almost invisibly through the brush, circumnavigating lakes and sloughs and following the banks of rivers. These trails were once very important when foot travel and dog packing were common during the summer, but today most foot trails are grown over with brush and their routes are remembered only by the old men.

Sled trails are intended primarily for dog team and snowmobile travel in winter, but those around the village are also used a great deal for summer foot travel. These trails are always several feet wide and are kept well cleared of brushy overgrowth and deadfalls. They tend to be more direct than summer trails, crossing over lakes, sloughs, rivers, and wet meadows, but they are by no means straight. Trail makers minimize their labor by winding around thick brush and trees instead of cutting their way through, and they angle their trails off a direct line of travel to cross as many frozen bodies of water and open areas as possible.

Cutting a trail through brushy country can be a major undertaking. This is why good trails are one of the most valuable assets of a trapline, and existing trails are maintained for generations. If a man wants to trap in an area that has been unused for many years, he will try to find an old trail that he can reopen instead of cutting a new one.

Trails are often very easy to follow because they are clearly defined corridors through dense vegetation. In some areas, however, it is hard to find a trail in untracked snow without some kind of markers. In open spruce forests, for example, the trees are blazed at frequent intervals by chopping a narrow strip of bark from a tree trunk, leaving a white mark which is easily seen. Markers are very important at places where a trail opens onto a river, lake, slough, or meadow, where travelers may have difficulty finding the trail's opening when they reach the other side. Large blazes are used here if there are big trees at the trail's edge, but the margins of lakes and meadows are often fringed with scrub, so instead of making blazes the Indians often hang something like a tin can or shred of cloth in the brush.

In open places, such as large meadows or lakes, the Kutchin sometimes mark the way by placing sticks in the snow; in a meadow where there are scattered willow bushes, branches may be stuck in the snow upside down so that markers are not confused with natural vegetation. Poles may also be leaned against bushes or placed horizontally in them to indicate the trail's location.

Knowledge of the Landscape

The key to successful exploitation of the subarctic forest is an intimate knowledge of local geography. Kutchin travelers must know the location of many trails, and of portages between lakes or across river bends. They should also know every hill, ravine, creek, or meadow—in short, every detail of the local landscape. This kind of knowledge is essential for two reasons: First, to exploit his surroundings effectively a man must know the location of every favorable microhabitat of the plants or animals he seeks. Second, efficient travel depends on a knowledge of trails, portages, short-cuts, lakes, and rivers. The longer a man travels in a particular region, the more adept he becomes at using the best routes and avoiding unnecessary expenditure of time and effort.

No man in Chalkyitsik has a thorough knowledge of the entire area exploited by the aggregate village population. Each has specialized in a particular area, usually where his trapline is situated, in which he is completely familiar with all trails and geographical features. Acquiring this thorough knowledge, even of a limited area, takes many years. A man learns to find his way around in an area after a couple of years, but it takes much longer to become highly efficient as a hunter-trapper. Knowledge of the landscape is almost as important to successful exploitation of the boreal forest environment as knowledge of hunting and trapping techniques.

Travel in the open upland forest and tundra country differs from travel in the dense lowland forest because it is not so dependent upon detailed knowledge of the landscape. An old Kutchin said that he could trap successfully far up the Black River even though the terrain is unfamiliar, because in that mountainous country it is easy to find the way. It is undoubtedly less difficult to learn to orient oneself by the configurations of a few dozen mountains than by an infinitude of local forest configurations.

The difference between boreal forest and open tundra may explain the Indians' concentration upon geographical knowledge for direction-finding as contrasted to the Eskimos' reliance upon indicators of the cardinal directions (e.g., compasses, stars, sun, wind direction). The Tranjik Kutchin always refer to trails, lakes, sloughs, meadows, rivers, direction of current, hills, and similar features whenever speaking of directions, and points of the compass are practically never referred to except for indicating wind direction. Thus, Fort Yukon is said to be "downriver," Vundik Lake is "beyond the Porcupine River," Ohtig Lake is "on the winter trail that way" (gesturing in the proper direction). Orientation with respect to local geography rather than navigational abstractions is also reported for the Peel River and Crow River Kutchin (Osgood 1936b, p. 102), the Tanana (McKennan 1959, p. 110), and the Kaska (Honigmann 1949, p. 261).

It is interesting in this regard that the Indians have very little knowledge of astronomical phenomena, with names for only a few stars and constellations. McKennan (1959, p. 110) points out that "small as the astronomical knowledge of the Upper Tanana is, it apparently is no smaller than that of the other Northern Athapaskan groups." This certainly holds true for the Tranjik Kutchin.

The Kutchin very rarely become lost, since they nearly always follow established trails or stay on frozen rivers and lakes, and they know the land so well that they seldom find themselves in unfamiliar territory. If a man should lose his way, however, he may wander around until he reaches a known landmark, sometimes climbing a tree to look around. If there are hills it is difficult to get lost because these are highly visible points of orientation, and from a hill it is easy to sight prominent landmarks such as rivers or lakes.

Daylight-Nightlight

Next to its potential for extreme cold, the North is perhaps most famous for the extraordinary length of its days and nights. Chalkyitsik, being just above the Arctic Circle, experiences twenty-four-hour daylight during the summer and very long nights in winter. This is more than a curiosity to the Kutchin, for the cycle of day lengths plays a paramount role in determining their hours of activity. During the summer the absence of darkness for months on end allows hunting and traveling without concern for time. Summer's freedom is paid for in the wintertime, however, as the Indians continually rush to keep ahead of darkness.

From about April 15 until August 15 there is no complete darkness in the Chalkyitsik country. The transition from long summer days to long winter nights occurs very rapidly. At both the spring and fall equinox (March 21 and September 23) the sun is above the horizon for only twelve hours, and twilight extends the daylength to about fifteen hours. During midwinter the days become very short, and on the shortest day of the year (December 21) the sun appears for only an hour. The long twilight extends the period of light sufficient for hunting and traveling to nearly seven hours, however. Cloudiness can shorten the day length almost by half during the winter, because the sun is below the horizon except at midday.

The moon is an important source of light in the winter, and is welcomed as a relief from the pitch darkness of prolonged nights. It appears for fourteen to twenty days each month between October and April, when the nights are dark enough so that its light has a significant effect. Throughout the first half of winter the moon rises just at sunset, giving the traveler a continuation of daylight. But from January on it favors the traveler in early morning, rising well after dark and setting with the sunrise.

The moon is full for about seven days of each lunar cycle, and during this time it remains almost continuously above the horizon. A full moon at these latitudes is almost like a lesser sun, because when it rises high in the crystal clear sky its light is reflected by the whiteness of snow. A bright half moon is enough for travel by dog team or snowmobile without using additional light, and a good full moon provides enough light so that the whole landscape, even distant mountains, is illuminated in a beautiful gray cast.

The aurora borealis, or northern lights, is another source of illumination on winter nights. Auroral bands appear in the sky here almost every night when it is dark enough to see them, but their brightness varies a great deal. Sometimes they are only a faint hazy glow, somewhat brighter than the Milky Way, but occasionally they are brilliant shimmering and twisting curtains of light, flashing a dull brightness across the snow. If the sky is pitch black, without twilight or moon, any aurora at all will lighten the landscape enough for easy walking without a flashlight.

Snow Conditions

Sometimes the season for winter travel opens before the first snow-fall. If a heavy ice fog accompanies near-zero temperatures the entire country may be whitened by a thick accumulation of hoar-frost. Every twig, spruce needle, and blade of grass is furred with a coating of frost crystals, and the ground appears to be covered by light snow. If frost accumulates thickly enough on the trails, dog teams and snowmobiles can run easily over it.

In early October, the Kutchin start watching and hoping for snow. Ideally, the snow will not come until after the river freezes hard, because if it arrives earlier its insulative cover makes the ice thicken slowly. Before snow arrives, the Kutchin can do almost nothing. Since the river is frozen, or may freeze at any time, they cannot travel by boat, and the bare land is usually passable only on foot. But when snow falls its lubricating cover allows them to travel anywhere at good speed and with little effort. And while the hunters and trappers are afforded high mobility, they can also read the passage of every animal on the snow surface. Thus, snow is the essential factor in winter activities.

After snow comes, trails have to be packed down to make a hard, slick surface. Once packed the first time, they are not so difficult to open after subsequent snowfalls. After every snow, especially if the temperature is below zero, toboggans run over the soft trails as it they were on sand. With a few days of travel over them, trails become very hard packed and icy. This is important for the dog musher because his team is much faster and can pull heavier loads on a packed trail.

As the winter progresses more and more snow accumulates, and it influences men and animals in many ways, especially if it is a winter of heavy snowfall. New trails become harder to open because it is difficult to pack deep snow enough for the dogs to pull through. It may be necessary to snowshoe over a trail one day, then drive over it the next day after hardening takes place. Sometimes snow becomes so deep that the Indians make no new trails, but stay on those which have already been used that winter.

The mean total snowfall at Fort Yukon, which receives about the same amount as Chalkyitsik, is 45.6 inches, or a little under 4 feet. Settling and periodic thaws usually prevent that much from accumulating on the ground at any one time. Snow depths of 3 to 5 feet are not unknown, but occur only during years of unusually heavy snowfall. Snow is usually deepest in the forest, where it remains fluffy and undisturbed except for a certain amount of settling. In large open places, such as lakes or meadows, it is blown around and packed by the wind. In some areas the surface may be completely free of snow, whereas along the forest edge drifts may pile up to depths of 10 feet or more.

Other factors also cause significant differences in the depth of local snow accumulations. For one thing, the snow is "always" deeper in the hills than along the rivers and flats, and it tends to be deeper up the Black River toward Salmon Village. Snow cover is also affected by regional differences in wind. The Porcupine River country is characterized by steady and powerful winds which drift and pack the snow, whereas the region south of Chalkyitsik, from Ohtig Lake to the Little Black River, has much less wind so that a traveler can generally expect to find deep, soft snow there.

With the coming of warm spring weather, around 40° to 50° above, the trails become soft and wet, making travel difficult for dogs and snowmobiles. Not only does everything sink into the snow, but the wet surface is also sticky for toboggans. Coating the toboggan bottom with melted grease, covering it with metal sheeting, or putting on iron-shod runners helps to relieve the stickiness, but nothing can offset the softness. The best solution is to travel at night after the temperature sinks below freezing, when the trails quickly freeze and harden, offering the best possible conditions for travel.

As the snow melts during April, bare places appear and steadily increase in size, first in the open country, then on lakes and rivers, and finally in the forest. At the same time puddles develop in the trails, and on rivers and lakes water and slush cover the ice beneath the remaining snow. Once the land is mostly free of snow, and the river and lake ice weakens around the edges, the season for overland travel is finished.

Ice Conditions

During the summer months lakes, sloughs, rivers, and creeks are major impediments to overland travel. This is especially true in the river flats, where there is almost as much water as land. But through the long cold season, when these bodies of water are frozen, they add to the ease of travel. For all its convenience, however, travel over the ice can be dangerous, especially during the fall and spring. There are basically two dangerous ice conditions, thin ice and overflow. Each is discussed separately here, because they are dealt with in very different ways.

Thin Ice

The first thin ice of the cold season forms on ponds and lakes, often before there has been any lasting snowfall. The Indians sometimes walk on thin ice in the fall and are quite skillful in judging its thickness and avoiding unsafe places. As long as the ice is not covered with snow or frost, it is fairly easy to judge its safety. Blackish colored ice which is highly transparent is generally thinner than whitish ice with many air bubbles in it. Right after freeze-up lakes tend to have whitish ice near shore, where the earliest freezing occurs, and clear ice farther out. The clear ice may be unsafe, but a person cannot be sure until he finds out how much it cracks or bends under him. Frequent and extensive cracking under a man's weight, of course, indicates danger. Where cracks occur in transparent ice, they show clearly how thick it is. Ice only an inch thick usually will not support a man, but two inches are sufficient if he walks carefully.

Ice can be especially dangerous in narrow sloughs connected to rivers. After a foot or two of ice covers them the water level falls (as it always does after freeze-up). If the ice does not drop with the water, it may remain suspended between the two shores, with a hollow space beneath. The weight of a dog team, snowmobile, or even a man on foot may be enough to break through this unsupported layer of ice. When the Kutchin travel on these sloughs they listen for a hollow, resonant sound which indicates this dangerous condition. There is usually another layer of solid ice underneath, but a man could be injured by the large chunks of ice that would fall through with him.

Any time snow covers thin ice it creates a dangerous situation, for not only is the ice hidden from view, but the snow prevents rapid thickening of the ice. The only way to judge ice safety now is to use a long (6- or 7-foot) pole to jab the ice. The Kutchin do not carry special poles for this purpose, but select one on the spot when it is needed. When they are ice fishing or beaver trapping they usually carry an ice chisel for chopping holes in the ice and testing its safety. Generally, any ice that breaks through with one firm jab is dangerous to walk on.

Lake ice is probably more dangerous in the spring than at any other season. After it has thawed for a few days a traveler who crosses a lake must watch for sharp depressions in the snow, because they usually mark holes in the ice. Not only are the holes a danger, but the ice surrounding them is often covered with a foot or so of water and slush. Travelers watch for them after any warm period, especially from March on, and are careful to give them a wide berth.

As spring progresses the snow cover steadily diminishes, and a thick layer of slush and water develops on the ice beneath the snow. Large puddles appear between the drifts, and as the water drains off through open holes and cracks the ice around these openings becomes dangerously thin. Then, after the snow is nearly gone, ice around the fringe of lakes and sloughs starts to grow weak, and small lanes of open water rim the shore, where warmth absorbed by the land melts the ice quickly.

The ice farther from the shore melts much less rapidly, and so travelers often cross very thin ice or open water to reach safe ice farther out. Under such conditions, however, a man must know the ice well to travel safely. When lake ice thaws, its ability to support weight depends not on its thickness but on how much it becomes honeycombed. The warm spring sun breaks the ice down into pencillike columns or needles, causing even thick ice to become weak. As this happens the ice darkens and millions of little pinholes penetrate downward into it. Dark ice is to be avoided. When it really becomes weak a man can hear a creaking, spongy sound with each step, and he should never remain on ice that makes this noise. Honeycombed ice 2 feet thick can disintegrate beneath a heavy weight.

Many of the techniques for dealing with thin or weak ice on lakes apply equally to rivers, but the existence of current creates a number of special problems. In places where the current is slow freezing occurs early, and if no snow covers the surface the ice may be thick enough to support a man in two or three days. In many parts of the river, however, the current is swift enough to cause slow thickening of the ice, especially around riffles, where open water may even remain throughout the winter.

Most swift places in the Black and Porcupine rivers gradually freeze over in early winter. Before ice completely covers them, they are marked by fog that steams constantly from their surfaces whenever the temperature is below zero; so travelers can avoid them by watching for plumes of fog ahead. When ice covers the riffles, it may remain thin all winter long, with nothing on the surface to indicate danger. The only way to travel safely, therefore, is to know the exact location of every riffle and swift place.

The Chalkyitsik Kutchin have traveled these rivers hundreds of times, summer and winter, and so they know where to expect dangerous ice. During summer and fall boat trips they note any changes in the location of fast water so that they can avoid it during the winter. Trails that follow river courses do not simply run down the middle or along one shore. They wind back and forth across the river, along sandbars, across portages, and on the ice in slow-water places. Obviously, a great deal of foreknowledge goes into their routing. An inexperienced person would certainly be courting disaster by striking out on his own with no trail to follow.

I recall one trip up the Black River with a man who owned a snowmobile. At one place he inexplicably raced straight across the river full throttle and drove directly up onto a rough bank, then stopped to check a trap. When I commented on his maneuver he said that the ice there was so thin that if he did not cross at full speed it might give way. The Kutchin say that the Porcupine River is more dangerous than the Black River; Moses Thomas said that a riffle in front of his cabin on the Porcupine sometimes has snow on the surface while the ice is completely eaten away underneath. Another man said he had lived on that river for over thirty years but still considers it too dangerous to travel on at night.

After the snow falls most thin-ice areas are well concealed, but in a few cases there are indicators of danger on the snow surface. These are usually depressions in the snow, similar to those described earlier for lake ice in spring but larger in extent. Riffles or narrow, swift channels are often clearly indicated by a much thinner snow cover than that on safer ice. The river traveler constantly watches the snow ahead for signs of unsafe ice or open water. If he wants to cross questionable areas, he can use a sharpened pole to poke the ice ahead as he walks along. He not only is concerned that it might jab through the ice, but he also pays close attention to the sound and "feel." Thin ice has a kind of resonating tone, whereas safe ice makes a solid, dull thud.

Most Kutchin have probably fallen at least partway through the ice several times in their lives. If a man falls completely through the ice he is in real trouble, because he may not be able to get back up onto the surface. This is especially true on lakes, where the water is more likely to be over a man's head than in the rivers. It is a good idea to carry a knife to help in getting back up on the ice if it gives way underfoot. With only bare hands it is almost impossible to get a grip on the slick ice surface and pull up onto it, but a knife can be used to make handholds. Thin places are usually localized so that a man can reach safe ice, except in springtime, when the surface becomes rotten everywhere.

The Kutchin stress that after a man falls through the ice, regardless of season, the first thing he must do is build a fire to warm himself and dry his clothing. This is why they suggest that anyone who travels on rivers or lakes should carry matches in several places. If he falls through and soaks his pants pockets, he could save his life with matches from his shirt pocket or from a bag in his toboggan.

One man reported that he once fell through ice about 7 miles from the village but did not try to dry out his clothing. He had fast dogs and was close to home, and so felt that he could make it safely. But by the time he got there his clothes were frozen hard, and he felt lucky to have arrived without serious injury. An old man suggested that even if he were only 200 yards from home he would build a fire before doing anything else if he fell through the ice in very cold weather.

Overflow

The second dangerous winter ice condition, overflow, occurs when water is forced up through cracks or holes onto the frozen surface. Although overflow may be encountered at any time, there are a number of factors that make it somewhat predictable. The most likely time to expect it is after a fresh snowfall. The weight of several inches of new snow can sometimes depress the ice enough so that water flows out over the surface. This happens mostly on lakes during the early winter, while the ice is still fairly new, but it can occur even on the thickest midwinter ice. The greater the snowfall, of course, the more overflow there will be.

If it were not for the deep cover of snow, overflow water would freeze immediately; but in most cases, especially on lakes, the water remains entirely beneath the snow. This insulates it from the cold, allowing it to spread widely over the ice surface and soak up into the snow to make slush. The time it takes to freeze may vary from a few days to a couple of weeks.

The middle of a lake is generally the worst area for overflow, because this is where the greatest amount of sagging takes place.

Rivers, on the other hand, seem to fracture and overflow more near the edges, perhaps because the ice breaks along the shore as it drops with the pressure of snow. After a heavy overflow it may be very difficult to get out onto the river ice without going through slush and water a foot or more deep. Overflow also tends to occur after periods of warm weather, when the temperature ranges above +15° or so. Warm temperature alone can cause overflow on lakes, although I do not know why. Most warm spells during the winter season are accompanied by snow, however, which insures that overflow will occur. The Kutchin are especially careful to stay away from muskrat pushups when such conditions prevail. Each pushup has a tunnel through the ice into the water below and is therefore an excellent conduit for the escape of overflow water.

The most frequent source of overflow on rivers is an increasing volume of flow, which causes water to pour out through cracks onto the surface, especially at shallow riffles which freeze clear to the bottom and obstruct the current. During any warm spell, even in midwinter, the current increases enough so that water cannot flow under the ice in certain places and must burst out and flow over the top. Certain spots predictably overflow each time there is a warm spell, and the Kutchin are alert whenever they travel across them.

Overflow occurs so frequently that travelers run into it many, many times each winter. They cannot avoid it because the water is often concealed by innocent-looking snow; and even where it is predictable, as along certain stretches of river, there is no way of telling exactly how widespread it may be. The problem is greatest for snowmobile drivers, because they are well into a concealed overflow before they can do anything about it.

Very often, especially on rivers, overflow water is so deep that it soaks up to the snow surface and is clearly visible, turning the snow a yellowish brown color that is easily seen from a distance. In the spring, when overflow can spread over miles of ice, some stretches of river may appear to have opened completely. As long as the temperature remains well above zero, exposed overflow will remain liquid or will freeze very slowly, but the cold weather that follows winter mild spells usually freezes exposed water or slush quickly.

Overflows are always an inconvenience and may be a real danger, because snowmobiles can easily freeze up if they run into a deep overflow at 30° below zero. When a driver runs into water he tries to go through it as fast as possible to avoid getting stuck in the rapidly freezing slush. Machines can run through 8 or 10 inches of water rather easily, but if it is deeper they are apt to stop. The frigid air contacting water suddenly deprived of its snow cover will cause very rapid freezing inside the vehicle and around it as soon as it stops moving.

Dog teams often turn aside when they reach an overflow, and of course they cannot get stuck in it. If the driver jumps onto his toboggan when he sees moisture in the dogs' tracks he can avoid wetting his feet, unless he has to help by pushing it through the slush. As soon as he reaches dry snow the driver must scrape the accumulation of ice off the toboggan bottom or it will be very hard to pull. Snowmobile drivers seldom do this, preferring to let the ice wear off.

No matter how well insulated they may be, all winter overflows eventually freeze. For a while they remain unsafe, but after they freeze solidly lake and river overflows are a real blessing for the traveler. Their effect is to make the soft snow much shallower than it was before or to eliminate it entirely. On rivers, frozen overflow may run for miles along the shore, making a perfect road. It is easily seen because of its dark color; and its glossy, frosted, or snow-dusted surface makes it distinguishable from areas not yet frozen. Since most overflows on a river happen at the same time, one solidly frozen stretch probably means that the rest are also safe.

Weather Prediction

The Kutchin trapper and hunter tries to read signs of change or continuity in weather patterns so that he can know what conditions to expect while out on the trail. Needless to say, this is important in a land where the temperature can drop to 70° below zero or howling blizzards can make travel almost impossible. The Indian's assessment of future weather conditions therefore shapes his plans for trapping, hunting, or other activities.

Unfortunately, accurate weather prediction is difficult here, given the kind of indicators the Kutchin must rely upon. Consequently, they seem disinterested in weather forecasting and take a defeatist attitude toward it. "Around here we just can't tell about the weather," they say. "If it snow, it snow. If wind, then wind. No way to tell what it will do." The indicators of weather change are not particularly numerous or well defined, and they often appear at about the same time as the change takes place. Thus even a reliable weather sign may give only a few hours' warning, if that. It is seldom possible to predict accurately a day ahead, and this inability to make reliable forecasts means that travel plans are always made very tentatively, subject to revision on the day of scheduled departure.

Old men report that the people used to watch the weather more closely than they do today and were better at forecasting it. This is undoubtedly true, since the indicators are so subtle that concentrated study would surely make for greater accuracy. What follows is a summary of the weather forecasting techniques used by the modern Tranjik Kutchin.

Long-range Forecasting

The Kutchin are more concerned with long-range weather prediction based on their knowledge of seasonal trends and the usual length of weather "spells" than with forecasting changes on a day-to-day basis. This is understandable, because long-term weather patterns tend to be fairly regular here, whereas more immediate changes are difficult to foresee. The same focus of interest on long-range forecasting is reported for the Kaska (Honigmann 1949, p. 222) and might prove to be rather general among northern Athapaskans.

The predictability of seasonal weather conditions is illustrated by the Indians' ability to expect with fair certainty that the Black River will freeze during the first part of October. About this time also, they say, the north wind starts to blow and usually continues steadily for about a month or so. Then a period of calm and intense cold sets in and lasts (with intermittent stormy spells) until February or March. The north wind starts blowing again at this time and continues for another month or so. People expect the onset of lasting warm weather around the end of April. Warm spells that occur before that time are considered deceptive, because they make it appear that spring has arrived when actually more cold weather lies ahead. But these are only trends which seem to recur over the years, and exceptional years are common, as one would expect.

Weather spells play a very important part in determining the activities of the Kutchin, especially during the long winter trapping season. The Indians have methods of predicting the onset of cold or warm spells, which are discussed below. Once a weather period begins they can forecast its probable length according to their knowledge of similar episodes during past years.

During the summer they know that cold, wet, and windy spells usually last for a certain number of days, then are followed by a period of warm and sunny weather. A few days of very warm temperature will usually give way to showers. During the winter, a month of very cold weather, reaching down to the −50° range, is considered a very long cold spell. Generally, the Kutchin start watching for warm weather signs after a week or so has passed, and after two weeks they strongly anticipate a change. I have seen men correctly predict that a cold snap just begun would last for a month, apparently basing the forecast on the time of year and the intensity of accompanying signs.

The Kutchin also know approximately how long winter warm spells usually last. When warm, cloudy weather appears, accompanied by strong signs, it usually lasts for about two weeks. If the signs are weaker, shorter warm periods are anticipated. Warm spells in midwinter are usually followed by intensely cold periods. On the spring and fall sides of midwinter, warm spells usually last longer and cold spells are briefer, and the Indians take this into account in planning their activities.

Sundogs and Moondogs

Every so often the sun or moon is surrounded by a halolike ring called a sundog or moondog. Farmers in the midwest recognize these coronas as signs of rain, the Eskimos watch for them as indicators of winter storms, and the Athapaskans use them to foretell a number of weather conditions according to differences in their appearance. Some of these differences are so subtle that only the old men can recognize them. Because they are so difficult to see, much less explain to someone who does not speak Kutchin, there are probably more distinctions than I have recorded here. One of the most reliable weather signs utilized by the Kutchin is a reddish or rainbow-colored sundog. This sign usually appears about twelve to twenty-four hours before the weather turns clear and sharply colder. It may also occur during cold spells, indicating that present conditions will continue. This sign is frequently accompanied by "false suns" (parhelia), bright spots in the halo on either side of the sun itself. These spots, which tend to be very red or rainbowlike in color, indicate a strong north wind accompanying cold weather.

Now a qualification must be added. Sometimes a sundog, whether or not it has this reddish or rainbow color, has a dark gray area around its inner margin. This is a snow sign, and if combined with rainbow colors it apparently indicates wind along with the snow. If the sundog is large, it means that snow will arrive later than if it is small, according to one old man. If this sounds fairly simple on paper, it is anything but simple in practice. The gray color is extremely difficult to see, and would never be noticed without special effort. The Kutchin themselves, especially those who are not old and experienced, have difficulty in seeing it.

The following example from my field notes will illustrate:

> Yesterday there was a rainbow-colored sundog with bright spots at its sides. Herbert Sam and David Simon both said that it meant clear skies and wind on the way. Then old William Sam said this was not a cold wind sign, but indicated clouds, snow, and perhaps wind, because the inner part was dark-colored. Today there was snow and a heavy wind.

Once in a while a double sundog appears, one halo inside another. When this happened in mid-May, an old man said it meant about two days of cold wind, then warm weather to follow. There were actually four or five days of wind, but then it turned very warm. Sundogs of this type, which very rarely occur, are difficult to learn about because people do not think of them until they appear. A hazy, gray sundog without color or spots is a good indicator of warm, cloudy weather with snow or rain. This type is often quite easy to see, but sometimes appears in an overcast and is very difficult to pick out.

A moondog apparently means only one thing—warm, cloudy weather and a good chance of precipitation. This sign does not precede all weather systems of this type, which come in from the south, but when it appears it seems highly reliable. If a warm weather system moves in during the winter, but no moondog occurs with it (provided the moon is present at the time), it indicates that the weather change will not last. But if a moondog appears, the warm and cloudy conditions will probably last up to two weeks or more.

Sundogs occur from time to time during the warmer months and are often considered a sign of rain. Rainbow sundogs are said to forecast cold, windy weather, but they tend to be unreliable in summer. In general sundogs are most reliable as a weather indicator during the coldest midwinter months, but even then miscues are not uncommon. It is always best to look for a number of weather signs occurring together, since forecasts based on one sign are often incorrect.

Wind

The wind not only is a part of the weather, it is also an important indicator of what weather changes are likely to take place in the immediate future. Whenever a breeze comes up the Kutchin take note of its direction and watch for signs of weather systems that usually move in with that kind of wind.

A northerly breeze, for example, generally means cool or cold weather, plus a good chance that the wind will become strong. Northeast winds usually bring long, powerful storms with clouds and precipitation. Winds from the southerly quadrant bring warm spells, often with clouds and snow (or rain). Even the slightest southerly breeze usually causes immediate warming, unless it is only a local air flow. Extremely cold periods are characterized by dead calm. North and south winds are the most common here, north being highly prevalent during the cold months.

One very interesting aspect of wind in the Tranjik Kutchin country is its tendency to be localized. The Porcupine River area, for example, is known as a very windy region. If it is calm at Chalkyitsik, there is probably a breeze along the Porcupine; and if it is stormy at Chalkyitsik, there will be a howling gale on the river.

Conversely, the area south of Chalkyitsik is referred to as calm country. When the snow has been packed into hard drifts around the village it may still be soft and undisturbed on huge Ohtig Lake, 10 miles south. These differences strongly influence hunting, trapping, and travel in the areas north and south of Chalkyitsik.

Cloud Movements

The appearance and movement of clouds often indicate the approach of weather systems with which they are associated. If fairly low clouds move in from the south, for example, there will probably be warm weather and perhaps snow. If they come in from the northeast, cold, windy weather and precipitation are likely to follow. Thus winds aloft, carrying clouds with them, sometimes move into an area before other changes in the weather occur.

There are certain types of clouds that the Kutchin call "wind clouds." These are high, wispy cirrus clouds, often called "mare's tails" by Outsiders. They are long clouds, obviously drawn out in the direction of winds aloft, sweeping into great curves near their downwind ends. These clouds are often followed by strong wind the next day, usually from the same direction as indicated by the elongation of the clouds.

There is an old mariner's saying, "Red sky at morning, sailor take warning; red sky at night, sailor's delight." This proverbial weather-word apparently applies for the dog musher as well as the sailor, if in a somewhat different way. The Kutchin say that red clouds in the sunrise mean warm, cloudy weather is on its way (presumably a southerly wind system). A bright red sunset, on the other hand, presages the approach of clear, calm, and cold winter weather.

Fog and Hoarfrost

Ground fog and the hoarfrost that it deposits everywhere on the winter landscape are good indicators that cold, clear weather is on the way. On some fall and winter mornings a thick fog hangs right down on the ground, not extending far above the treetops. This fog is practically infallible as an indicator of cold weather, with temperatures falling well below zero. An Indian who sees this

might well decide to stay at home and watch the weather instead
of leaving for his trapline.

This kind of fog is not to be confused with the atmospheric haze
that appears before warm weather. Some nights, before a warm
spell begins, the stars are barely visible or twinkle a great deal.
At the same time, the moon may have a hazy glow or a moondog
around it. These phenomena result from atmospheric haze, which
seems to increase considerably as a warm weather system moves
in from the south.

Animal Behavior

Sometimes animals are more clever than men about foreseeing
changes in the weather. Muskrats, for example, are able to anticipate cold weather in the springtime. One to three days before a
cold snap they start plugging and relining the walls of their little
houses or pushups with mud and vegetable matter. Men who open
these houses to set traps anticipate cold weather when they see
fresh lining inside.

The arrival of migratory birds, particularly waterfowl, is watched
carefully as an indicator of the beginning of warm spring weather.
Around late April, ducks and geese will fail to show up during
warm spells if there is to be another period of cold weather. And
when they do arrive in large numbers, the Indians say that the
weather will remain warm.

An old man who has fished the Black River country for the better
part of seventy years said that in his experience fish come out of
the streams early if there is to be an early freeze-up. If there is
to be a late freeze-up, on the other hand, they come out later than
usual. Thus he has learned to predict the season by watching the
dates when his fish traps start producing.

The Kutchin also say that black bears know if it will be a warm
or cold winter. If it is going to be mild, they make their sleeping
places right near the openings of their dens, and if it will be cold
they make them far back toward the rear. According to the
Koyukon, snowshoe hare tracks in the fall can tell a man if it will
be a winter of light or heavy snow. If the tracks are very wide,
indicating well-furred hind feet, there are heavy snows ahead (G.
R. Bane, personal communication).

Radio Forecasts

All of the Chalkyitsik Kutchin own radios which can pick up stations at Fairbanks and Anchorage. Since Fairbanks is only about 200 miles away and in a similar interior location, there is a definite correlation between the weather there and at Chalkyitsik. Thus by listening to forecasts on the radio the people have an idea of what conditions to expect, especially for warm weather systems moving up from the south, which frequently reach Chalkyitsik two or three days after they move into the Fairbanks region. The correlation is less marked in regard to other weather patterns.

Temperature

Very few people in Chalkyitsik use thermometers, though the temperature is an important means of forecasting weather. The Indians are adept at judging the temperature just by the "feel" of it when they step outside. An increase of a few degrees, especially during the evening or night when the temperature should normally fall, may be a good sign that warmer weather is on the way. Conversely, if the temperature falls during the day it probably means that a cold air mass is moving in. Rising temperature can also precede the beginning of a windstorm. Like the weather indicators discussed above, this one is most reliable when used in conjunction with a number of other signs. For example, during very cold weather the slightest breeze will cause an immediate rise in temperature. But this is usually temporary, and the temperature falls again as soon as it is calm.

Summary

There are three types of weather systems which are of considerable importance to the winter traveler. It is worthwhile to summarize their characteristics here, noting the signs that forewarn of their approach.

The most clearly defined weather pattern here is the warm, southerly type that moves in periodically throughout the months of winter. This kind of weather is often preceded by a sundog which is plain gray in color, a rainbow sundog with a dark inner margin, or a moondog. The wind usually shifts to a southerly direction, fairly low clouds move in, and the temperature rises. There is generally a marked increase in atmospheric haze ahead of such systems. Warm-weather forecasts on Fairbanks radio stations always indicate a chance that this kind of weather may come in. A reversal of any or all of these characteristics after a few days indicates the probable approach of a weather change.

Cold spells are a second important weather type, equally distinctive in character but somewhat more difficult to predict. Rainbow or reddish-colored sundogs without a dark area inside are good signs of the approach or continuation of a cold snap. The wind is usually light and highly variable in direction, decreasing to a calm as the temperature drops; cloudiness disappears and the sky becomes extraordinarily clear before and during this weather. The sky may be blocked from view, however, by very heavy ground fog, which leaves hoarfrost everywhere. Fairbanks radio stations forecast cold weather. Again, reversal or moderation of these weather features indicates a change in the offing.

The third distinctive weather type is the winter windstorm, generally coming in from the north or northeast. Rainbow sundogs and "false suns" are a good indicator that stormy and cold weather is on its way; the breeze usually picks up early and may rise to storm force very quickly. There is often some change in cloud cover along with this pattern; the sky may clear, or clouds may come in on the wind. Snow often accompanies winter storms, sometimes only flurries, sometimes heavy amounts. There may be a rise in temperature before and during this kind of weather, but it is never really warm, as in southerly systems. As with the other weather systems, these characteristics fade or reverse themselves when a change is imminent.

Effects of Wind and Cold

The effects of weather on activities of the Black River Kutchin have been discussed in this and earlier chapters. This section deals briefly with the importance of wind and temperature as determinants of winter travel and related activities. These are by far the most important elements of winter weather, as one would expect in this environment.

The effects of wind vary somewhat during the winter according to the temperature and snow conditions. A 15 mile per hour wind severely curtails activities if the temperature is −20° but has much less effect if it is +20°. If there is a fresh, soft snow blowing before the wind it is much harder to travel than if the snow is hardened and does not blow into new drifts. Unless the temperature is above zero, a wind 10 to 15 mph or stronger has some curtailing effect on activities of the Kutchin. Such winds can be rather common. In the winter of 1969–70 (between November 1 and March 31) there were fifty-two days with winds over 10 mph and twenty-four days when it blew 15 to 20 mph or more. This was an unusually windy year, but wind certainly plays a significant role in Kutchin activities every winter.

Temperature is of course the most pervasive aspect of the winter climate in interior Alaska. At first glance it might appear that cold temperatures would have a preponderantly negative effect on outdoor activities, but this is only partly true. If the fall is warm, the people become impatient for the arrival of cold weather so they will have snow to travel on and their cached meat will not spoil. But when it does turn cold they say that it takes a while to acclimatize themselves.

The effect of cold temperature changes as winter progresses; weather that keeps people inside in October would seem pleasant for outdoor activities in December. Several men in Chalkyitsik appear to be relatively insensitive to cold, and are more likely than others to visit their traplines when it ranges between −40° and −50°. Every man has been on the trail at one time or another when it was −60° to −75°, but this is always exceptional. By and large, −30° to −35° is the accepted winter cutoff, and anything below −50° is considered extremely difficult traveling weather.

The following field note, written in mid-November, illustrates the effects of extreme cold:

Today it was minus fifty. The supercooled air stung your nose and cheeks like pricking needles, and chilled your lungs with each breath. It found every opening in your clothing and eventually seeped inside to surround you. The only way to keep warm was to exert yourself in some way—chopping wood, running behind the dog sled, or any work that would not make you winded. If you overexerted, you found yourself quickly exhausted and short of breath, as if the cold had sucked away the air. It became almost frightening when this happened; your body seemed to forbid breathing deeply enough to get sufficient oxygen.

At minus fifty the air was crystal clear and utterly calm, carrying the least sound a great distance. Only around the village was the silence and clarity disrupted. The cluster of houses sat in a cloud of fog produced by the hot smoke and steam from chimneys spreading out beneath a temperature inversion 30 or 40 feet above the ground. The fog settled down among the houses, dissipating slowly in the still air. Ice-fog created a hazy glow around the sun, turning orange and vermilion as the sun moved lower in the sky.

Few people moved around outside. Snowmobiles would not start, and dogs were reluctant to leave their houses and pulled without enthusiasm when put into harness. Whenever they stopped on the trail, they would curl up on the ground and only got up again with some urging. When they stood they repeatedly lifted one foot, then another, to relieve the stinging cold. Even the wild animals would not move. In a tree behind the village a gray jay roosted in a young birch, feathers puffed into a ball and its feet tucked up underneath, and refused to fly when I walked right beneath it.

Trappers prefer to head for their lines when signs indicate lasting warm weather, and if the temperature is dropping or any cold weather signs appear they will wait and see. During this study there was very little activity in the entire month of January because of a protracted cold spell, but the first sign of a warming trend immediately sent men off to run their traplines before the temperature dropped again. The ideal temperature for winter travel is between $-25°$ and $+15°$.

Incidentally, the Kutchin and Koyukon Athapaskans seem much more affected by cold than the North Alaskan Eskimos. Indians are not unwilling to complain about the cold, to admit that they are chilled and uncomfortable, or to decide against travel because of low temperatures. The Eskimos virtually never complain about temperature or about being cold themselves, and they rarely alter their travel plans because of low temperature alone. When they say it is "cold," they mean it is windy, and only extremes such as $-30°$ with a 25 mph wind keep them from traveling. When there is little or no wind, they will carry on normal activities at $-40°$ to $-50°$ (cf. Nelson 1969, p. 99).

Winter Clothing

Anthropologists working among the northern Athapaskans have repeatedly found that it is almost impossible to learn about their aboriginal dress because it disappeared so rapidly after contact with the white man. This nearly immediate change resulted partly from a general receptiveness on the part of the Indians to everything the newcomers had to offer, but other factors were also involved. When he established Fort Yukon in 1847, Murray noted that:

> Blankets, axes, knives, powder horns and files went off rapidly enough, but it was hard to dispose of the clothing, as they consider their own dresses much superior to ours both in beauty and durability, and they are partly right, although I endeavoured to persuade them to the contrary. [Murray 1910, p. 56]

The fur trader was attempting to introduce a change in clothing styles, obviously because he wanted the Indians to save their valuable furs for trade. Coupled with this effort to discourage the use of traditional apparel, however, a genuine desire for European clothing seems to have emerged. The old-timers tell how people used to wear their warm fur clothing out on the trail, but when they were approaching a village they shed their warm outfits and put on suits of fancy European dress. Thus it appears that their initial negative reaction was soon displaced by a positive one based on status associated with imported clothes. By 1919, Cadzow (1925*b*, p. 295) found that the last vestiges of traditional Kutchin dress had disappeared. Descriptions of aboriginal clothing are available, however, for the Chandalar, Peel River, and Crow River Kutchin (McKennan 1965, pp. 44–46; Osgood 1936*b*, pp. 38–44).

The modern Kutchin trapper or hunter usually wears a homemade cloth parka with a wolf or wolverine fur ruff. Underneath the parka he wears a jacket, if it is very cold, plus a heavy shirt or sweat shirt. Most men use some kind of long-sleeved underwear beneath it all. The multilayer arrangement applies to lower garments as well. Trappers often wear two pairs of pants and a pair of long underwear. Heavy cloth flight pants are used during cold winter travel. Trappers always wear a pair of cloth or leather gloves, and while traveling they put heavy mittens on over the gloves for extra warmth. Gloves become damp and cold after a while when used inside mittens, and so one or two extra pairs are carried.

Footgear is usually the moosehide and canvas boot, made on an essentially Eskimo design. The sole of the boot is of tanned moosehide, and the 8-to-10-inch top is canvas. A pair of long ties secures each boot around the ankle, and another tie closes the top snugly around the calf to keep out the snow. Since "canvas boots" give little warmth in themselves, the wearer must have good protection inside. The women sew inner boots of quilting or other warm material, and these are worn over several pairs of heavy wool socks. Hare-skin "socks" may be used as one of these layers. Good insoles, either manufactured felt types, hare skin, muskrat skin, or other fur, are essential protection against the cold undersurface.

Some of today's hunters and trappers use commercially manufactured cloth boots with rubber soles. These boots are considered too heavy and clumsy for regular wear, but are very good during periods when the snow is wet or there is much overflow. Moosehide soaks up water like a sponge and is really unsatisfactory for above-freezing temperatures or other wet situations.

In general, the Kutchin are careful to keep their clothing dry. After each day's journey they build a good fire in the cabin stove and hang everything up near the ceiling where it will dry thoroughly. This is absolutly essential for northern travel, because clothing always becomes moist from perspiration and snow during the day's activities, and this wetness markedly decreases its insulative qualities.

Frostbite and Freezing

No matter how much clothing the Indians wear, they are resigned to the fact that they are often going to get cold. Being chilled is simply a fact of life in the subarctic, and the people do not take it seriously unless there is danger of frostbite or freezing. Snowmobile travelers are the most likely to suffer from extreme cold because they travel at high speeds in low temperatures. Yet surprisingly few suffer from frostbite. This is largely because they stop whenever someone feels chilled, either just to stand around and warm up or to light a fire and make a pot of tea. Travelers are also careful to rewarm numb or stinging flesh by holding their hands against it. They always avoid breathing on their hands or into anything held against the face, because this moistens the flesh and causes deeper chilling.

Partners watch each other's faces for the telltale white spots that indicate freezing, and a man traveling alone will check his face in a mirror as soon as he gets home. When temperatures sink to 60° below and colder, the Indians say it is difficult to avoid frostbite when traveling or even walking outside for very long. Nevertheless, serious cases are very rare. Everyone will get a few nips each winter regardless of how careful he is. Once a person is frostbitten that place will be highly sensitive to cold and easily reinjured for the rest of the season.

The Tranjik Kutchin state emphatically that their method of curing frozen or frostbitten flesh is to apply handfuls of dry snow to it. As soon as the snow becomes wet, the skin is dried and another handful is applied. Another method is to hold the affected member in ice water. The Kutchin always use these techniques and say that if heat is applied the flesh will become sore. My first impression on hearing this was that the Kutchin had gotten the idea from white men who held this to be an effective cure. But the fact that other Athapaskans (including the Koyukon and Kaska) use the same technique may indicate otherwise (cf. Honigmann 1949, p. 245).

This same idea has long been held in American culture, but medical evidence clearly demonstrates that it is anything but a cure for frostbite or freezing. In fact, applying cold water or snow to a frostbitten limb is analogous to treating burned flesh by placing it inside an oven (Washburn 1963, p. 692). The method used in modern medicine, and employed for centuries by the Eskimos, consists of immersing frostbitten parts in water at about 110° F. or applying moist heat. The Eskimo treatment usually involves placing affected flesh against the warm body of another person.

Although frostbite has always been a common minor problem here, serious freezing and freezing to death were extremely rare in the past and are virtually nonexistent today. The old-timers say that they have never heard of anybody freezing to death around the Black River country, where it is always easy to build a fire to keep warm. In the mountain regions above timberline, however, there is always a danger of being caught with no way to make a fire.

The Chalkyitsik Kutchin and the Koyukon, again in direct opposition to the practice of Eskimos and white explorers, believe that if a man gets lost or is caught on the trail without shelter, he must never permit himself to fall asleep. If he does he will freeze to death without awakening. The Indians warn that a man should not overexert himself or work up a sweat. If this happens, he should stop and build a fire, then dry his clothing. But men who have become lost in cold weather often say that they did not dare to stop and rest, fearing that they would fall asleep, and so they walked themselves to utter exhaustion, which in some cases nearly caused their death. Yet they still feel that they would never have survived had they stopped to rest and sleep.

Here again is a belief that coincides with a theory widely prevalent in white North American culture but is in direct contradiction to the practice of the Arctic Eskimos. In their tundra and sea-ice environment the Eskimos have had to cope with more severe weather, if somewhat less intensely cold temperatures, than the Athapaskans. Eskimos have regularly found themselves unable to get their bearings in the powerful storms which are so frequent in their country, and in countless cases they have survived because they sat down and went to sleep. Rather than walk themselves into exhaustion, they conserve their strength and warmth, moving around only when necessary to generate body heat (see also Stefansson 1944, pp. 345–46; Nelson 1969, p. 101).

12 Mink

Introduction

The mink, or *chiihdsuu* (*Mustela vison*), is common throughout the forested parts of North America, including the country of the Black River Kutchin. This small member of the weasel family measures some 18 to 24 inches in length, weighs only a pound or two, and is generally rich brown in color except for white patches under the chin.

Mink are semiaquatic creatures, preferring to live around the margins of lakes, sloughs, ponds, creeks, and rivers. Their tracks are not often seen far from water, summer or winter; but since there is water almost everywhere in the flats, mink are common here. The Kutchin say that a special kind of mink, which they call mountain mink, or *chiits'uu*, lives in the hilly or mountainous country. This animal is distinctly smaller and darker than the mink of the lowlands, and it is apparently uncommon.

Mink are predatory and scavenging carnivores with a diversity of tastes. They feed heavily on fish and prefer to live where the supply is plentiful. They also eat a variety of small mammals and perhaps an occasional bird, but their favorite food, according to the Kutchin, is the muskrat. The Indians say that the mink population tends to fluctuate somewhat in accord with the number of muskrats and fish, but this is certainly not always true.

In 1969–70 the official mink season opened on November 1 and closed on January 31. Trappers try to set their lines early, because during November the mink are very active and easy to trap. By December they seem to become scarce, perhaps because the arrival of really cold weather makes them inactive, but for some reason they become active again after the first of the year. Unfortunately, mink pelts tend to lose quality beginning in January because the bright winter sun bleaches them. Thus, although mink become increasingly active and easy to catch their value decreases rapidly. A certain percentage that are taken between January and April remain prime, however, and this tempts some trappers to stretch the season beyond its legal closing date.

Locating Trap Sets

The trapper's first problem is deciding where to make his sets for mink. To some extent his choice of trap sites is based on a knowledge of certain places that are for one reason or another attractive to mink, but to an even greater degree the trapper locates his sets on the basis of fresh mink sign.

He travels along each lake, slough, and creek in his territory watching the snow-covered ice and banks for mink tracks. Once he finds them he follows to see what the animals have been doing. Mink travel considerable distances along banks and over the ice, leaving their singular tracks as evidence of their explorations. They investigate each little irregularity of the shoreline, moving into the brush, up the bank, back down onto the ice, along the grass, up the bank again, and so on.

The trapper is especially interested in areas where mink tracks are fresh and abundant, because the more tracks there are in a certain place, the more likely it is that a burrow is nearby. If a track shows that the mink has killed and dragged an animal, a special effort is made to follow it to the place where the carcass has been cached, the idea being to find an area where the mink tends to remain or which it is likely to revisit, since a trap set there has a good chance of being found by the animal. A good trapper also watches for places where fresh tracks appear several times during a winter, indicating that one or more animals occasionally use that route. More than this, however, he examines the country surrounding the area where tracks occur to find out where the mink are most likely to live.

Mink occupy a burrow or den, often an old muskrat hole, which they generally use throughout the winter. Mink dens are sometimes at the level of the ice, but most often they are on the bank several feet from the ice edge. Once a trapper has found a mink's trail, therefore, he watches for places where it goes up the bank into the brush or where it disappears into a hole.

There are many old muskrat holes along lakeshores; so if the tracks enter and leave a hole only once it is probably not a den. A trap may be set in such a place, however, because each time a mink passes it is likely to go in for another look around. An occupied den will probably have many tracks around it and perhaps one or two well-defined trails leading into it. It is worth the effort involved to find dens, because once they are located mink are almost certain to be caught in them.

One of the most interesting methods of locating places to set for mink is to follow the animals' tracks as they go from one muskrat pushup to another looking for a meal. Muskrats enter these little mud and vegetation houses to feed on plants brought up from the water underneath. Mink dig their way inside and wait there for the unsuspecting "rat" to enter, when it is easily killed. Sometimes a mink's trail goes from one pushup to the next, but the tracks leading away show that no kill was made. If the trapper is lucky, however, there are deep footprints, drag marks, and spots of blood to show that the mink has pulled a rat from its house and taken it to shore. He follows the tracks off the ice and into the brush until he finds where the kill has been taken into a hole and cached. A trap set at such a place is almost certain to catch a mink within a few days, and there is a good chance it will catch one or two more when it is reset.

A good mink trapper sets out many traps, from fifty to a hundred or more at the peak of the season. If a particular lake or area has many tracks, he makes a number of sets there. One trapper had seven traps around the shores of a small lake which usually produced good catches. The same man will place up to six traps around one small spot to make sure he catches a mink that has been frequenting the area. Most of the Chalkyitsik Kutchin are less ambitious, however, and do not use so many traps.

Trap-setting Methods

Mink can be taken with almost any trap, from the smallest size to the largest, but number 1½ is considered best. Number 1 traps are a bit too small, and numbers 2 and 3 are generally used for larger animals but can catch mink. If a large trap is set for mink, the pan (which triggers it) is depressed partway so the animals' light weight will spring it.

When an Indian sets out on his line he carries several dozen traps and a container full of odorous bait. The bait is essential in trapping because its odor attracts animals into the sets. Each man prepares his own bait mixture. Most Chalkyitsik Kutchin use rotten fish as the basic ingredient of mink bait, the idea being to get a strong fishy odor that the mink can detect at a distance. A second important addition is beaver castor, a strong-smelling fluid (from the castor and oil glands of the beaver) that attracts several kinds

Setting a trap in the opening of a mink burrow. Sticks at each side of the set narrow the entryway, forcing animals to step onto the trap.

of fur animals, including mink. Some men use a scent taken from the muskrat, since mink are enticed by the odor of their prey. Fluid from the musk gland of the mink itself is sometimes mixed into trap bait.

A man I watched preparing bait mixture started by mashing up some rotten fish, entrails, and eggs in a tin can. Then he added beaver castor and heated it on the stove. Later he decided to add muskrat scent. This bait was a crumbly mass that remained somewhat gummy even at 30° below zero. It was smeared onto strips of dried salmon (several inches long), hind feet of snowshoe hares, parts of duck wings, or flat splinters of wood. A fur or feather base is preferred for baits, apparently because it holds the scent for a long time.

Some men replenish their mink baits each time they run a line, to insure that a good fresh scent is always there. Old baits are carried off by animals like weasels or lose their smell and become ineffective. Careless trappers may allow the sets to become useless by not replacing the bait. If a squirrel, hare, or gray jay is caught in a trap, its carcass can be added to the set for an extra bait. Commercial mink baits are generally scorned, though most of the Indians have tried them.

A number of different trap sets are used for mink. The most common of these is called the cubby set, because the trapper makes a little cubby or "house" and puts a trap at its opening. When he has found a promising spot, the Indian first looks around for a small natural cranny, usually a little cleft in the bank, an overhanging tangle of roots, or a shelter formed by a bunch of alder or willow trunks at the edge of a frozen lake or river. Any natural enclosure is good, as long as the mink will have to look inside to investigate the smell.

Once a trapper finds such a place, with a fairly narrow opening, he puts the bait inside toward the back of the cranny, then finds a branch or pole 5 or 6 feet long and fastens the trap chain to it. This acts as a toggle to prevent the trap's being dragged away. This done, the trap is placed in the middle of the opening with the toggle laid on the snow in front of it. The enclosure must be fairly tight, so that to get at the bait the mink must come in through the front opening, where it steps on the trap. Since most natural crannies are fairly open, a number of sticks are pushed into the snow alongside the trap and around the sides of the cranny like a small fence, leaving only one entryway for the mink.

The Chalkyitsik Kutchin do not attempt to bury or conceal their traps. After a set is completed they take a small handful of dry snow and sprinkle a dusting over the pan and spring of the trap to make it appear less out of place. Years ago they buried their traps completely by making a little depression in the snow, placing the trap inside and laying tissue paper on it, then putting a thin layer of snow over that. Today it is not considered necessary to do this, except for wolf, wolverine, and fox sets.

Mink and some other fur animals in this region do not seem to be particularly frightened of human scent or other unnatural signs around a trap set, a marked difference from the behavior of the same species in the "lower forty-eight," where trappers must go to great lengths to conceal all scents and other indicators of human activity around a set. Perhaps animals in the Chalkyitsik region have had so little contact with man that they have not learned to fear him. Chalkyitsik trappers make no effort whatsoever to construct natural-looking sets or to eliminate tracks and other signs of their activity, though they do attempt to minimize the amount of foreign odor that gets onto their traps.

Another good way to catch mink is with a burrow set, which is made when a trapper finds a hole that is being used by mink or is likely to be investigated by them. Snow is cleared from the hole entrance to make room for the trap, to provide a bare spot for it, and to make the hole conspicuous so that a passing mink will notice it. Then the trap is placed on bare dirt, or occasionally on a bed of dry grass or twigs, to keep it off the snow. Otherwise it may freeze in an open position. The trap is always put right at the burrow entrance, but not inside. A few sticks or twigs are pushed into the snow on both sides of the hole and trap, so the mink must step right onto the trap to get inside, and a little snow is sprinkled on the trap's pan and spring. Bait is often used with hole sets, placed either inside the opening or beside it, though this is unnecessary for active dens.

Trappers are usually very good at remembering where each set is, for every spot along their trails is known to them and stands out as a place different from any other. In some areas, however, especially around the edge of sizable lakes, sloughs, or rivers, it is extremely difficult to remember the exact location of every trap. All an Indian needs to remind him is a small blaze on a tree near the set, or a stick put in the snow alongside his trail. Markers like this are most important after a heavy snowfall or a windstorm that causes drifting, when a set may be completely hidden under the snow.

Weasels (*Mustela erminea*) are sometimes caught in traps set for mink. No special effort is made to catch these little animals, worth only about a dollar apiece, but they often frequent willow and alder thickets adjacent to water and it is not uncommon to find one in a mink set. When this happens a man will probably take the animal home so that his son can sell the skin. Young boys sometimes trap weasels (usually called ermine in their white winter coats) around the village, and may get one or two each year.

Checking Sets

Several days to a week after he sets out his mink traps, or after his last previous check, the trapper runs his line. Checking traps simply involves driving along the trail between sets, looking at each one to see if it has been disturbed or if anything is in it. A careful trapper stops at each one and walks over to it for a close look to see that everything is all right. He might also put in a fresh bait. Sometimes a man finds mink tracks going right by the set, the animal showing no interest in it whatsoever. The Kutchin say that in some years, or parts of some years, mink become wary of traps or disinterested in them, whereas in other years they are easily trapped.

If there has been a wind or fresh snow between checks, some or all of the sets will have to be repaired. To do this, the trap is pulled out of the snow by its chain, then replaced after the new snow is cleared away and a firm base prepared. Heavy snowfall or (especially) hoarfrost can freeze small traps so they will not snap or will do so only if the animal steps on them directly and firmly, and so each trap may be snapped and reset to be sure it is not frozen. This is not necessary with large traps, such as those used for lynx. If a snowfall, windstorm, or heavy hoarfrost occurs soon after a man runs his line, he will probably have a poor catch next time around because the sets have been spoiled.

Mink sometimes live for many days in a trap, unless the weather is cold enough to freeze them to death quickly. When a trapper finds one alive he strikes it on the head with a long stick, which knocks it unconscious but seldom kills it. A few more blows may finish it off, but some trappers prefer to pinch the animal's heart.

After a mink is killed and removed from a trap, the set is rebuilt. Once an animal has been taken in a particular trap set the chances are said to be much better for getting more in it, since mink leave a heavy scent around the place where they are caught, which apparently attracts others of their kind. Of course not all animals that get into traps stay in them. They may chew or twist off a foot that is in a trap, or manage to pull a poorly caught foot out relatively unscathed. Indians always look for hairs on the trap to see what kind of animal has escaped.

Uses of Mink

Mink brought in from the trapline are usually solidly frozen, and so a trapper hangs them up to thaw when he reaches his cabin. They are hung near the roof, where they soften in an hour or two. Skinning an animal of this size is fairly simple, but requires some practice. Using a well-sharpened pocketknife, the trapper makes a cut along the back of each hind leg, from the anus to the "ankle." The skin is pulled and cut away from the legs, and the feet are cut off and left attached to the skin. The tail is skinned by grasping the hide in one hand and the carcass in the other and stripping the skin off with a strong pull.

Once the hide is removed from both hind legs and the tail, it is gradually skinned toward the head, turning it inside out. The knife is used to cut between flesh and skin, leaving as little fat as possible on the hide. Each foreleg is skinned to the "wrist," where the foot is severed and left attached to the pelt. Then the skin is peeled down and cut free around the ears, eyes, nose, and lips. This technique, known as casing, removes a pelt in the same way a child pulls off his sock by turning it inside out.

The hide is now put on a stretcher, a tapering board 2½ to 3 feet long and 3 to 4 inches wide, cut down the middle and hinged at its pointed end so it can be spread apart and held open with a wooden peg. The pelt is slipped onto it, inside out, and the boards are spread to stretch it tight. Mink are always scraped to remove the adhering fat before being put up to dry. This is done with a scraper made from the sharpened leg bone of a moose, which takes off the fat but will not cut the skin. Scraping is hard work, but it takes only five or ten minutes to clean each mink, after which the stretcher is set up on poles or rafters near the cabin roof, where the heat dries the hide overnight.

After a pelt is thoroughly dried it is turned right side out so its fur can be examined by the purchaser. Prices vary according to the size, color, and quality of the fur, and a man never knows what he might get for any pelt. During the year of this study large, prime pelts brought twenty-five to thirty-five dollars, whereas those of lower quality netted from five dollars up. The fur is the only valuable part of a mink, and the carcass is simply discarded. Individual trappers caught anywhere from two or three mink to about twenty-five during the 1968–69 season.

13 Marten

Habitat and Season

The marten, or *tsuk* (*Martes americana*), is another member of the weasel family. It is very similar in appearance to the mink, but usually is a few inches longer and weighs a little more. This graceful creature is yellowish brown to dark brown in color, with light, almost orange, fur under its neck. It is best known for its ability to chase and catch red squirrels in the trees, and squirrels are undoubtedly an important part of its diet. It also eats other small animals, such as hares, mice, lemmings, and an occasional bird. The Kutchin say that marten will also eat berries.

Marten are one of the most important fur animals in the country exploited by the Tranjik Kutchin. They occur everywhere, but are most common in the hills flanking the Porcupine River and Black River valleys. Anyone interested in trapping specifically for marten has to go into the larger and steeper hills, because in other areas they are not common enough to make the effort worthwhile. They seem to prefer country that is forested with spruce or mixed spruce and deciduous trees.

Although he knows quite well what habitat they prefer, a trapper can never be sure of finding marten at a given time because they are so mobile. Marten are great travelers, able to cover up to 25 miles in a single night (Rhode and Barker 1953, p. 31). The idea

218

of a home territory apparently has little relevance to them, since they can move out of an area almost completely and not return to it for some time. Trappers are well aware of this propensity because it greatly affects the size of their catch. Wanderings of individual animals have little bearing on trapping success, but they sometimes move in or out of a particular area en masse.

The Tranjik Kutchin say that two things will cause an emigration of marten from an area—caribou and lynx. If caribou move into an area to winter, the marten for some unknown reason leave immediately. Lynx have the same effect, apparently because they prey on marten. Some trappers have poor years or are forced to pull their traps early when the marten leave their territory.

Locating Trap Sets

Marten traplines are usually farther from Chalkyitsik than any other type of line, because marten are common only in the hilly country that flanks the Yukon Flats. Men who trap marten usually travel out to a main cabin near the hills and from there operate one or more side lines which run into the good marten country. This means that Indians who want to catch marten have to run their lines with dogs, on foot, or both; if a snowmobile is used at all, it is only to reach the main cabin.

One of the keys to success in marten trapping is to make a large number of sets. A good trapper puts out a total of 100 to 150 sets today, and in the past this figure was probably doubled. In country where marten are common, traps are usually set at regular intervals along the trail, ideally every hundred yards, "so you always see the next trap from the one before it." Since this is done in areas where marten abound year after year, little attention need be paid to the presence or absence of tracks. But in most areas traps are spaced more widely, and tracks are important for deciding where to make sets.

Trappers generally watch for tracks when making any kind of sets. A place where the tracks show that several marten have passed by is always a good spot for a trap, and in some cases a trapper remembers that a certain place has been good year after year—either he has caught marten there many times or they tend to pass by several times each winter. Trapping is a game of probabilities, and the idea is to set in places where there is a good chance that an animal will come by sooner or later.

Trap-setting Methods

Marten are usually taken with number 1 traps, which are strong enough to catch and hold them and light enough to haul in rough terrain. Number 1½ traps will also take marten but are too large and heavy to carry around in the hills. They are sometimes caught in larger traps set for lynx, fox, or wolf.

Marten could perhaps be attracted to a set by almost any kind of meat, but the Kutchin seem to prefer strong-smelling rotted fish. Beaver castor smeared on a duck's wing, hare's foot, or piece of furry moosehide also makes a good bait, especially if the castor is old and smelly. A number of mixtures like those described for mink trapping are also used. Marten are easy to trap because they are curious, unafraid of human scent, and strongly attracted by the smell of baits. "Marten is just like a rabbit," the people say, "he'll go right in your trap."

The basic type of set used for marten trapping is the cubby set. The cubby is usually made against the trunk of a fair-sized spruce tree (12- to 18-inch diameter) alongside the trail. Two parallel walls of sticks, about 7 inches apart, extend outward some 10 to 15 inches from the tree, making a little enclosure with its open end usually toward the trail. The walls are 18 to 20 inches high, made from six to eight stout sticks (1 to 4 inches in diameter) pushed into the snow. Sometimes heavier sticks, split lengthwise and with the flat part facing in, are used to make the walls.

The walls are usually vertical but sometimes slope inward creating a sort of gabled effect, which keeps snow off the trap. Marten cubbies are always tightly built, with narrow spaces between the sticks, in contrast to the loose, almost haphazard construction of cubbies made for other animals. Careful trappers often cut two to five spruce saplings, remove the lower limbs, and lean the trees over each cubby, forming an umbrella or canopy to keep snow off the set. If no saplings are handy, spruce boughs will serve the purpose.

Once a cubby is built the trap is placed just inside its open end, with the toggle laid across in front of it. The trap just about fills

A cubby set for marten, with a spruce bough "roof" to keep snow from covering the trap. The toggle is concealed beneath the snow.

the opening, and if there is much space around the edges sticks are put alongside it, forcing any animal that enters to step on the trap. Snow is sprinkled lightly on the trap, but no further effort is made to conceal it. Bait is wired or nailed onto the trunk of the tree or otherwise placed at the cubby's far end.

Hares, squirrels, and shrews sometimes damage fur animals that die in cubby traps, and this is especially common with marten. Hares and squirrels pull the guard hairs out of a dead marten, apparently for "nesting" material, leaving large patches of exposed underfur, which, of course, ruins the pelt. Shrews are even more original. They make a little hole through the skin and eat the flesh inside. Given enough time they can hollow out a carcass, leaving just a shell for the trapper. The perforated hide is worth little.

One method for keeping marten safe is to make pole sets. Two poles 4 to 5 feet long are laid side by side against a low tree branch or a bush, with the upper ends 3 feet above ground, and a trap is put on them a few inches from the top. Its chain is fastened to another pole, a bush, or a branch above the trap. Bait is fastened to the tree or bush several inches above the set, and the marten steps on the trap as he goes after the bait. In short, the set consists of an inclined plane or ramp which the animal follows when it is attracted to the bait. When a marten is caught it eventually falls off the ramp, but since the chain is fastened above it hangs there and dies quickly. Chalkyitsik trappers seldom use pole sets, however, because marten too often pass them by.

Marten lines must be checked often, because animals should be removed quickly to prevent damage to their pelts. This is especially true when a line has just been set; the first and second checks are generally very productive, then the take falls off considerably. A man who wants to bring home good fur and to keep his sets "working" removes the game frequently. This principle applies to all trapping but is especially true for marten.

Uses of Marten

After they are brought in off the trapline, marten are skinned and their pelts stretched and dried in much the same way as was described earlier for mink. The skin is "cased" by peeling it off so that it is inside out and is slipped onto a drying board. After drying it is turned fur side out so the buyer can easily appraise its quality. The carcass is nearly always discarded, though it might sometimes be used for dog food.

As the country becomes less heavily exploited, there seem to be increasing numbers of marten. Some areas, for example, are trapped only briefly each winter, or are left untouched for several

A pole set for marten. The arrow points to the trap. A moose-skin bait is affixed to the tree above the trap.

years at a time. Men who go into the wilder areas make exceptionally large catches. Several years ago an old man returned to his former territory and took some two hundred marten in a month. Other trappers, perhaps not as highly skilled as this man, are lucky to catch seventy-five in a season in the more heavily exploited country nearer Chalkyitsik.

Trappers can usually count on fair catches of marten year after year, unless they happen to be in an area affected by a local emigration like those described above. Beyond this, the size of the catch depends in large degree on the trapper's ambition, which often hinges on the price the pelts will bring. In the year of this study marten were worth ten to twenty-five dollars apiece, which was considered fairly good; but since lynx brought more and were particularly abundant, many trappers went after them instead.

Marten are the most important fur animals for those of the Chalkyitsik Kutchin who own traplines extending into hilly country to the north and east. These men have probably earned more from marten than from any other animal, especially in the past when they lived in line cabins on the upper Black River and along the Porcupine. Other men have spent most of their lives trapping out in the flats, and as a consequence have caught relatively few marten. In general, this animal has been of great importance to the Black River Kutchin; although small in size, it has generally brought a fairly high price and has been common enough to assure large catches year after year.

14   Lynx

Introduction

The lynx, or *ninjii* (*Lynx canadensis*), closely resembles the familiar bobcat of more southerly regions. Lynx have long legs and large paws which are partially webbed to help keep them on top of the deep, soft snow; their fur is dark gray, becoming light colored in late winter and early spring. A beardlike ruff fringes their neck behind the chin, and each ear is topped with a long tassel of black hair. They measure 2 to 3 feet in body length and weigh 15 to 30 pounds. Lynx are found throughout subarctic North America, their distribution coinciding fairly well with the limits of the boreal forest; they are common throughout the Black River and Porcupine River country but seem to favor the forested river valleys and the Yukon Flats.

Lynx feed primarily on snowshoe hares, perhaps almost exclusively when hares are abundant. In fact, the population of lynx and hares may fluctuate in concert, so dependent is the predator upon its favored prey. The Indians say that when there are many rabbits the lynx get thin, because they cannot build up fat eating nothing but lean rabbit meat. During years when hares are few, lynx sustain themselves on other prey, such as voles, grouse, and ptarmigan.

The population of lynx in the Black River country, and in North

225

America as a whole, is subject to marked cyclic fluctuation. The population cycles have averaged about ten years in length at the continental level over the past two hundred years (Keith 1963, p. 118). Coupled with these long-term changes in lynx population are localized movements which cause dramatic shifts in abundance. During the winter of this study, for example, trapline success and frequency of lynx tracks in certain areas indicated that a number of such movements took place throughout the region. On a trapline that ran for some 20 miles along the north side of the Porcupine River, lynx were abundant early in the season, disappeared almost completely for about two months, then became fairly common late in the season.

Lynx often seem to disappear during spells of extreme cold. Apparently they can stay in one place for long periods at such times. They also go up into the hills in cold weather and move down along the rivers during warm spells. Perhaps they go to the uplands when it is cold because temperature inversions make higher areas warmer.

The legal trapping season for lynx is rather long, running from November 1 through March 31 (in 1969–70). The men like to start setting for lynx by mid-November, because they often make good catches early in the season. The skins become fully prime after the first of the year, however, and remain so into the early spring. Lynx are also rather active during the latter part of the season, making for large takes when the skins are most valuable. By March, however, some are past their prime.

Locating Trap Sets

Most of the Chalkyitsik Kutchin have been using the same traplines for many years, and know from long experience the best places for lynx sets. They often leave some of their traps out in the woods during the off-season, hanging them in trees near the spots where they are to be set again next year. A trapper may use the same setting places continuously over a very long period, perhaps for a lifetime.

Trap sites are usually associated with some geographic peculiarity that tends to funnel lynx through a certain place, such as a narrow isthmus of forest between two open areas, or the end of a forested point jutting out into a lake or meadow. A narrow V-shaped ravine, creek, or slough is good, because it is a constricted natural pathway. The top of any steep river or lake bank is also attractive to lynx, because they like to walk along in the woods at the edge of an open area.

A toboggan or snowshoe trail is often used as a route for travel by lynx and other animals, especially when the snow is deep and soft, and so trappers can make sets right alongside their trails. Wherever there is a naturally attractive feature in the landscape, the presence of a packed trail doubles its value as a trap site. In effect, the area becomes a crossroads. The place where a long, steep slough bank and man's trail intersect is ideal, for example, because lynx following either the bank or the trail will encounter a trap set here.

Each trapper makes a large number of sets in places where he has caught lynx previously, but also keeps his eyes open for fresh tracks indicating that lynx are active in an area. Trappers usually do not make sets where they see only one lynx track, because the chances are not good that the animal will pass by again. They look for areas where there are two or more sets of tracks within a short distance, going in opposite directions. If all the tracks go in the same direction they probably record the passing of a lynx family, since one to three kittens usually stay with the mother through their first winter.

Another way to find good trap sites is to watch for a place where several lynx pass by during the course of a month or two. There is always a good chance they will come through there again. One expert trapper said that it is extremely difficult to identify good lynx crossings just by looking at the landscape; places that look good are actually not, and others that appear in no way different from the surrounding country are excellent. A man has to consider both landforms and sign, always watching closely and remembering what he has seen from week to week and from year to year.

Trap-setting Methods

Lynx do not have a particularly acute sense of smell but can be attracted to trap sets with a number of different kinds of bait. Most important of these is fluid from the oil and castor glands of the beaver. "Lynx are crazy for the smell of castor," the old-timers say. "When they smell it they just can't pass it by." Some men use straight castor as a bait, but many concoct a mixture with castor as a basic ingredient. Additional components of these mixtures include rotten fish and the musk from mink and muskrat scent glands. Chalkyitsik trappers often use the same bait for lynx, marten, and mink.

Although lynx do not have an acute sense of smell, this weakness is apparently balanced by exceptionally good vision, which the animal relies on for much of its hunting (Pruitt 1967, p. 64). Trappers often take advantage of this and of the cat's curiosity by putting bits of a red ribbon on a tree or branch above a set. The Huslia Koyukon rely almost exclusively on visual attractants. Most commonly they draw a little face on a blazed tree trunk behind the trap, or on a piece of wood that is put in the set.

The best trap for lynx is a number 3; the larger and more powerful number 4 trap is also good, though the Kutchin use very few of that size. Number 1½ and 2 traps are a bit small for the big feet of a lynx. Most lynx traps are set in cubbies similar to those described for marten but somewhat larger and more loosely built. Once the cubby is put together, the bait, which has been smeared onto a hare's foot, bird wing, or piece of fur, is fastened to the tree trunk inside the cubby. The trap chain is fastened to a large, heavy toggle, usually a dry branch 6 to 10 feet long. The toggle is laid on the snow in front of the cubby, and the trap is placed on a bed of dry twigs or grass just inside the cubby's opening. Some powder snow is sprinkled on the trap pan and springs, but no further effort is made to conceal it. Lynx are more curious than wary.

Small twigs 5 to 8 inches long are stuck into the snow around the trap to keep small animals away from it and to guide the animal's foot onto it. Sometimes only four twigs are used, two in front of the trap and two behind it, angled into the snow to form a shallow V, but most trappers prefer to poke about a dozen little sticks into the snow in a circle, like a small "fence" with the trap inside. The twigs slant sharply outward from the trap, so they funnel the animal's foot down into it.

By far the major part of lynx trapping is done with cubby sets, but some simpler techniques are occasionally utilized. Most important of these is the trail set, which consists of a trap placed in

A cubby set for lynx. The trap is encircled by small sticks at the cubby entrance. The toggle is buried by new snow.

the middle of a side line trail (one that is checked on foot) or in a lynx trail. The trap is toggled to a branch, which is laid alongside the path out of the way. Four small sticks are poked into the snow, two on either side of the trap, making a shallow V or X that helps to guide the animal's foot onto the pan. This arrangement of sticks is identical to that used for some cubby sets.

The trail set is something of a gamble, because a lynx can easily get over or around it. Some bait is usually rubbed on a tree trunk alongside it to increase the chances for a catch. When a man comes to his trail sets he always steps over them, not around them, because if an animal sees tracks going around a set it will do likewise. The trap is not concealed in any way, except for the usual sprinkle of snow.

The Tranjik Kutchin undoubtedly use other kinds of lynx sets besides those described here, but these are by far the most common. Much more could be said about individual variations, since every man has his own style. Indeed, it is often possible to tell who made a set just by looking at it, since particular methods or arrangements are used so regularly by certain individuals. There are also differences in the care and skill that go into making sets. Some men are inventive and experimental, others are routinized and unimaginative, and these differences in approach are probably reflected in the size of a man's catch, especially when they involve care and attention to details.

Checking Traps

The method of checking lynx traplines is essentially the same as that described for mink and marten. It simply involves walking or riding from trap to trap inspecting, removing catches, and remaking sets. Lynx traps should be checked regularly, every ten days to two weeks, so that traps are emptied and kept "working." There is a definite chance that animals will be lost if they are left in traps too long. Lynx often drag the trap and toggle a fair distance if they remain alive for some time. It is easy to track them unless a fresh snow or a windstorm obliterates their tracks, when they can easily be lost for good.

Trappers are especially anxious to get out to their lines during warm spells and after windstorms, because at these times lynx tend to move around more, which increases the chances for a good catch. During warm weather they also tend to remain alive in the traps. The Kutchin say that trapped lynx sometimes live for a month. When an Indian finds a lynx alive in a trap he is not afraid of it, but he does treat it with great respect. There are three really dangerous trapped animals—lynx, wolf, and wolverine. Lynx are probably the least dangerous of these, but their knifelike claws can do considerable damage.

The best way to kill a trapped lynx without damaging the hide is to snare it. A cable snare is fastened onto the end of a 5- or 10-foot pole. Then, keeping at a safe distance, the trapper slips the snare around the lynx's neck and pulls it tight, lifting the animal from the ground as much as possible. It fights wildly for about two minutes, then finally goes limp. The pole is leaned against a tree for several minutes to make sure the animal is dead, then the snare is removed from the pole and left, still locked tight, around the animal's neck. The prospect of having a lynx "come to life" while it is being hauled in the toboggan is not at all pleasant, and the Indians make sure it does not happen.

Sometimes it is difficult or impossible to snare lynx in this way. If it is so dark that the animal is only a shadow in the brush, or if the bushes are too thick to get a snare to the animal, it is killed by clubbing it across the back of its neck with a long, stout pole. Some men strike lynx on the head, but this causes blood clots under the hide which make for difficult skinning. Lynx are rarely shot because the bullet does considerable damage to the hide. If a man comes across a lynx in another man's trap, he kills the animal and hangs it up in a tree or bush so nothing can disturb or damage it.

Snaring

The Kutchin have been using snares for catching lynx since aboriginal times and are highly skilled in methods of setting them. Snares are inexpensive, easy to transport, easy to set, and very effective indeed. Lynx die quickly in a snare, almost without a fight, so there are virtually no escapes. Although the Chalkyitsik Kutchin set considerably fewer snares than traps, the number of catches per set is probably higher in snares.

The snares used today are commercially made "patent snares" that are ordered through the mail. These snares are made from double-twisted steel cable with a locking slide that will not permit them to loosen once they have tightened around an animal's neck. They come in a number of sizes, depending on the thickness of the cable; Chalkyitsik trappers use numbers 0, 1, and 2 for lynx.

Snare sets are located by somewhat different criteria than traps.

Since snares are usually positioned where animals will walk into them during the normal course of their travels, bait is not necessary. Nearly all lynx snares are set in trails, usually a man's own snowshoe and toboggan trails, which the animals like to follow. These trails are narrowly bordered by vegetation on both sides, very dense in some places, so that animals are more likely to walk into a snare than try to go around it in the brush and deep snow.

Sometimes a man will make short side trails into the brush on snowshoes, placing snares along them. Lynx like to follow side trails that branch off a main trapline trail, "because they're curious to see what is there." A trapper may prefer this kind of set because it is off the main trail where he does not have to move it every time he passes by with a dog team or snowmobile. In some places lynx have their own trails, which are excellent locations for snares.

Most trappers put snares in their line trails "every so often,"

A typical snare set for lynx. The snare may be tethered to a loose pole or to a young tree growing alongside the trail. Sticks in the snow beside the snare guide animals into it.

anywhere from a few hundred yards to several miles apart. The number of sets depends on the length of a line, the ambition of the trapper, and the number of good areas. Snares are usually set in a place that is close to a natural lynx crossing or lynx trail, though sometimes a man just makes a set on a "hunch" with no special reason to believe that place is better than any other. In any case, a snare is nearly always put in a spot where the trail is narrow with thick vegetation on both sides. Willows and other shrubby plants often grow partway into a trail, narrowing it enough so that a dog team or snowmobile brushes them as it passes. These are good places because a snare works best at a narrow spot where it almost fills the gap without need for artificial means of blocking the way around.

When a trapper finds a fairly narrow place he fastens a snare onto a slender tree growing alongside the trail, or to a 5- to 10-foot pole that he lays in the brush either across or beside the trail. Each snare is twisted onto a 2-foot piece of stiff wire, which is used to fasten the snare to its toggle. Since the toggle is usually alongside the trail, the wire sticks out horizontally into the pathway, with the snare hanging from its outer end. The snare itself hangs 15 to 20 inches above the trail's surface. Its loop is 7 to 9 inches in diameter and must be no larger—otherwise the incredibly agile lynx may jump right through it. Care is taken to keep strong odors such as dog scent or gasoline off the snare, because lynx will smell them and walk around the set.

Once a snare is tethered, opened, and adjusted to the correct height, it is usually necessary to put some slender twigs alongside it to guide the animal into the noose. Three or four twiggy willow or alder withes, 2 or 3 feet long, are set in the snow on each side of the loop, making a fairly natural-looking barrier with its only opening through the center where the noose hangs. A foot-long stick is usually placed right under the snare as well to discourage animals from going under the set.

Lynx snares are occasionally set in cubbies, more or less the same as those used for traps. The cubby is 3 to 5 feet long, making a narrow passageway with a bait fastened inside. The snare is toggled to a heavy pole and set in the opening, where it will catch a lynx as it enters. Cubbies can also be made from a small circle of short poles with a bait inside and a snare set in the narrow opening. Similar arrangements are made in a number of situations such as a natural recess in a lake or creek bank or a natural enclosure among the bushes. Sticks are set up in the snow to make one narrow entryway and the snare is placed there, usually about a foot off the ground.

Uses of Lynx

Snared animals are nearly always dead when the trapper checks his line. The snare is removed from its tether, since it is solidly frozen into the animal's flesh, and another one is put in its place to remake the set. Back in his line cabin or at home in the village, the trapper must hang frozen lynx from the rafters to thaw them for skinning. Because they are fairly large, they usually take all night to soften. If a lynx has not frozen solidly it will be infested with biting fleas, and so a man first kills them by sprinkling a powdered insect killer into the fur and wrapping the carcass tightly in a bag for a couple of hours.

Lynx are skinned about the same way as marten and mink, except that considerably more work is involved for an animal this size. The carcasses are rarely discarded after skinning, because lynx flesh is considered good eating. The fat ones are preferred, and thin or old ones are fed to the dogs. Not enough lynx are caught to add much bulk to the diet, but they are considered a treat or at least a variation from the daily fare.

The season's catch of lynx for the active trappers in Chalkyitsik ran between twenty and forty per trapline in 1969–70, some of which was divided between partners, halving the individual profit. Lynx prices vary according to the size and quality of the pelt, and in this year they brought from twelve dollars to almost forty dollars apiece. Several men caught over twenty lynx in a single check of their lines, but this good luck was balanced by times when they took few or none at all.

15 The Minor Fur Species

Introduction

This chapter deals with four species of fur animals of minor importance to the modern Tranjik Kutchin. They are considered together partly because it was impossible to obtain a large amount of information regarding them and partly because the methods of trapping them are for the most part very similar. Only one of these species, the red fox, is common in the Black River and Porcupine River country; wolves and wolverines are about as common here as anywhere, which means only that they are scattered and seldom encountered; and otters are very rare in most of this region.

Because they are generally uncommon, wolves, wolverines, and otters have never been economically important to the Black River people. Wolves and wolverines are significant in the people's lives, however, because they habitually plunder caches and cabins and steal fur from traplines. Few men trap red fox today, despite their relative abundance and the increasing value of their hides, but in early times, when they brought a very high price, great effort was put into fox trapping.

The accounts of wolverine, wolf, fox, and otter trapping which follow are less complete than those for other fur species. There was little opportunity to study the actual construction of trap and snare sets for these species, and less was said about them in the course of conversations, which is particularly unfortunate since these are among the most fascinating animals inhabiting the boreal forest.

Wolverine

The Animal

Even trappers who spend a lifetime out in the bush rarely see more of a wolverine than its tracks. Few animals are more adept at avoiding man while still managing to get a free meal at his expense now and then. The wolverine (*Gulo luscus*), which the Kutchin call *naah-tryaa,* is a large and extraordinarily powerful member of the weasel family. It is 3 to 4 feet in length, weighs 20 to 35 pounds, and looks almost like a small bear. It is dark brown, sometimes almost black, with a pair of yellowish stripes from the shoulders to the rump. It has large feet and a short, brushy tail (Burt and Grossenheider 1952, p. 42).

Wolverines are found throughout most of the boreal forest and tundra country of Alaska and Canada. Their tracks are likely to be seen anywhere in the region exploited by the Chalkyitsik Kutchin, but they are most common in the hilly flanks of the Yukon Flats and in heavily forested areas along the Little Black, Porcupine, and upper Black rivers. They are solitary wanderers, so widely scattered that a man will rarely see more than a track or two when he runs 50 to 100 miles of trapline. Where they are most common, a trapper can figure on several being around his line each year, sometimes just passing through and sometimes making a practice of stealing fur from his sets.

The Indians say that wolverines are scavengers in the strictest sense of the word, rarely killing any food for themselves. They sniff out carrion beneath the snow or follow wolf packs to clean up their leavings. Beyond this, the Kutchin know little of how wolverines make a living except when they get into a trapline. Trapped animals and trap baits are prime attractions for these freeloaders, which sometimes follow a man's trail emptying each set of its bait or catch cleverly enough to avoid being caught. What they cannot eat at the moment they carry off and cache for later use. They are even said to make "false caches" by piling up snow here and there, so that it is difficult for a man to find his fur and reclaim it.

The strength of wolverines is legendary, and in this case the legend seems basically correct. They haul away chunks of carrion several times their size and weight. Both Indians and Eskimos say that wolverines are not afraid of bears, and perhaps on the strength of their ego alone will back them down and send them on their way. Few caches or cabins are safe from their entry, and once inside they will eat all they can and defile the rest.

Some white trappers nurture an almost pathological hatred for wolverines and try to destroy as many as they can. The Kutchin try to catch any that are around their traplines, but do not appear to bear a grudge against the species in general. Wolverines were worth little on the market until recent years, and the main reason for catching them was to protect the trapline. But they have become increasingly valuable in the fur trade over the past few years, and so the incentive to catch them is increasing. A single hide might bring thirty-five to fifty dollars now, compared with five dollars several years ago. Wolverine pelts have always been valuable to the people themselves, because they make fine ruffs and trimming for parkas. Wolverine carcasses might be used for dog food, but beyond this the meat has no value. The trapping season for these animals is very long, from November 1 until July 15 (in 1969–70). There is also a legal hunting season, from September 1 until March 31, but rifle kills are limited to one animal per person. Chalkyitsik trappers caught about six wolverines in 1969–70.

Trapping and Snaring

There are several criteria for deciding when and where to make wolverine sets. The routes of the wolverine, like those of other animals, tend to be funneled through ravines and narrow sloughs, along ridge tops, and so on. Traps set in such natural corridors or crossings may catch not only wolverines but also wolves, foxes, or lynx. Wolverine sets are sometimes put near the ends of a trapline, to help protect it against possible raids. Moose-kill sites are another good place to set for wolverines (as well as wolves and foxes) because they attract these scavenging animals. Finally, tracks are an important indicator in locating wolverine sets, especially if there is fresh sign in the same area on more than one occasion. Traps are not often set specifically for wolverine because it is so difficult to prevent them from escaping, but any set that is made for wolves is also considered a wolverine set. Perhaps the best method for catching wolverine is the post set. A small tree is cut off 3 or 4 feet above the ground, and a piece of moose skin is nailed or wired near the top of the stump. A trap is toggled onto the tree and set at its base, usually on the side toward the trapper's trail. The trap must be concealed by placing it in a little depression, covering it with tissue or a bit of cloth, then sprinkling snow over the top. If there is hard snow around, a chunk may be cut and placed over the jaws, then shaved very thin with a large knife; snow is then dusted over the springs. When a wolverine (or wolf) tries to steal the moose-skin bait, it steps on the trap.

Wolverines are very difficult animals to keep in a trap once caught. A powerful trap, number 3 with a double spring, is always used, but once its trapped foot freezes the animal will chew it off and escape. The only sure way to get a trapped wolverine is to reach it before this happens. Once a wolverine has escaped it will never be caught again; it may continue to raid sets but now it knows where the trap is and avoids it. If a trapper finds a live wolverine in his set he keeps a very respectful distance and shoots it.

Snares are probably more effective than traps for catching wolverines. They will apparently enter a snare with little hesitation, but there is a good chance that they will twist and chew it relentlessly until it snaps. Number 1 and 2 snares are the preferred sizes for wolverines. They are generally placed in a man's own trail, in a well-used animal trail, or near a bait or kill site. In the last case, snares are placed in small natural passageways between shrubs or bushes around a moose or caribou kill. Some meat, entrails, bones, or hide are left behind to attract animals. A good method is to nail or hang the skin of a moose in a tree, then set snares around the area.

Trail snares for wolverine must be set very carefully, because the animal will avoid a set that does not look perfectly natural. A trapper must not step off the trail in the area and must avoid disturbing the surroundings in any way; he looks for a narrow place in the trail where brush extends into it far enough so that sticks are not required to block the way around the snare. There must also be a small (about 1½-inch diameter), limber tree nearby for the toggle, because if the tree is stiff and stout a wolverine will break the snare when caught.

The snare has a long, heavy wire so it can be fastened high, 2½ to 3 feet above the ground, and it is simply hung between the narrow bushes, about a foot from the surface, with no sticks or other artificial surroundings. The only changes in the natural setting are the man's trail or tracks and the snare hanging from its long wire. The snare is fastened high to take advantage of the flexibility of its tether. Once a wolverine is caught it tends to go round and round the tree, wrapping the snare on the trunk until it becomes so short that the animal's feet can hardly touch the ground, which helps to kill it quickly. But even when all these extra steps are taken a good percentage of snared wolverines escape.

Deadfalls

The Kutchin say that the deadfall, made according to an aboriginal pattern, is the most effective device for catching wolverines. Some of the older men still make deadfalls, but only when tracks show that a wolverine is around the trapline. For all other animals they rely completely on traps or snares.

The only type of deadfall used in recent years by the Chalkyitsik Kutchin is the samson-post deadfall, made as follows: A small cubby, roofed over with sticks, is built against the trunk of a spruce tree, and a log perhaps 10 feet long and 10 inches in diameter is placed on the ground crosswise in front of it. Long stakes are driven into the ground on both sides of the log, two at each end, and another log, about the same size, is placed on top of the first, held between these same stakes. The top log is raised at one end, making an open space about six to eight inches wide between the two logs at the cubby entrance.

A samson-post trigger is now set in place to support the upper log. This consists of a slender round stick that rests horizontally on the lower log and extends into the cubby. A piece of bait is placed on the cubby end of this stick. Another stick, about 6 inches long, is set vertically on the end of the horizontal bait stick, and props up the top log. Thus the vertical stick rests precariously on the small, rounded bait stick, and if anything disturbs the bait the vertical stick is dislodged so the top log crashes down. The animal's head or upper body will be caught between the two logs, killing it instantly. This same type of deadfall, in a smaller size, was formerly used for marten. (See Osgood 1940, p. 249, and 1937, p. 97, for illustrations of similar deadfalls.)

Deadfalls formerly existed in an almost bewildering variety, and many were very clever indeed, but practically all are variations on the same basic theme. The one described here is fairly representative, since all operate in much the same way. Any kind of deadfall can be built on a different scale to catch virtually every animal found in this or any other environment.

Despite their versatility and general effectiveness, deadfalls have all but disappeared in recent years, because steel traps are as good or better for catching almost all species and are immeasurably simpler to set and use. It takes all of a short winter's day to make four deadfalls, whereas a man can set many traps in that time. Even repairing and resetting deadfalls at the beginning of the season is a relatively slow job. Further, deadfalls are not portable and therefore cannot be placed where they might be most productive at a given time.

Wolf

Perhaps the most famous northern animal is the wolf (*Canis lupus*), which the Kutchin call *zhoh*. Wolves look much like oversized dogs, weighing anywhere from 70 to 170 pounds and standing about 2 feet high at the shoulder. They usually travel in small groups or packs, but solitary individuals are not rare. Wolves are fairly common throughout the territory of the Chalkyitsik Kutchin. Their tracks are frequently seen during winter travel along the lakes and rivers but are not so common that the Indians do not take special notice of wolf sign whenever they come across it.

Wolves are well known to everyone, but few people really understand them. They are much maligned as predatory killers of valuable wildlife, and unfortunately many people (the Kutchin among them) do not understand the crucial role of predators in maintaining a balanced and healthy population of prey species. It has been proved time and again that in wilderness areas a good measure of predation is beneficial or even essential for the well-being of moose, caribou, and other prey species.

So wolves, like the people who share the land with them, are predators. They depend in fair measure upon small animals, such as hares, squirrels, voles, and birds. They kill large game as well, but are generally incapable of overtaking or subduing healthy adult animals. During the course of their wanderings wolves "test" each moose and each caribou herd, trying to find animals they can kill. Healthy moose can easily fight them off, and caribou leave them behind with little effort. But the old or infirm animals weaken quickly and eventually fall prey to the wolves.

Wolves are also scavengers, cleaning up whatever carrion they come across and sometimes getting into trouble when the carrion is a trapped or snared animal. Young wolves that have not yet become wary of man are likely to raid traplines. When this happens the Indian is sure to set for them, and if they remain in the area long enough he gets them.

Trapping

It is difficult to anticipate the movements of wolves, except in the broadest sense. They often wander along open areas such as frozen lakes or rivers, and these are particularly good places to make sets for them. A man usually sets for wolves without seeing any tracks; he just knows that sooner or later a pack will probably come along on the ice and investigate the trap. Sometimes, however, wolves move through a particular area more than once, and he decides to set for them in case they return. This may be along his trapline, where he is almost required to set if he is to prevent losses from his traps.

When they kill a moose, the Indians usually leave behind certain parts such as the viscera, skin, or head, knowing that they will be very attractive to wolves. Or better still, they sometimes run across moose remains which are being eaten by wolves, and in this case sets made around the site are virtually certain to make catches. When wolves are attracted to a bait or carcass, they seem far more cautious if there are human signs around. But if sets are made long beforehand, so signs of human presence are gone, they are less cautious; and if sets are made where they have already been feeding they are not at all careful.

When traps are set around a kill site, they are placed right next to the bait, so a wolf (or wolverine or fox) will step on the trap as it sniffs or eats. The traps must be covered by a layer of snow and toggled to a solid stump or heavy log. One man said he toggles his traps onto the antlers of a bull moose head, setting one trap on each side. He also stakes the hide out on the ground and sets about a dozen traps around it. The more sets there are around a kill site the greater the chance of catching animals. Baits like moose heads are best placed out on the river or lake ice where they are visible from a distance. Wolves are very cautious and clever animals, however, and even the best sets often fail to fool them. They may circle around and around a tempting bait without a single animal's coming up to sniff at it.

Another way to catch wolves is to freeze a stake into the ice early in the fall and toggle a trap onto it, concealed under the snow at its base. Wolves are attracted to such landmarks because they urinate on them to leave a scent mark. Wolves should be taken with number 3 double-spring traps, or larger ones if available, for they are very tough and powerful animals and can escape from any but the heaviest trap. The Kutchin generally kill trapped wolves by shooting them.

Wolves were subject to a fifty-dollar bounty until 1969, when they were declared a game species. At this time a season (October 1 to April 30) applied for both trapping and hunting. Wolf hides once brought very low prices, but now are worth thirty-five to seventy dollars or more. Trappers sell the hides to fur houses, to local traders, or to villagers who want them for sewing. Wolf skins are sometimes tanned and cut into strips several inches wide for parka ruffs.

Snaring

Only five to ten wolves are caught each year by Chalkyitsik trappers, at least half with snares, for wolves are more likely to get into a snare than a trap and are less likely to get out of it. Number 1 or 2 snares are used for these animals. The smaller size is not as strong but cuts more deeply into the skin for a quicker kill; the larger size is stronger but may be broken because the animal does not die as quickly.

Trail snares for wolves are set by much the same technique as described for wolverine and lynx. The snare is about 15 to 18 inches above the ground (measured to the bottom of the loop), and the noose is 10 to 12 inches in diameter. A stout toggle, 5 to 8 feet long, is placed in the brush alongside the trail. The set should be natural looking, like wolverine snares. Wolves rarely get into lynx sets, because they are too artificial for this animal's keen eye. Another method of snaring wolves is to make sets around kill sites. Snares are placed in natural openings through the brush around a kill, as described for wolverine sets, many snares being placed around the area to maximize the chances for success.

Besides snares in the brush, a kind of cubby set is made at kill sites. A piece of the dead animal is set inside a circle of brush or sticks, often at a place where bushes grow in a partial circle. Open spaces are closed with sticks or pieces of brush, except for a narrow opening where the snare is placed. The snare is a foot or two from the meat, about 12 to 14 inches above the ground.

Shooting and Poisoning

Wolves are rarely seen because they avoid open areas during the day and are extremely wary of a man's approach. Most of the men living in Chalkyitsik have seen few wolves and have been able to shoot only one or two. This happens more by accident than design. For example, a man might be sitting in the brush at the edge of a frozen lake or river when a wolf walks into the open within shooting range. The Kutchin do not set out to hunt wolves, for it would be foolish to do so in this region, where the brush is so thick that wolves can disappear into it and a man cannot hope to follow.

In more open country, however, it is another matter. Along the Koyukuk River the vegetation is more scattered, especially in the hills where wolves are most common, and with high-speed snowmobiles hunters can simply chase the animals down. In the first few years after machines came to this region the Indians greatly increased their catch of wolves and wolverines, because where the country is open the tireless machines can be driven in the tracks of fleeing animals until they either reach a den or can run no more. The number of wolves and wolverines has apparently declined significantly as a result of this practice.

The most deadly method of killing predators like the wolf has been outlawed for many years. Formerly the people killed those animals by setting out meat garnished with strychnine. Anything that fed on the bait staggered to its death somewhere nearby, and the trapper simply tracked it to where it lay. Many of the Chalkyitsik Kutchin have used poison in the past, but today they seem to fear and despise it because poison is extremely dangerous for user and animal alike. In the words of one old man, "Poison never dies." Any animal that eats a poisoned bait will die; scavengers which feed on animals killed by the poison will be killed in turn, and so on, until hundreds of animals may eventually die from one poison set. It is not surprising that the Indians are opposed to its use since they are always averse to senseless killing of animals.

Danger toward Man

Few beliefs are more popular in American wildlife lore than the idea that wolves are nearly as willing to pursue a man as any other prey. In this light the experiences of the Kutchin, who have inhabited wolf country for innumerable generations, are of considerable interest.

For all their ability to avoid traps and snares set for them, and to stay out of sight almost completely, wolves sometimes have a strange fearlessness of human settlements. There is little question that wolves, presumably lean and hungry ones, have often come right to the edge of Chalkyitsik and have approached occupied out-cabins in the surrounding country. Each year wolf tracks are seen within half a mile of the village. Sometimes these animals have stolen rabbits from snares, but usually they have just gone on their way.

A certain number of wolves have been attracted into the village or camps, apparently with the idea of killing and eating dogs. In some cases they were frightened away by people or barking dogs, but on two remembered occasions they entered villages and attacked dogs. A lone wolf was once shot in Chalkyitsik, and at Fort Yukon another solitary wolf dragged a dog away and killed it. Interestingly, almost all stories of approaches by wolves involve single animals, not packs. Lone wolves are said to be dangerous to man, probably because they are old or infirm, thin, and perhaps ready to die. They have been left by the others to make a living on whatever they are able to kill or scavenge.

None of the Indians I asked could recall an actual incident where a man was injured or attacked by wolves. When wolf packs approach humans they apparently do so out of curiosity, and a shout or a rifle shot will frighten them off. Clearly, wolves are not afraid of dogs, but except in rare instances of starving or rabid animals they nurture a respectful fear of man.

Red Fox

The red fox (*Vulpes fulva*) is familiar to everyone, since it is common over most of the United States and Canada. It is actually better termed the colored fox, because it has three very distinct color phases—the typical red phase (red fox), a black phase (silver fox), and a cross phase which is brownish in color (cross fox). The red and cross phases are common throughout the Chalkyitsik region, whereas the black phase is relatively uncommon. Foxes will eat almost anything. They hunt rabbits, squirrels, ptarmigan, grouse, and voles; they are sharp-nosed scavengers; and they consume a variety of plant foods, especially berries.

The legal season for trapping and hunting foxes runs from November 1 to February 28. It is best to catch them before the New Year, because they tend to rub their fur after that time, leaving patches with few guard hairs. If there is a long spell of intensely cold weather in December their fur will remain prime later in the year, because when it is cold they stay holed up and do not rub the fur off.

Foxes tend to favor open areas such as broad meadows and frozen rivers or lakes; so these are the best places to trap them. To a certain extent the location of sets within these areas is random, because there are few natural "crossings" which foxes use repeatedly. The best place for sets is near naturally attractive features, such as mounds, muskrat houses, or beaver houses, where foxes often urinate to make scent posts. Tracks are somewhat important but only in the sense that they indicate the local numbers of foxes. If a particular meadow or lake has many tracks on it, or is often crossed by fresh tracks, it may be a good place for a set.

Foxes seem unable to walk past a muskrat pushup on a lake or slough without approaching to sniff at it and perhaps to mark it with urine. A trap set beside a pushup will often catch a fox

sooner or later even without any bait. The trap and toggle must
be carefully buried, however, because foxes are too wary to go
near the place otherwise.

Another way to set fox traps is to make a small mound of snow
(about 8 inches high) at the edge of an open field and put a bait
on top of it. The trap is placed in a small depression on the downwind (south) side of the mound, covered with a piece of tissue
paper, and sprinkled with snow. The toggle and chain are also
buried. When a fox passes downwind of the set he smells the bait,
approaches it, and steps on the trap as he sniffs the top of the
mound.

A somewhat different technique, called the blind set, is also made
in open meadows and on ice-covered lakes, rivers, or sloughs. The
trap and toggle are simply placed in a flat area, well concealed under
the snow, and bait is "sprinkled around" the set. The foxes are
caught as they step around the spot sniffing or eating the bait.
Small chunks of meat or rotten fish are effective for this type of
set. Fox sets must be made carefully, avoiding unnatural scents
or appearances. Cubby sets apparently will not catch foxes, even
if the trap is buried. Number 1½ traps will hold them, but numbers
2 and 3 are the most effective sizes.

It is fairly easy to snare foxes, using the same method described
earlier for lynx sets, and trappers commonly find foxes in snares
put in their line trails for lynx. Any snare (or trap) set for wolf
or wolverine is apt to catch a fox, especially around kill sites, which
often attract them. Since they are more common than the larger
predators, many of them are taken in these sets. Number 0 snares,
which usually hold lynx, may be broken by the harder-to-kill fox.
Number 1 or 2 snares are preferred.

Trappers and hunters often see foxes as they travel in winter,
especially in the large meadows. The animals usually run for the
brush, but occasionally they just sit and watch. Snowmobiles sometimes excite more curiosity than fear. If an Indian gets within rifle
range of such an animal, he will often try to shoot it. Often it
is too small and too far away for an easy shot, however, and the
firing only frightens it away. On one occasion several men I was
with had come across a moose and were firing repeatedly at it.
In the midst of all this shooting a fox walked right between the
hunters and the moose. A hunter shot it, then resumed firing at
the moose.

Although foxes were abundant in 1969–70, and prices for good
pelts ran from twenty to twenty-five dollars, very few men made
an effort to trap them. It is difficult to understand why this was
so. One man said that he did not care to trap fox because they
so often drag the trap and toggle away, then snow or wind obliterates
the tracks so nothing can be found. Another said that fox are difficult
for him to catch, and so he sets for other animals. A third man
took exception to the common opinion that they are hard to trap.
He felt that people do not go after fox because to be successful
they must set many large-sized traps, and in a year when lynx are
abundant and bring high prices no one wishes to use his large traps
for fox.

Probably no more than twenty-five foxes were taken by Chalkyitsik trappers in 1969–70. Men who trapped during the years when
fur prices were high sometimes caught one hundred foxes, even
up to two hundred in a few cases. Today fox pelts are usually sold
to fur dealers, though the women sometimes use them as trim on
parkas or mittens. Fox carcasses may be fed to the dogs, but otherwise they are not used.

Otter

The otter (*Lutra canadensis*), called *tryaa* in Kutchin, is an aquatic
member of the weasel family. It bears some resemblance to a mink,
but is much larger and has very small ears, a broad snout, webbed
feet, and a thick, closely furred tail. Otters range from 3 to 4 feet
in length and weigh 10 to 20 pounds (Burt and Grossenheider 1952,
p. 42). They are found over most of the United States and Canada,
but their distribution is spotty. They are extremely rare in the Black
River and virtually absent from the Porcupine. Otters are said to
like swift water, such as the Salmon and Sucker rivers, where the
water remains open all winter. They are common in the Koyukuk
River country.

Otters are highly aquatic animals, never ranging very far from
water, but they travel long distances following the rivers and
streams. They are partial to fish, but also eat muskrats, clams, water
insects, and perhaps beavers. There is some disagreement among
the Kutchin on the relationship between beavers and otters. A few
say they are good friends, often living together in beaver houses;
others say that otters enter beaver houses only to prey upon the

occupants. Strangely, none of the protagonists has ever opened an otter's stomach to examine its contents for beaver remains.

The Chalkyitsik Kutchin rarely trap otters today, but the Huslia Koyukon catch a fair number each year. These animals are very hard to trap, because they are intelligent and extremely wary. The Koyukon often set for them in very narrow streams, only 2 or 3 feet across. Traps are placed in the water along each side, never in the middle, toggled to stakes driven solidly into the ground. Otters scull along in the stream with their paws out toward the sides, and catch a foot in the trap as they pass it. Traps are also set in the narrow spillway on a beaver dam, which otters swim through to enter a beaver pond.

The Koyukon also make trail sets on land. During the summer Indians watch for otter trails, which often run along a lakeshore or portage across a neck of land between two bodies of water, and when the otter season is open (November 1 to March 31 in 1969–70) they set traps in these trails, concealing them under the snow. There is presumably a chance that an otter will just slide over a set on its belly, but they walk enough of the time so that they are likely to step on the trap.

Otters can also be snared, and the Chalkyitsik Kutchin occasionally find one in a snare set under the ice in front of a beaver house. They are tough animals, however, and frequently escape by twisting the snare until it breaks. Peter James caught an otter in 1970 when he heard it growling at him from inside a burrow. He put a snare at the opening, went away, and returned to find the otter in it. A man from Hughes described an otter snare set in a narrow creek bed which the animals follow back and forth on top of the snow or ice. The lower edge of the snare is about 3 inches above the surface and the noose is about 10 inches in diameter. Number 2 snares are best, though otters often break them.

The otter has a very high-quality pelt with durable fur, but does not bring a good price today. One of the two otters taken by Chalkyitsik trappers in 1969–70 brought fifteen dollars. Apparently they are so hard to catch that few men ever take them. Even around Huslia, where there are more of them, twelve was a very good catch for one season in the heyday of trapping, and a good percentage of these were taken by shooting rather than with traps or snares.

16   Beaver

The Animal

The beaver, or *tsee'* (*Castor canadensis*), is another familiar animal found over most of the United States and Canada. It is the largest North American rodent, measuring 2 to 4 feet in length and usually weighing 30 to 50 pounds. Beavers are thickset and have webbed hind feet and a flat, paddle-shaped tail; their fur is rich brown and of very high quality.

The most remarkable thing about beavers is their ability to construct elaborate, effective houses and dens and to stock a whole winter's supply of food nearby. Beaver houses are made by piling sticks and mud into a large mound, sometimes 12 feet across and 6 to 8 feet high and with several rooms. The size of the beaver house and number of rooms depend upon how many animals occupy it. There may be only one or two beavers in a house, but more often there are six or seven, and occasionally as many as twelve. Experienced trappers can estimate how many beavers live in a house by looking at its size, the associated feed pile, and the amount of tree-cutting in the area. Beaver houses are sometimes occupied by three generations, including two large old animals, a couple of younger ones, and some smaller ones born the previous spring.

Beavers usually have one or more dens in the river bank which, like the house, are entered through underwater tunnels. The dens may be used for sleeping and the house for feeding, but this is not always so. They are also refuges in case the house is disturbed or destroyed. Some beavers live in marshy lakes with no steep banks and must do without dens. The Indians say that beaver houses are often occupied, continuously or intermittently, for twenty years or more.

Beavers feed mostly on the bark of trees or shrubs such as birch, poplar, aspen, willow, and alder; and they also eat some types of underwater vegetation. The area around a beaver dwelling usually has many well-worn trails leading into the woods, where the animals climb up to feed. Beavers fell trees and bushes by gnawing around the base, then cut them into handy sections and take them to the water or to the house. Travelers often see beavers swimming along in a river or lake with a branch in tow, heading for home.

Some of the wood that is cut is added to the feed pile, which is several yards out in front of the lodge. This underwater stockpile for the long winter season is usually about 20 feet long and nearly that wide, extending from the bottom to the water's surface. Feed piles are clearly visible during the winter because the sticks and branches protrude above the snow. This is often the most obvious indicator of beaver, since the lodge may be small and deeply covered by snow. In the Chalkyitsik region nearly all lodges are built against a steep bank, not in the water, and they are difficult to see in winter.

Underwater runways or channels lead from the beaver lodge and bank dens to the feed pile. These are habitually used pathways, narrowly defined near the dwellings but less so farther out. They are used all year around, though more heavily during the winter months when the animals apparently spend considerable time going back and forth from house to feed pile. With this elaborate underwater layout of feed pile, runways, and lodge entrances, beavers must have a fairly constant water level, and so they sometimes build dams to insure that the water does not drop so far that it is all destroyed. Beaver dams are often found where houses are built in sloughs, creeks, and lakes with outlet streams.

Beaver trapping (and snaring) has traditionally been a springtime activity, carried on when long days and high sun begin to erode winter's cold. The legal season ran from November 1 through April 15 in 1969–70. A few beaver were taken during the fall, but most trappers were busy setting for "winter fur" (such as mink and lynx) at that time. The principal beaver season begins in February, when the frigid temperatures begin to ease off. It is very difficult to set for beaver in extreme cold, because too much hard work and discomfort are involved. Men usually trap beaver until dwindling snow makes travel difficult, they fill their legal limit, or they tire of the hard work and frequent trapline checks.

Snaring

An old Kutchin once commented, "I spent my whole life studying beaver. Finally I know enough about them, but now I'm too old to trap." He was not joking. The beaver is a unique animal with complex patterns of behavior, living in an environment it has modified to its own needs and concealed most of the time from human eyes. If a man is to catch beaver, he must become familiar with the animal and its underwater world and learn complex, specialized

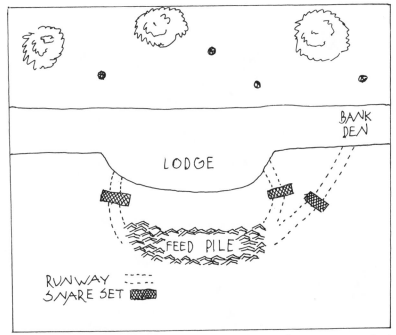

Schematic view of a beaver lodge from above, showing position of lodge, bank den, feed pile, runways, and snare sets.

trapping methods which differ completely from those used for land animals.

The apprentice trapper is completely confused the first time he watches a man setting beaver snares. Unable to see what is going on under the ice and lacking verbal instruction, he must slowly acquire a "feel" for the process. In his mind he eventually can visualize the relationship of lodge entrances, bank dens, runways, and feed pile and thus achieve a basic understanding of how snares should be positioned and why. This kind of fundamental knowledge comes over a period of weeks, but it takes years to develop the thorough understanding that makes for expertise in beaver snaring.

Beavers were not taken with underwater snares in aboriginal times, and so this is perhaps the only snaring technique that originated after contact. According to the Chalkyitsik Kutchin, the modern technique of beaver snaring was originated by "some white man" around 1940. Before that time they were taken only with gaff hooks and steel traps, neither of which is in use today.

Men who go beaver snaring usually devote a great deal of energy to it during a month or two of intensive activity. Making sets requires a considerable expenditure of time, checks are made frequently, and special equipment must be carried—all of which precludes nearly every other concern. In addition to the usual equipment and supplies, beaver snaring requires shovels, ice chisels, fleshing bones, chain saws (generally used today), and a large number of snares. Two men snaring beaver in 1970 carried 200 snares and used about 125 of them to set a total of 12 houses.

Locating Snaring Sites

Men who go after beaver know the location of most or all of the beaver houses on their trapline. During winter activities they get a chance to look at most of them to see if they are occupied, which they do by checking for a patch of twigs sticking above the snow or ice which shows that a feed pile is there.

Each year there are changes; an old house is vacated, an abandoned one is reoccupied, or sometimes a new house has been constructed. When the season arrives a trapper already has a good idea which houses he will set and what route he will travel between them. When he looks the houses over, the trapper estimates how many beavers may be in each house. His enthusiasm and effort depend on his guess as to the number of occupants.

The ideal place to find a beaver house is in a small, deep, round lake surrounded by timber, with steep banks and a creek running from it. Since such a lake is relatively free of wind, the snow lies deep and soft, providing a thick layer of insulation which keeps the ice thin over the runways. Steep banks mean deep water, which is best for snaring. If the lake is not narrow the feed pile will generally be well away from the house, making for clear runways, whereas in a restricted spot the feed pile and house are close together and the runways are clogged with sticks, making it hard to set snares. If there is a creek running from the lake the beaver will dam it, thus maintaining a deep water level.

Although there are many beaver in the rivers, they are hard to catch. The water is often so deep that runways are not restricted to a fixed course, making it hard to place snares accurately, and thick ice develops above the runways, making them hard to locate and requiring much chiseling to make sets. The river animals are also thought to be extremely wary.

Locating Runways

A trapper's first job is to find the runways in which he will place his snares. The Indians know approximately where to search for runways by looking at the relationship of the lodge and the feed pile. Most houses are set against a bank with runways leading from two entrances, one on each side, angling out toward the ends of the feed pile. Runways also lead from bank dens toward the feed pile, and these should be found.

There are two ways to pinpoint the location of runways. One is to shovel snow away from the ice between the house and feed pile and carefully inspect its surface. The ice over a runway is often full of little air bubbles, which gives it a whitish color. Indians also look for bits of vegetation frozen into the ice, since beavers apparently expel air and chewed plant material as they enter or leave the lodge.

A second way to locate runways precisely is with an ice chisel. This is a 4-foot wooden pole bolted to a 2-foot bar of heavy iron sharpened at the end to make a keen, flat blade. As he walks around a beaver house, the trapper jabs his chisel firmly into the ice. When he strikes the ice over a runway there is a different "feel," as if the usual brittle hardness is lacking, and there may be a different sound, perhaps caused by the thin ice and an air space beneath. None of these differences is easy to detect, and some experienced trappers have never mastered this technique.

When a trapper thinks he has found a runway, he tries to chisel through the ice to test its thickness. Ice over a runway tends to be thin, because the regular movements of beavers prevent it from thickening normally. Thus, if he finds ice that is more than 12 to 18 inches thick the Indian will generally assume that he is looking in the wrong place. Runways usually have only 6 to 12 inches of ice covering them, and even less if there is deep snow on the surface. If a trapper finds thin ice and if a "whoosh" of air comes out when

Two men setting beaver snares in a runway. The man on the right holds a curved stick, used to feel the configuration of the runway beneath the ice. Note the chain saw, used to cut the set-hole.

he chops through, he has found a good runway. Well-used runways often have a hollow space between water and ice, filled with compressed air.

When a trapper locates a runway he may use a 4- to 6-foot curved stick to probe beneath the ice, feeling for the runway's direction and width, depth of the water, bottom configurations, and position of any sticks that might be in the way of a set. The runway can usually be detected as an arch in the undersurface of the ice, which may be only 6 inches thick in the runway and 2 to 4 feet thick at the sides. By feeling this arch it is easy to tell in which direction the runway goes.

Making Snare Sets

The number of sets made at each beaver house depends on the number of runways, how well defined they are, the number of dens found, and how many beavers the trapper thinks live there. An effort is made to set at every runway, so that the animals must pass snares wherever they go, but it is usually impossible to find them all.

A small beaver house is likely to have two sets, one where each runway leads from it. Very large houses, on the other hand, may have considerably more, including sets in the lodge and den runways, and perhaps near the feed pile. Because runways generally go from the lodge or bank den toward the feed pile, a trapper orients his sets to intercept animals swimming in that direction. Snares are usually put near the lodge, dens, or feed pile, seldom in the open area between. If a house contains many beavers, however, a man can put his snares almost anywhere in the area and still make catches.

To make a set the trapper first cuts a rectangular hole through the ice over a runway. This is often done with a chain saw as well as a chisel, especially where the ice is thick. Beavers are caught with number 2 snares which are fastened onto pieces of heavy wire 2 to 3 feet long. The snare wires are twisted securely around a dry pole 6 to 10 feet long, and are adjusted so they extend horizontally from it. Snares can be hung from one or both sides of the toggle and are usually arranged in two or three tiers depending on the depth and width of the runway. The trapper tries to figure out

A cross section illustrating beaver snares set in front of a beaver house which is
built against a bank.

the runway's exact shape so that his snares nearly cover its entire
width.

Once the snares are arranged on the toggle, it is carefully lowered
into the water through the opening. Its sharpened lower end is
pushed several inches into the bottom so the lowest snare hangs
a few inches above the mud and the top snares are 6 to 12 inches
beneath the water surface. The average number of snares per toggle
is five or six, and most houses have two or three sets around them;
so ten to twenty snares are used for each house. The number can
be far higher, up to fifty or sixty for a large house.

These sets are sometimes baited, sometimes not. Beavers will
swim into the snares when they go to and from the feed pile, but
most trappers increase their chances for a catch by placing freshly cut
branches in the water alongside the snares. These are pushed into
the bottom, usually at the outer edge of the snares, where beaver

Setting beaver snares at a hole cut through the ice above a runway. Note ice chisels stuck in the snow.

will "fool around" with them and increase their chances of becoming ensnared. Beavers love any kind of fresh bait during the winter, but are especially attracted to species that do not occur in their territory. For example, if willows grow nearby, aspen or poplar make especially good bait. After he has made his sets and baited them, the trapper shovels snow onto the water in the opening and piles it a foot or two high. This insulates the set, preventing thick ice from developing in the hole and thereby reducing the labor of checking snares. If it is relatively warm or checks are frequent, little or no ice may develop.

It takes about an hour to make all the sets around a beaver house, depending on how many men are working, how large the house is, ice thickness, and other factors. The number of lodges set in a day also varies, depending on the distance between them and the time spent on each one. In 1970 three men traveling by snowmobile set five houses in one day, a very high number, two or three being more common. Snowmobiles and chain saws do much to increase the speed of setting and traveling.

Checking Snares

Newly set beaver snares are usually checked within one day, sometimes by the evening of the day they are put out. After the first or second check they are left for two to three days, because success usually diminishes rapidly from that time on. When a house has been set for about a week, poor returns can be anticipated, because the less clever animals have been caught and only the wise ones remain. Sets are usually kept in place for two to three weeks, however, and are always checked regularly, because when a dead animal hangs in a set for several days other beavers avoid it. Also, snared animals may float up against the ice and freeze into it if not removed.

The method of checking beaver snares is quite simple. The snow is shoveled away from the set-hole, the ice is chiseled out until the hole is restored to its original size, and all the slush is removed with a shovel. Then the toggle is lifted from the water very carefully so that snares will not be disturbed if they remain empty and unsprung. If all remain open and set, the pole is slipped back into the water. The snares are usually sprung, indicating that the set is in a good runway and that some beavers remain in the house. Sticks are often found in snares, where they were caught as beavers carried them in or out of the lodge. If a beaver is pulled up, it is removed by taking the snare off the pole, then it is dried by rubbing it back and forth in the granular snow found a foot or so beneath the surface powder.

Bait Set

One other common method used for snaring beavers near their houses involves attracting them to a bait rather than setting in the runways. The bait set is made by chopping a hole about 2 or 3 feet square near the feed pile or elsewhere within 20 to 30 yards of a beaver lodge. A freshly cut trunk of poplar, aspen, or other suitable bait is pushed into the lake or river bottom, so that it stands in the middle of the opening. Four stout toggles are selected, each about 3 inches in diameter and 4 feet long, and one snare is attached to the middle of each toggle.

The toggles are laid on the ice over the hole, one on each of the four sides, with the attached snares hanging straight down into the water a foot or so away from the bait and about 3 or 4 inches beneath the ice. Since the set is not made in a runway, the snares may extend below 2 or 3 feet of ice. The Koyukon make similar sets, but slide the bait in at an angle, and extend the snares a few inches farther under the ice. The Koyukon depend almost exclusively on bait sets. They are familiar with runway sets but reject them because they catch too many small beavers. Bait sets are selective in favor of the larger, more valuable animals, though they do not catch as many. They are also said to catch the beavers that are too smart to be taken with runway snares.

Uses of Beaver

The technique of skinning a beaver differs from the casing method used for all other furbearers. After the carcass has thawed, the four paws are cut off at the ankle and wrist joints, and the tail is removed where the fur and scales meet. A slit is made along the belly from chin to tail, and the hide is fleshed away using a well-honed knife and a sharp, flat piece of bone. The skin is removed from the abdomen, toward the flanks, and around to the back. The legs are skinned at the same time, using both the knife and bone fleshing tool. Throughout the skinning process the trapper cuts adhering fat off the hide with deft strokes of his knife. Great care is required to avoid making holes in the skin.

Skinning a beaver may appear simple, but great skill and care are essential to do a job that will not diminish the hide's value.

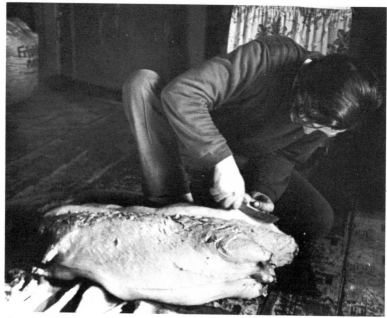

A trapper skinning a beaver. The white color is a thick layer of fat that surrounds the animal's body.

Men who are very good at it are often paid (or given meat) to skin these animals for others who are less skilled. Once the skin is removed and cleaned of adhering fat, it is stretched by nailing it onto a large board. Beaver pelts should be as nearly circular as possible.

The beaver is exceptional among fur animals for the high value of its meat. It is edible throughout the year but is best through the winter until about June. The meat is tender and delicious, especially that of a young animal. It is usually boiled but may be roasted in an oven or cooked over a fire on a stick. The tail, which is mostly fat and a favorite of many people, is burned on a stick over the fire until the skin can be peeled off, then roasted or boiled. The liver is also good and is usually prepared by boiling.

Another valuable product of beaver is castor, which has been mentioned many times in the preceding chapters. Beavers of both sexes have two pairs of glands near the anal opening. One set of glands, the castors, secretes a yellow fluid, castoreum. The animals use this substance for making scent posts on the shore around their habitations. The other set of glands, called oil glands, secrete a cream-colored oil that is used on their fur. The Black River Kutchin dry both sets of glands by hanging them in a warm place and use their secretions as bait for trapping most terrestrial fur species. They refer to both sets of glands as castors and, as far as I know, mix their contents together for bait. The fluid has a unique and pervasive odor.

The number of beavers taken by Chalkyitsik trappers has varied considerably over the years, largely according to the dictates of law. These animals are particularly susceptible to over trapping, because they are in high demand, their houses and feed piles show exactly where they are, and their mobility is extremely limited. Unlike most fur species, therefore, they have been protected by take limitations. During years of heavy trapping a total catch of ten was sometimes permitted, for example, and restrictions on methods of trapping and hunting made this quota difficult to fill. Today, the legal limit in the Black River area is twenty per trapper, which is not difficult to achieve by modern techniques.

Until three or four years ago beaver trapping was a major springtime activity among the Chalkyitsik people, but today very little of it is done. One reason is a lack of interest, since the beaver season comes at the end of the long winter when men are getting tired of trapping; and another is the spring carnival, with dog races and other festivities, which falls in the middle of the beaver season. Since preparations may take two weeks and the carnival lasts almost a week, it is a major deterrent to trapping.

In 1969–70, three or four men did limited beaver snaring during the fall season. In the spring two men put a major effort into beaver snaring, and two or three more pursued it in a limited way. This may have been fewer than usual, but indications are that unless beaver prices soar very high few Kutchin are going to bother with them. The prices are rather good now, and two men who caught thirty-nine beaver made nearly a thousand dollars between them. Thus, it is difficult to explain the low interest in beaver snaring, since a man can earn as much in a month as he can from several months of trapping winter fur.

17 Muskrat

The Animal

The muskrat, or *dzan* (*Ondatra zibethica*), is in many respects a miniature version of the beaver. It is an aquatic rodent, about a foot in body length, with rich brown fur. Its tail is a few inches shorter than its body, naked, and flattened vertically. The tail is used, together with webbed hind feet, for paddling around in the water. Muskrats are found in lakes, ponds, sloughs, and sluggish rivers over most of the United States and Canada. They are herbivorous, feeding on a wide variety of aquatic and shoreline plants, but they occasionally eat fish and clams.

There is a remarkable similarity between the housing arrangements that muskrats and beavers provide for themselves. Muskrats build houses either along a lakeshore or out in shallow water by making a pile of vegetation, then digging up into it from under the water and hollowing out a room just above water level. Where there is a bank several feet high along the lake or river, they live in dens made by burrowing a tunnel from under the water up into the bank, making a very secure hideaway. Bank dens are far more common than houses in the Chalkyitsik region. Their entrances are near shore, several inches to a few feet under the surface, with clearly defined runways leading from them.

Muskrats also build little shelters or houses on top of the lake

262

ice after freeze-up. While the ice is still fairly thin, they gnaw a hole through it and make a pile of vegetation on the surface, which is hollowed out inside to provide a feeding and breathing spot well away from the shore. These little houses, or "pushups," 18 to 24 inches long and 8 to 10 inches high, sometimes stipple the surface of a lake which has a large population of muskrat. The Kutchin say that "rats" chink any openings in the pushup walls before cold weather arrives, making sure that it remains well insulated so the tunnel entrance will not freeze. In the spring they feed in the open on top of the ice, and later on at little flattened places in the vegetation along shore.

Muskrats are found almost everywhere in the territory exploited by the Tranjik Kutchin, being fairly common in the rivers and sloughs and abundant in many of the lakes. The muskrat population varies from place to place and from year to year. Declines in population are usually explained by the Kutchin in terms of an environmental condition that causes a large-scale die-off. The most dramatic population declines are caused by severe winter cold, which may kill them by the thousands. For example, a bitter cold winter with little snow may cause the tunnel entrances of pushups to freeze solidly, with disastrous results for the muskrats.

Trapping Methods

The legal season for muskrats runs through the winter and into early summer (November 1 to June 10 in 1969–70), but only part of this season is actually utilized. No effort is made to take rats during the late fall, and since it is difficult and uncomfortable to set muskrat traps during cold midwinter weather, the Indians prefer to trap other species. If the animals are plentiful some men set out as early as February, but they usually wait until sometime in March, when a good warm spell sets in.

The season continues for one to two months, depending on weather conditions. Eventually warm temperatures thaw the ice and collapse the pushups, ending productive trapping. If it remains warm, muskrats come out through the pushup holes to feed on top of the ice, where they can be shot or (sometimes) trapped, but if it turns cold again, the holes freeze over and there is no way to take them. After the ice melts around the lakeshores, muskrats can be trapped on the banks.

The muskrat trapper's first problem is to locate pushups, and this can be difficult if the snow is deep. So he may stake them out in early winter before they are covered, by going around on the lakes and putting a long stick in the snow next to each pushup. Few men bother to do this anymore, feeling that they will be able to find pushups easily enough when the spring thaw arrives. The ones least likely to freeze during the winter, however, are those most deeply covered with snow. A certain percentage of the pushups will be frozen and no longer in use by spring, the number depending on temperature and snow depth the preceding winter. Some lakes may suffer more than others. Large lakes, exposed to heavy winds that sweep away the snow, are worse than small, sheltered ones.

Once a pushup is found it must be examined to see if it is being used. The trapper uses his shovel to cut away at the house until he opens a small hole into the interior, then peeks inside or probes into it with his chisel handle or a small curved stick until he locates the tunnel entrance and feeding platforms. If he has opened the house near the entrance, he carefully replaces the moss, puts slush or snow over it, and seals it well. Then he makes a hole about 6 inches in diameter at one end of a feeding platform (a small, flat place inside the pushup), where he will place his trap.

Once this opening is made, the trapper uses a small chisel to cut out a depression for the trap, chipping enough ice away from the platform so that the trap will be covered by 1 to 2 inches of water when set inside. The trap bed, as it is called, must be level but is roughened on the bottom to keep the trap from slipping around. A little moss is sometimes placed under the trap to help prevent slippage. Before the trap is set in, a small scoop is used to remove all ice chips and slush from the water.

The trap is ready to be set in place after it is fastened to a toggle. This is usually a 5- or 6-foot branch with twigs left on it so that when placed outside the pushup it is easily seen from a distance, marking the set's location. Muskrats are nearly always taken with number 1 traps, preferably the "jump" type which has no large spring extending out from the side, for it must be small enough

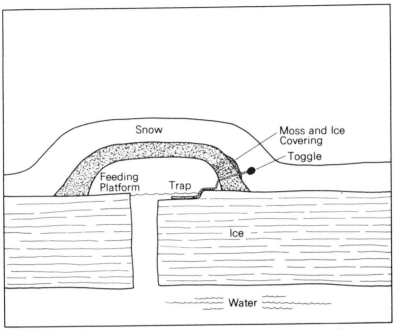

Diagram of a muskrat pushup atop lake ice, showing method of setting a trap inside.

to fit within the narrow confines of a pushup. It is best to have a double-length chain, or to extend a normal chain with a long wire, to allow the muskrat to dive into the water and drown after it is caught; otherwise it is likely to twist its leg off.

After setting his trap the Indian usually dips a little twig into a jar of strong-smelling bait, either beaver castor or a commercial scent, then places the twig beside the trap. This masks any foreign odors and attracts the animal toward the trap. It seems to be especially important to use bait after one or more muskrats have been caught in a pushup.

When the trap, toggle, and bait are in place, the trapper carefully replaces the moss he removed when he opened the pushup. Sometimes he carries along extra moss or takes pieces from other parts of the pushup to make an especially good covering. The hole must be sealed tightly to prevent cold air from entering and freezing the tunnel and to keep the animal from becoming wary. During subfreezing weather slush produced by scooping water out onto the snow is packed over the house, freezing into a tight seal. It is then covered by shoveling a foot or more of snow on top.

During the latter part of the season pushups deteriorate, but traps can still be set in them. When they have partially fallen in, the walls can be rebuilt using a few sticks and excess material removed from this or another house. Rats will use a pushup that is partially open, but it is a good idea to pack snow over a deteriorating pushup to protect it from further thawing. As long as the ice stays safe a trap can be set around the hole that remains after a pushup has fallen in completely. The technique is the same, except that there is no structure to deal with. Success tends to diminish as pushups deteriorate and collapse, but trapping is easiest at this time.

Muskrat traps are checked by removing the snow, slicing open the hole in the pushup, and peeking inside at the set. Some trapped animals will dive and drown in the water below, but others remain inside the pushup and must be killed. Muskrats bite fiercely and hang on stubbornly, and so they are handled carefully. The best method is to lift a muskrat by the trap chain, then kill it by clubbing it on the head. Since this is often not fatal, the trapper steps on its head and pulls its tail until the vertebrae separate. After the trap is emptied it is replaced in the pushup, a new bait is prepared, the hole is closed, and a good cover of slush and snow is put on.

Muskrat traps are usually checked daily to prevent losses and to keep the sets empty and "working," and the trap is replaced after each catch until it is empty for about two days in succession. Pushups are generally used by two to six animals, but if a man gets three or four he has done well. One trapper claimed to have caught fifteen in one set, but this is very unusual. A man is able to tend 35 to 40 sets a day in cold weather, and as many as 60 when it is warm. Up to 250 sets have been made on a good lake, and a single trapper may have many good lakes in his territory. Muskrat trapping is done with a dog team or snowmobile, or occasionally on foot. Machines of course enable a man to cover a large area in a short time, increasing the number of sets he can make.

During the late spring, early summer, and fall muskrats can be trapped at little feeding platforms they make in the grassy vegetation along lakeshores and river banks. These are most often used for sets when the ice is melting away along the margins of lakes and before there is enough open water to hunt rats from a canoe. The trap is simply placed on a platform with a little grass over it for concealment, and the chain is toggled to a bush or stake.

Hunting Techniques

Before trapping in pushups was invented, the Black River people caught muskrats by clubbing them. A pushup was broken down and one man stood watching it while several others went around disturbing the other pushups in the area. The animals were driven to the one that was being watched, and when they surfaced there they were clubbed. This technique could only be used on lakes where there were no banks suitable for dens, so that the muskrats could not seek refuge away from the disturbance. Up to twenty a day were taken in this way.

The Kutchin formerly took muskrat during the fall using a dip net made from babiche. After thin, clear ice covered the lakes they walked along the shore where the bank was a foot or less in height, looking for runways heading out into the water. Whenever one of these underwater trails was found, they made a hole and pushed sticks into the bottom on each side, making a small fence with a narrow opening for the runway right in the middle. Then a dip net was placed in the opening.

One man went up on the shore 5 or 10 feet from the water's edge and jumped up and down, frightening the muskrat so it swam full speed through its tunnel into the runway and into the net. Several animals might be caught in succession from the same den. Today's old-timers can remember when this method was used to get a supply of skins for winter robes and clothing.

Muskrat shooting became important after the introduction of firearms, and though it was undoubtedly done with the bow and arrow before contact, it became a major technique for obtaining muskrat pelts until it was finally outlawed in 1969. Muskrat shooting began in April or early May, depending on the weather. On warm, sunny days the animals came out on top of the ice to feed on green plants cut underwater. Except when it was windy, they were not difficult to approach to within easy range for a .22 rifle. They were shot in the neck, to minimize damage and so they would not convulse and fall back into the water. Thirty or more could be shot in a good day.

Hunters must be very careful when walking around rat holes at this season, because the ice may be very thin. It may also be covered with deep slush and water, and so waterproof footgear is essential. Although it may sound incredible, the aboriginal Kutchin had no waterproof boots. They put several layers of hare skins inside their moosehide moccasins, and although water soaked clear through them the heavy insulation kept their feet bearably warm. Surprisingly enough, the people knew that beaver skin and bearskin were waterproof, but the old-timers say these were not used to manufacture boots. Needless to say, the rubber boot was a very welcome introduction. There was also no waterproof clothing during aboriginal times, except for the slightly resistant caribou and moosehide apparel. Here again, the Kutchin simply got wet when it rained.

Spring trappers and hunters also face the problem of snowblindness when high sun and snow combine to brighten the landscape. The Indians traditionally used snow goggles made from pieces of skin or carved wood pierced with small holes, and also put an inch-wide streak of charcoal across the face beneath the eyes and over the bridge of the nose, "to scare snowblindness away." Few Indians today are afflicted with snowblindness, because they wear sunglasses on bright days.

Until recently the Indians hunted muskrats from canoes during May and early June, after the ice was gone from lakes and rivers. Since muskrats tend to be most active through the dusky night, the hunters often lived by an upside-down schedule that kept them up all night. The bobbing heads of muskrats were easily spotted from a distance when the water was smooth, and hunters paddled toward each one they saw, attempting to get within range for a .22 rifle. If a muskrat dived it was fairly easy to predict where it would reappear.

Muskrats could also be attracted by pressing the lips together and making a series of low squeaking sounds, mimicking the noise they make during the spring mating season. When a hunter came close to one, he aimed carefully and shot it in the head. If it was hit well, the animal floated lifelessly in the water. Missing or wounding was common, and sometimes a long chase was necessary before success or failure was decided.

A tradition grew up around spring "ratting" in the days when most Indians concentrated their efforts on muskrats for about three months of each year. Each family had its own "rat camp" on the shore of a good lake and near a number of other lakes that could be reached by easy portages. This was the best time of the year for everyone, with plenty of fresh ducks and muskrats, outdoor living, long days, and warm sunshine. When there were many rats to skin it meant hard work and long hours for everyone, but since each pelt brought a dollar or more it was worthwhile. The "rat camp" began to fade ten or fifteen years ago, but its final disappearance did not come until the past few years.

Gun-shot muskrats never brought as much as trapped ones because the skins were damaged; but they were worth something, and the meat was a great delicacy. The recently passed law which prohibits shooting muskrats means that hides with bullet holes cannot be sold, and so the people have lost a major reason for hunting them. They might take a few for meat, but seem to feel that it is best not to shoot fur animals if the pelt is wasted. This is an unfortunate loss for the people, whose activities seem to have little effect on muskrat population. The money obtained from hunted rats was not much, but it helped, and the meat was worth a great deal.

Uses of Muskrat

Muskrats are fairly small animals which are easy to "case out." Their skin is removed much like that of other fur animals, by peeling it off inside out from the rear end toward the head. A sharp penknife is used for cutting the skin free in certain places, and a bone blade serves as a scraper for removing all the adhering fat. Muskrat skins are stretched and dried on small drying boards made specifically for them. An active trapper owns a large stock of these boards and keeps them full for weeks on end in a good year. He is able to skin and flesh a rat in a few minutes, with a deftness that results from handling literally tens of thousands of them in a lifetime.

The little carcasses are tasty and fat, good eating for people and nourishing for the dogs as well. They are skinny and poor eating from June until around November, but by January they have become very fat and remain so until late May. Muskrats are boiled or roasted; the meat is very tender and tastes delicious.

Muskrats have only about a pound of meat but are sometimes taken in such great numbers that they make up a sizable volume of food. They may have been fairly important as a food species in the past, especially in the spring when other meat supplies ran short. The muskrat season comes at a time when big game like moose are difficult to hunt and transport, and before the fish and waterfowl become abundant. Muskrats are widely distributed, tend to be prolific, can be taken by a variety of modern and traditional methods, and have rich, fat meat. Furthermore, they can be trapped by women and older children. Some Chalkyitsik women are very successful muskrat trappers.

The best muskrat catches by individual Chalkyitsik Kutchin have run up to 2,000 animals. Most good trappers have taken 750 to 1,000 rats during their better seasons, and when the pelts brought between one and two dollars apiece this meant a great deal of money for some people. In 1969 one man took 250 muskrats from a single fairly small lake near Chalkyitsik and got about a dollar apiece for the hides. By contrast, the best catch made by any Chalkyitsik trapper in 1970 was not over 40 muskrats. This reflects an extraordinarily low population and a correspondingly low interest in muskrat trapping. Pelt prices in 1970 were a dollar apiece or less.

IV PROBLEMS IN ADAPTATION

18   History, Environment, and Settlement Pattern

This chapter briefly examines the changing pattern of settlement among the Black River Kutchin and its relationship to historical and environmental phenomena. It begins with the time of first contact, when the people followed a largely nomadic hunting and gathering way of life without permanent habitation. Then it describes the emergence of traplines or trapping territories in response to the development of the fur trade, when tiny settlements were scattered widely over the land. And finally it traces the decline of these trapline settlements as the Kutchin moved into villages, examining some consequences of life in the new towns.

Traditional Settlement Pattern

Their habits of life differ somewhat according to locality, but none have settled villages—carrying their deerskin lodges wherever food is most abundant. [Dall 1870, p. 109]

When the oldest living Tranjik Kutchin describe the days of their youth, they always speak of the wandering. "When I'm a kid we're always moving. Never stay around one place for long. We got to move, otherwise we find no food. Even then sometimes there's no food for a while, so people in camp go hungry. Wherever there's food, well, we got to move to that place." If they found a good

273

fishing lake, for example, they would stay there until the catches became poor, then move on. Small groups of people might split up and go in different directions, and if one group found a good resource a messenger was sent for the others so they could rejoin and take advantage of the temporary abundance.

The degree of mobility described for the early days is particularly striking; small bands of people might cover hundreds of miles in a season. Although there was some tendency to remain within a vaguely bounded "tribal" region, the Kutchin were free to move beyond these boundaries at will. Black River Kutchin not only wandered throughout their own region, but also moved up and down the Porcupine River, into the Old Crow Flats, across the Yukon Flats, and into the Chandalar country. Thus, Kutchin tribal groups were perhaps better defined culturally than territorially or ecologically.

People from all the Alaskan Kutchin tribes, and from the Crow and Peel River tribes of Canada, were often encountered by the Black River Indians. Individuals or families might decide to spend a season, a year, or more in the area of another tribe. These large-scale movements were of course less common than the more limited travels in search of localized food sources, which were usually sufficient in a given area to permit a stay of weeks or perhaps months at one place. When game was killed hunters used pack dogs and hand-pulled toboggans to haul it into camp, rather than moving to the site of the kill.

It is clear that under aboriginal conditions the Kutchin could not have delineated any form of territory for the exclusive use of an individual, band, or tribe. The resource base was not uniform enough, spatially or temporally, to support a population whose mobility was restricted by local or regional territories. The situation here is the same as that described for the precontact or early postcontact Algonkians of eastern Canada, where "any hunting-trapping group that was forced to remain on a particular 'hunting territory' sized tract would probably starve to death, at one time or another, within a generation" (Knight 1965, p. 33).

Two key ecological factors in this environment precluded the development of a territorial system during aboriginal times. First, the resources are highly scattered and localized; and second, they are subject to marked cyclic or noncyclic variations. These two factors have been noted many times in the preceding chapters, with regard to almost every major resource utilized by the Black River Kutchin. Variations in availability may occur only on a local basis or may affect an entire region. Snowshoe hares may die off everywhere or salmon might not appear in good numbers, creating a universal shortage; but the localized shortage is more common, such as failure of the whitefish run in a particular creek or movement of the moose out of a certain area.

The situation in this region, if not in the boreal forest generally, is much the same as that in the arid Great Basin.

All of the plant and animal foods had in common the extremely important characteristic that the place and quantity of their occurrence from year to year were unpredictable. . . . A locality might be very fertile one year and attract large numbers of families, but offer little food for several years thereafter. Few localities had foods in sufficient quantity and reliability to permit permanent settlements. Throughout most of the area, the families were concerned predominantly with warding off potential starvation by moving from place to place. These movements were determined by reports from friends or relatives about the probable quantities of foods to be had. [Steward 1955, p. 105]

In the Great Basin, resource variability largely depends on rainfall and the availability of water, but in the boreal forest it results from a number of different factors. One might be tempted to speculate that all marginal environments are characterized by localization and variability in the resource base, but this is not the case. For example, coastal Eskimos of northern Alaska live in a marginal environment, but it is subject to significantly lower variability, with far less localization of food sources. The marine animals, such as seal, walrus, and waterfowl, are much less concentrated in specific, limited areas; and the same holds for caribou, which occur in some-what localized herds but wander freely over the tundra and might turn up anywhere.

The Eskimo devotes a lifetime to learning more and more about the habits of the animals and about the mobile sea ice on which he hunts, whereas the Kutchin spends a lifetime learning more and more about the landscape. The key to hunting success in the high Arctic is knowledge of the game, current, ice, and weather—the major factors influencing resource availability; but in the boreal forest the key to success in hunting and trapping is knowledge of the landscape. The Indian must know where to find the trails, lakes, hills, valleys, forests, and meadows and the most stable concentrations of edible plants and game.

The marked cyclic or noncyclic fluctuations in almost every significant food resource probably had an important effect on population levels of the aboriginal Kutchin. Four potentially critical resources—moose, fish, snowshoe hare, and muskrat—experience changes of considerable magnitude, and waterfowl and caribou are subject to changes in annual availability resulting from prevailing weather conditions or migratory patterns.

During a given year some species are likely to be abundant, others uncommon or rare; but there is usually some resource to fall back on. There were times, however, when all of the important food sources coincided in a low ebb, leaving the Indians without sufficient food. The ensuing starvation might cause a substantial decline in native population. There is no doubt that starvation has occurred in the past, and it is equally certain that low points in animal populations have all coincided from time to time. In 1969–70, every species except the snowshoe hare was at a fairly low ebb, and if the people had been forced to live on hares alone they would have starved.

The Fur-Trade Era

At some time after the development of a regular fur trade, I cannot say just when, the Kutchin began establishing relatively permanent family settlements with associated private traplines. These traplines may have been developed at the suggestion of white traders, or in imitation of white trappers who moved into the area, or perhaps they arose spontaneously out of a need to avoid conflict over rights to particular territories. As they exist today, traplines are not tracts of land with recognized encircling boundaries, but networks of trails and lakes that are used by a particular individual or family year after year. Ownership is based on uninterrupted use, and is therefore not permanent; should a trapline be left unused for several consecutive years it could be taken over by anyone who wanted it. By the early twentieth century this system was well established; traplines were being bought and sold, and permanent settlements of one to three families had been established where traplines adjoined navigable rivers.

Families remained on their traplines for most of the year, which meant that the old nomadic pattern had been abandoned. The principal movement was between trapline and trading center, usually during a month or so in the summer. Thus an ancient pattern of mobility was abandoned, while the population still remained widely dispersed over the country. If anything, there was probably less concentration now than there had been during the aboriginal past, except for the annual trading gatherings in Fort Yukon or Old Rampart.

Since the resource base continued to be localized and variable after the Kutchin established permanent trapline settlements, they must have found it difficult to extract as much food from the land as when they were free to wander. The trapline was an exclusive territory only for exploitation of fur resources, however, because there were no private hunting rights. Any man could take moose, bear, caribou, waterfowl, small game, or fish wherever he pleased, on a first-come, first-served basis.

The Kutchin were no longer able to move where the resources were, but compensated for this lack of mobility by adopting more effective means of utilizing their resources and transporting their catch. A man could now hunt with a repeating rifle instead of a bow and arrow or muzzle-loader, and could fish with gill nets obtained through trade. And he could use dog teams and toboggans for hauling game back to the cabin instead of using hand-pulled sleds or pack dogs, or back-packing. Dog teams provided greatly increased individual mobility to compensate for the loss of group mobility that resulted from establishing trapline settlements.

The Kutchin now had access to foods obtained through trade with white men, an important dietary supplement to compensate for the possible loss of hunting productivity (cf. Leacock 1954, pp. 27–28). Trapped animals, including beaver, muskrat, and lynx, assumed a larger role in the diet than they ever had before. Muskrats alone were sufficiently abundant in this region to form a significant addition to the food supply. In the eastern subarctic, very large beaver catches contributed substantially to the native food intake (Knight 1965, p. 35), but this was probably never true of the Black River region.

The kind of trapline-territoriality that has emerged among the Black River Kutchin apparently also characterizes neighboring

Kutchin groups in the Yukon Flats, Crow River, and Peel River regions, though the descriptions available for these areas are not clear and detailed enough for accurate comparisons. The Koyukon and other Athapaskans west of the Kutchin seem to have well-defined, individually owned traplines, but the Athapaskan groups to the east along the Mackenzie River and into the Great Slave Lake region apparently have poorly defined family territories, if any at all. The Snowdrift Chipewyan, for example, seldom trap in the same area for more than five years and generally utilize a territory for only two or three years before moving. Some men have trapped over most of the region within a hundred-mile radius of their village at one time or another, and they obviously exercise considerable freedom in choosing the areas which they feel will be most productive (VanStone 1965, p. 163).

The Indian who owns a trapline will naturally tend to concentrate most of his exploitative activities—hunting, fishing, and trapping—in that area. Although this might be viewed as somewhat restrictive, it may in fact result in more effective utilization of the area. As we have seen, exploiting the boreal forest environment requires a thorough knowledge of the landscape. The Indian must know the precise details of local geography, the favored habitat of each species of useful plant and animal, and all physical features important for travel and safety, knowledge which it takes many years to acquire.

The trapline-territory gives its user an adaptive advantage because it tends to restrict all his exploitative activities to a limited region, and the longer a man utilizes the same area the better he will operate within it. One old man put it this way: "I trap in the same country every winter now for fifty years. That line is a hundred miles long, I guess, and I know every lake, every little pond, all the creeks, all the beaver houses, every trail, all the best places for any kind of animal, and darn near every single tree in it."

Another interesting consequence of the development of trapline-territories is that within each line one or two fur species tend to be particularly abundant. Some men have spent the greater part of their lives in "beaver country," for example, or "marten country," and as a result tend to be more interested in these animals than others, speak about them more often, and appear to know them better. One man trapped in beaver country, caught more beaver than anything else, and is considered an expert on that animal; another prefers to trap exclusively in the river valleys of his territory and therefore knows more about lynx and beaver than about marten. It seems likely that this localization and consequent specialization of knowledge might increase a trapper's skill and effectiveness in exploiting the resources of his particular area.

Another aspect of territoriality in trapping, perhaps the reason traplines were originally established, is competition. Because proceeds are not shared, individuals are competing with one another for game. Hunting, by contrast, is a cooperative endeavor in which the proceeds are divided among members of the group (Leacock 1954, pp. 6–7). Establishing recognized family-owned tracts of land eliminated the kind of hostility that was sure to arise when different individuals attempted to exploit the same localized resource without sharing.

Even with established territories, a certain amount of hostility arises between persons trapping in adjacent areas. An undercurrent of resentment occasionally emerges when men talk about neighboring trappers because of real or imagined territorial infractions. In earlier times the competitive spirit reached such extremes that trappers carefully hid their individual trapping techniques from one another. They would break up their trap cubbies in the spring so that if someone walked along their trail during the off-season he would not see how they made sets. Competition has diminished today, now that trapping is less important and much of the country is underexploited, and so most trappers are fairly willing to help one another.

The Emergence of Villages

The beginning of village life in this region can be traced back to the middle of the last century, when the first trading posts were established. During the first ninety to one hundred years after contact, settlements such as Fort Yukon and Old Rampart assumed great importance in the Indians' lives, though relatively few established permanent residence in them. Most remained scattered across the land except in the summer months, when they came in for trade and festivity. All of today's adults grew up on the trapline, following lifeways developed before the turn of the century.

About twenty to thirty years ago this pattern gave way rather rapidly to a new one, as the Kutchin began moving into large permanent settlements. Many families from the surrounding region took up residence in Fort Yukon, but a number of the Black River people went to the new village of Chalkyitsik, the primary attraction being a school for the children. In Chalkyitsik a new school had been built by 1941, though Fort Yukon had had facilities long before that. At first the tie between people and school was fairly loose, but as the children became estalished in schools the families found it increasingly impractical to remain away on the trapline. The last families to live out on the line all winter were those without children, and even they have moved to town within the past five years. This pattern has been followed all over the western subarctic, though it occurred earlier in some areas (central and western Alaska) and later in others (northwestern Canada).

Once the Indians accepted permanent residence in a village they were forced to alter their trapping and hunting routines. Men did not like staying on the line for long periods without their families, and so they began making briefer excursions to set and check traps and to hunt. During the first ten or twenty years the average length of stay outside the village was probably two to four weeks, but it has recently decreased to between three and fourteen days. In order to trap effectively under these schedules the men have had to shorten their lines drastically and to increase their mobility. It is reasonable to guess that the number of dogs per team increased as the Indians became more and more tied to sedentary village life. Larger teams would enable trappers to reach and check their lines more rapidly, allowing them to spend less time away from the village.

The importance of high individual mobility has steadily increased since the Kutchin abandoned group mobility in favor of permanent settlements. This has been underscored all over Alaska in recent years with the overwhelming acceptance of snowmobiles. The Kutchin have been able to maintain fairly long lines in the face of waning interest in trapping because machines allow them to cover great distances. Similarly, the North Alaskan Eskimos have greatly expanded their exploitative range since the introduction of snowmobiles, and they now travel far beyond the previous limits of their activity. In order to remain effective, the taiga and tundra hunters must cover a large territory, and with dog teams this could only be done by increasing the time spent. But the high speed of machines greatly reduces the time factor. Motorized boats probably had a similar effect when they were introduced years ago.

The emergence of village life has contributed to a waning interest in the subsistence economy by forcing trappers to remain away from their families. Snowmobiles are helping to slow that trend somewhat, but other factors (such as welfare income and availability of wage labor) will continue to pull the Indians away from the land. Villages have had other effects as well. They have created a social environment far different from any that existed in the days of nomadic family groupings and scattered trapline settlements. The adjustment to large, permanent social groupings has not been easy, as one might expect where people have nothing comparable in their background.

A major problem facing the people of Chalkyitsik is their inability to develop a real sense of community. The Kutchin are pervasively individualistic—each family prefers to function autonomously—which makes it virtually impossible to institute a well-organized, cooperative village life. In the old days camps were small and their membership was fluid, and so there was little opportunity or need to develop a formal community structure. There were men called "chiefs," who wielded considerable authority over an encampment. But groups were never permanent, so no one had to follow any particular leadership for more than a few months, and it was always easy to move away if a person grew tired of a particular chief. It is interesting to note that the modern Kutchin unquestioningly obey their white "bosses" when they have jobs but many retain their individualism by quitting so frequently that one boss rarely holds sway over them for long.

Community functioning is also made difficult by the high level of interpersonal hostility that pervades village life. In aboriginal times membership in encampments and two-family dwellings was very fluid, as families continually shifted their associations to reduce hostilities (Osgood 1936*b*, p. 111). With a scattered population and small groups there was little need to develop mechanisms for minimizing hostility resulting from continued close association. But today, large permanent settlements force people to associate day after day for years without effective means for reducing hostile feelings.

The North Alaskan Eskimos appear to have moved far more easily than the Kutchin to a permanent community existence, although the adjustment is by no means perfect. Eskimos are far more adept at carrying on a smooth, relatively friendly social existence. They are compulsively, almost passionately, sociable. They gravitate to crowds, taking any opportunity to interact with one another; and the larger the group, the better. I have seen hunters detour miles across the tundra just to see who another traveler is and say hello, even though they were just out of the village for a few hours. Eskimos seem to have an extraordinary ability to suppress hostilities and maintain friendly relationships.

The Kutchin do not share this sociability, having little apparent preference for groups larger than the family, and they seem to enjoy each other far less than Eskimos do. I have seen boat crews pass each other far up the Black River without exchanging a word. The Kutchin also lack the Eskimos' skill in the nuances of easy social interaction. They seem to have considerable difficulty just coping with one another on a permanent basis, whereas the Eskimos apparently derive considerable pleasure and fascination from their village associations.

The coastal Alaskan Eskimos traditionally lived for part of the year in fairly large settlements. Families lived alone or with one or two other families only during certain seasons, gravitating toward larger, permanent coastal settlements whenever resources permitted such a move. The Kutchin were unable to maintain a village or encampment of this type, largely because of the nature of their environment, and thus were not preadapted for village life to the degree that Eskimos were, in terms of either formal organization or interpersonal relationships.

But there is also an unexplainable difference in Eskimo and Kutchin personality. The Indians not only were less *able* to establish large, permanent encampments, but were perhaps less *willing* to do so as well. The Eskimos' compulsive sociability attracts them to gatherings, whereas the Indians react in the opposite way. It is not unlikely that Eskimos established villages whenever possible because they wanted to live together, and although the Indians might have afforded larger gatherings their independent individualism gave them no urge to do so.

It is pure speculation, but perhaps one group developed settlements that were above the optimum size for the resource base, whereas the other remained below the optimum. The potential for cooperative activity must always be balanced against the danger of overstressing local resources, which makes this question extremely difficult to answer. Do people sometimes congregate in groups which are above or below the most adaptive size in order to satisfy their particular social propensities?

This question is of considerable importance in ecological formulations, which usually hold that size and distribution of the resource base, plus the exploitative efficiency of the culture, determine the distribution and concentration of the population; and that this in turn exerts a powerful influence upon the organizational features of the social group. Earlier in this chapter I discussed the ways in which the boreal forest environment influenced the size of social units among the Kutchin. Although there is undoubtedly a strong environmental influence, it is well worth considering the factor of sociability, which may tend to exaggerate or minimize the effects of environment. There is a good chance that both factors were at work in determining settlement pattern and group size among the aboriginal Kutchin and Eskimo. Obviously, both cultural and environmental phenomena determine settlement, encampment, travel, and other exploitative patterns today, and there is little reason to believe that this was not true in the past.

19 Acculturative Patterns and Exploitative Skills

Acculturation and Attitudes toward Change

I saw so much harmless fun and amusement among these Indians, and they evidently find so much enjoyment in hunting and fishing, that I could only wish they might never see much of the white man, and never learn the baneful habits and customs he is sure to introduce. [Whymper 1868a, p. 232]

More than a hundred years have passed since this passage was written, and the Kutchin have become a very different people during that time. Previous chapters have illustrated changes in subsistence and settlement. This chapter will examine the pattern of change more generally, with comparative notes on other Athapaskan groups and the neighboring Eskimos. It will focus particularly on the causes and consequences of a recent turning away from life on the land.

So many aspects of Kutchin culture have undergone great change in the past century that it is impracticable to mention more than a few examples. The preceding chapters are filled with accounts of technological changes that took place very rapidly after contact. One of the most notable was the acceptance of firearms, a case in which the underlying practical motivation is eminently obvious. There are many instances, however, where change seems to have been favored for its own sake. A striking example is the disappearance of traditional winter clothing in favor of decidedly inferior white man's apparel.

Among the Kutchin and other Athapaskan groups, the aboriginal dress vanished so rapidly that anthropologists have been unable to learn much about it. As was true in many other aspects of culture, the Indians apparently favored something new over something old, regardless of how good or bad it might be. Thus Stefansson (1962, p. 26) notes that the Mackenzie Athapaskans "would rather shiver in fashionable attire than be comfortable in furs which are cheap and therefore unaristocratic."

The desire for change continues today among the Kutchin, coupled with a generally negative view toward all things of the past. The only people not completely negative about traditional life are the oldest and most conservative individuals. They say that in the old days people were happier, got along better, and had not acquired the evils of drinking. "Today everybody walks around like half asleep all the time. Something wrong with them." But although they feel that some things have taken a bad turn, they are very happy that other changes have occurred. They like the security of modern times when people live without fear of scarcity. "Long time ago we were poor. No good that time. Sometimes ten men got only one rabbit to eat between them. We lived out in the brush, just like wild animals."

Today's adults and young people are much more negative about traditional Indian life, often expressing a mild shame or disgust toward ancestral lifeways. Aboriginal religion and taboos are ridiculed, folklore is said to be untrue, old customs are considered stupid, and the general state of existence in former times is looked upon with disfavor. The old people have spoken of hardship and starvation and have described hunting methods that appear difficult and ineffective. Thus the modern Indians feel lucky to have missed the "bad old days," and care little to hear about them. "Far as I can see all that old time stuff is a bunch of nonsense. We're damn lucky it's not like that today." The only continuity with the past remains in areas which are deeply rooted in the Indian personality, do not conflict with white culture, or are essential for successful exploitation of the environment.

Similar attitudes toward the past occur among other Athapaskan peoples. Some of the older Chandalar Kutchin, for example, said that in previous times life was so hard that the Indians were lucky to pull through at all, and "when the old people talked of it they would burst into tears" (McKennan 1965, pp. 28, 78). Similarly, the Chipewyan generally place little value on things of the past and retain little to show a continuity with aboriginal life (VanStone 1965, p. 111; personal communication). And among the Kaska:

> Informants repeatedly referred to the hard life under aboriginal conditions where people lived in the bush "same like game," when there were "no clothes, just skin," and hardly any food but fish and meat. Today there is no tendency for people to idealize the ability of their grandparents to adapt to the environment with the resources of aboriginal culture. The past is done with and nobody wants to abandon technical improvements to return to former patterns. [Honigmann 1949, p. 51]

A notable contrast to this pattern is found among the Koyukon, who are almost as acculturated as the Kutchin but retain a strong interest in traditional Indian culture. They talk often and with enthusiasm about previous times, events, and customs; but their concern is largely historical, and they maintain a sense of identity with the older lifeways while still moving quite readily away from them. The Koyukon are more aware of their Indian identity and feel more positively toward it; yet they are not conservative regarding acculturative changes. In some important respects, such as language, values, and economic life, they are more acculturated than the Kutchin.

Coupled with their negativism about the past, the Kutchin tend to be relatively satisfied with modern life. One old man who spoke of the general disharmony today was asked if the Indian might not have been better off without the white man. "Oh no," he said, "It's *good* the white man came along. Otherwise I guess no Indians going to be left. All starved to death by now." Another very old Black River man living on relief said, "Look here, today I got dollar every day from government. I never worry, nothing. Lots of grub. Old times everybody worried about food all the time. Oh yes, today is way better." Even the history-minded Koyukon feel that these are better times and that people are happier now than in the early days.

Younger adults generally feel that they should enter more and more into the white man's world—that things are better than ever today but can be improved further by continuing change. They stress the value of education as a primary vehicle for change, and speak only English to their children in the hope that it will improve their ability to master the new way of life. During a discussion of village improvements at a meeting a woman argued, "We don't just want to stay Indians. We got to do something to change things here."

The Kutchin generally appear to like white men and admire their abilities, partly because they are indebted to whites for bringing them greater abundance than they knew before. There is an effort to emulate most aspects of white culture and an almost total absence of criticism of it. In marked contrast to the North Alaskan Eskimos, the Kutchin (and Koyukon) have no negative feelings about having white blood in their ancestry, and are generally willing to credit whites with developing modern exploitative methods and technological devices, sometimes even those which are probably of Indian origin.

From the time of earliest contact the Kutchin seem to have treated the white man's coming as a windfall, and particularly so because of their well-developed sense of business. The Indians' relationship to white men has stemmed largely from a mutual desire for trade or exchange. The Kutchin have a long tradition of trade relationships and receptivity to new ideas and objects, which has made them most amenable to the presence of newcomers in their land.

But there is something more to it. The Kutchin call themselves *Dinje-ju,* which means the smallest or youngest people and may be taken figuratively to mean the "least people." As one man put it, "The Indian thinks that everybody else is smarter than him." When a Kutchin does something incorrect or irresponsible, he is likely to say, "Too much *Dinje-ju.*" A similar attitude characterizes the Koyukon, who admire both the whites and the neighboring Eskimos. The Indians have a very low and negative self-image, feeling that others' lives are probably better than their own.

This is a remarkable contrast to the Eskimos, who sum up their self-image in the term they apply to themselves, *Iñupiat,* which means the "real people." The following statement summarizes the way North Alaskan Eskimos in general feel about themselves:

The Nunamiut quite plainly considered themselves to be distinct from, nay better than, their neighbors. One Nunamiut informant expressed this by saying that the Nunamiut were better wrestlers, runners, hunters, and lovers than any other people they had encountered, coastal and river Eskimos, Indians and white men included. [Campbell 1968, p. 3]

Whereas the Eskimo is proud to a fault, the Indian is overly self-critical. Athapaskans seem to recognize their weaknesses and strengths, whereas Eskimos see their own strengths and focus upon the shortcomings of others. This is partly because white men have gotten along far more successfully in the interior environment than on the Arctic tundra and sea ice. Given time for learning, Outsiders have a tendency to equal or even surpass the skills (or at least the success) of Indians in their own country, whereas among the Eskimos they always remain inferior in their ability to get along on the land.

Receptiveness to Change:
Athapaskans and Eskimos

It should not be surprising, in view of what has just been said, that Athapaskans and North Alaskan Eskimos have reacted quite differently to acculturative influences. When the Indians (Kutchin or Koyukon) encounter something belonging to the white man's culture, they tend to accept it on the general assumption that all things of the white man are good and ought to be accepted. Eskimos, on the other hand, tend to react with interested skepticism. They do not follow a general precept that all things from the white man's culture are good, and so each item is evaluated individually. This is not universally true, and the decisions to accept or reject do not always appear wise, but initial reactions usually lean more in this direction than toward the openness of the Indians.

If Eskimos do accept something from white culture, they generally reinterpret it so that it fits into the Eskimo world, rather than molding their world to fit into that of the white man. Eskimos operate from the position that their culture is superior; thus, newly accepted items are likely to be given Eskimo names, or the English terms will be Eskimoized. This characteristic of reworking terms is one of the clearest manifestations of their desire to fit the Outside world into an Eskimo framework. These people seem so closely bound to their own conceptual framework that it is very difficult for them to develop great flexibility in dealing within frameworks which are completely different.

The Athapaskans take an entirely opposite position, feeling that they must mold their world, their culture, to mesh easily with that of the white man. When they accept something from the Outside, they make an effort to interpret it as Outsiders would. They seldom Athapaskanize things that are not Athapaskan. The two worlds, Indian and white, are to be kept entirely separate conceptually, with the former decidedly the less valued of the two.

An important aspect of this is the Athapaskans' relativistic philosophy, as illustrated by this description of the Kaska:

> One characteristic of epistemological thinking stands out clearly, the relativistic nature of truth. The Indian does not regard his thinking in absolutist, or universal, terms of validity. "That's what Injun believe," Old Man would say, implying the realization that white and other people have conceptual systems which differ from that held by the Kaska. Knowledge to the Indian is derived from experience and tradition. Since not all peoples have the same experience nor identical traditions, there follows the readily accepted assumption that the world contains different kinds of knowledge and different truths. [Honigmann 1949, pp. 215–16]

Eskimos take a far more absolutist and ethnocentric view, which generally classifies their own way as correct or "genuine" and other ways as inferior or invalid. Hence the suffix *-piak,* which means "genuine," is frequently appended to the terms for traditional Eskimo items. For example, *umiak* means "boat" and *umiápiak* means "Eskimo boat," to set the real article apart from all the rest. I was once assured that Eskimos are the only "real" human beings, and all other people are "something else, I don't know what."

Eskimos accept culture change more slowly than the Indians, almost reluctantly at times. They are following the difficult course of attempting to change while still remaining *Iñupiat,* "real people," which is unsettling when each change moves them further away from what they would define as an Eskimo. They are acculturating rather "successfully," in that they adapt well to wage labor and school environments, but they are bothered by inconsistencies between the new life and the old value system. An Eskimo hunts—that is what makes him an Eskimo—so how can he be a wage laborer and still retain his identity? The Eskimo is torn by inner conflicts because he is losing what he values most highly, his "Eskimoness," and becoming something that he considers to be of a lesser order.

The Kutchin accept change willingly and enthusiastically, moving toward something they feel is better. They are often frustrated, not because they are losing their traditional culture but because they are not losing it fast enough. They appear to be trying to shed their own culture and lifeways, and to a great extent they are succeeding.

A broad overview indicates that similar acculturative responses hold true for Athapaskans and Eskimos throughout Alaska. An interesting example is found in postcontact sites excavated in southwestern Alaska. VanStone and Townsend find that Tanaina Indians occupying the Kijik site were extremely receptive to Russian and American trade goods, whereas Eskimos inhabiting the Crow Village and Tikchik sites showed a marked conservatism toward acceptance of trade goods. In the Kijik site "there is little about the collection of artifacts or the excavated living structures that suggest continuity with the past at all." By contrast, in the Eskimo sites "the collections clearly indicate continuity with emphasis on the retention of traditional forms" (1970, p. 145). This is true despite approximately equal access to trade goods among both groups.

The kind of receptivity described for the Kutchin, Koyukon, and Tanaina seems to characterize northern Athapaskans in general, and some early anthropologists describe receptiveness to change as a general attribute of Athapaskan-speakers. For example, Goddard finds that wherever Athapaskan peoples have spread, from the subarctic to the Pacific Coast and southwestern United States, they have undergone drastic changes by adapting to new environments and assimilating elements of the cultures already present in these environments. Athapaskan peoples, he notes, seem to "show great willingness to give up their own modes of life and thought and to adopt those of others" (1906, p. 338).

Morice, who lived many years among northern Athapaskans, also found this quality of receptivity one of the most outstanding characteristics of all Athapaskan, or Déné, peoples. He noted that Indians of this family have a great propensity for borrowing from foreigners supposedly higher on the social scale, customs and mythology, industries and technological items. In fact this national trait is . . . glaringly apparent throughout all their tribes, in the south as well as in the north. [Morice, n.d., p. 110]

The Carrier are remarkably fond of white people, he notes, and the eastern Déné strive to imitate the manners of voyageurs and traders. The Ingalik have adopted customs from neighboring Eskimos, and the Chipewyan borrow heavily from the Cree. Farther south, along the northern California coast, the Hupa have almost completely assimilated the culture of neighboring tribes, and groups living close to Northwest Coast Indians have borrowed heavily from them.

in the same way as children naturally imitate their elders, even so do these aborigines instinctively allow aliens to play over them the role of superiors whose manners they must ape and models whom they must copy. [Morice, n.d., p. 111]

Although his wording is much in the style of his time, Morice is making an important point. Instead of reworking an essentially Athapaskan adaptive framework when they moved into different environments, the Indians adapted by borrowing techniques and technology from peoples already present in those environments. This could have resulted from adaptive superiority on the part of indigenous peoples, from an unexplainable propensity to borrow on the part of the Athapaskans, or (most likely) from a combination of both factors. Certainly, the Kutchin have increased their exploitative efficiency through borrowing from Eskimos and whites, but they have also accepted many cultural elements which brought them no practical gain whatsoever.

Acculturation and Adaptive Skills

Since the time of first contact there has been continuous change in the lifeways of the Kutchin, but until about twenty years ago they remained heavily dependent upon the land. In 1949 nearly 70 percent of the people in Fort Yukon were supported principally or wholly by hunting, fishing, and trapping. One-quarter of the population received some kind of relief (Shimkin 1955, p. 228). Today there are probably no people who derive over half their subsistence from the land in that community, and most indulge in only very minor hunting or trapping activities. Similarly, the Black River people have moved strongly away from a subsistence economy over the past one or two decades. Each year the effort put into hunting, fishing, and trapping diminishes as people turn their backs on the land and look toward new ways of making a living.

When today's old people were young, the Kutchin depended as heavily upon the land as their aboriginal ancestors had. "In those days men get up first thing in the morning, go out to check snares, and hunt all day. Sometimes they come home late at night. Every day they hunt." The growth of the fur trade shifted attention from game to fur, with some decrease in reliance upon wild foods, but kept the people closely tied to the land. Men in their forties today started running their own traplines at fifteen, but accompanied their elders on the line when much younger. Theirs was the last generation to learn trapping in this way, however, and today there are few men under thirty who know how to trap at all. The younger Kutchin are no longer learning exploitative skills, and the older people are becoming less interested in putting their skills to productive use. About twenty years ago this decline started, and within the past ten years it has increased precipitously.

The Kutchin have not consciously decided at one point or another to find new ways to make a living; instead they have simply lost interest in hunting and trapping. They are more concerned about affairs in the village, for example, than being somewhere out in the forest. Old people complain about this trend, because in most cases subsistence activities are not being replaced by any productive endeavors. "They hardly try for game nowadays," one man said, "because they don't care about hunting. Everybody knows government will always take care of them."

VanStone (1963, pp. 166–71) draws comparative data on the trend away from a subsistence economy throughout the Canadian subarctic, and finds that the same patterns of change are occurring throughout much of this region. These trends are particularly marked in the western subarctic, as shown by studies of the Chipewyan, Slave, and Dogrib. In the eastern subarctic the Algonkian-speaking peoples do not show this clear pattern, and changes are less pronounced. Historical differences, plus a greater tendency toward conservatism, have slowed the decline among the Algonkian Indians. In general, the Alaskan Athapaskans seem to be further along in the trend away from a subsistence economy than their counterparts in Canada.

Five basic factors have led to a decline in exploitative activities among subarctic Indians in Canada and Alaska. These factors, set forth by VanStone (1963, pp. 163–64), include the hardships and uncertainty of trapping, improvements in housing (attractions of village life), wage employment, payment of family allowances, and establishment of schools. The following discussion will consider each of these factors as it applies to changes in subsistence activities among the Chalkyitsik Kutchin.

Hardships of Hunting and Trapping

The Kutchin see hunting and trapping as a hard way to make a living, and they generally look forward to the day when they can give it up for good. I once asked an old man which is a better way to live, by hunting and trapping or by working for wages. He replied, "Oh, job is *way* better. When you hunt you got to go out in rain, cold, any kind of weather. Sometimes you get nothing for it, too. If no animals around, then you get nothing except hard work. When you got a job, then you got money, you just stay inside the house. No tough time." This opinion is universally held in Chalkyitsik.

The Kutchin do not take great pride in themselves as hunters or trappers, viewing these activities merely as one way to make a living, and now that there are alternatives the Indians are ready to accept them. It is important to bear in mind that it is not only the hardships of the subsistence life that help to cause the modern decline, but also the people's attitude toward these hardships. Eskimos face an even more difficult environment and the same general acculturative forces, but are much less concerned about physical hardships as a negative aspect of outdoor life.

Attractions of Village Life

The desire for material comfort and a settled existence with family close at hand is a major factor in keeping the modern Kutchin away from the land. The men consider it a great hardship to go out for days or weeks at a time, away from the ease and convenience of their settled village existence. Even though they may have comfortable line cabins they still miss their families and the social routine back in town, for life out on the line is profoundly boring compared with the excitement of daily goings-on at home. Their exploitative range and effectiveness is being curtailed sharply, and although the arrival of snowmobiles has caused some stabilization in this trend, other factors continue to draw the Kutchin away from a heavily subsistence-based livelihood.

Desire for Wage Employment

For well over a century the Kutchin have been hunting for monetary gain; and trapping, the main occupation here since contact, has always been done primarily for the sake of acquiring money. Thus an essential reason for going out is the money rather than the game itself. In this light it is not difficult to understand why the hunting and trapping economy is given up when better sources of money become available. The Kutchin place a high value on money and dislike the discomforts of life out in the bush; so when hunting and trapping are superseded by wage labor, which pays more for less difficult work, it is small wonder that the Indians are happy to change.

The adult Kutchin, who grew up exclusively as hunters and trappers, are almost as ready to drop that way of life as any city man is to change jobs when a better opportunity presents itself. There is little sense in clinging to an "out-of-date" way of making money when new and better ways present themselves. Thus the Kutchin are somewhat dominated by an interest in jobs and money, unlike the North Alaskan Eskimos, who also seek wage labor but value hunting above practically all else.

The Kutchin are able to find jobs in a number of ways. There are a few opportunities in Chalkyitsik itself, such as school maintenance man, postmaster, and store manager, but jobs ordinarily can be obtained only by leaving the village to work in Fort Yukon, Fairbanks, Anchorage, or other areas in Alaska. A few find "permanent" jobs, which they keep for a year or more before returning to the village, but most work only for a few months at a time, usually during the summer.

It is curious that despite their high valuation of wage labor the Kutchin are apparently less successful on the job than North Alaskan Eskimos. Honigmann (1968, p. 3) found that Indians (mostly Athapaskans) in the community of Inuvik do not perform as well on wage labor as Eskimos living in the same village. Yet they do not compensate by pursuing the more traditional life, and so more Indians than Eskimos receive welfare. Indian children, on the other hand, do somewhat better in school than Eskimo youngsters.

These differences may relate to the Eskimos' ability to work better in a cooperative situation, to do their part toward a communal gain. Most Kutchin are so highly individualistic and independent that the job routine appears to make little sense to them except as a means of getting money; and few consider a job more than a temporary arrangement. They work effectively when they feel like it, but quit or stay home as the fancy strikes. There is no real goal beyond acquiring some money, and little value is placed on doing a good job for its own sake or achieving a long-range goal by working together.

So a contradiction emerges. The Kutchin value money and jobs highly, more so than traditional pursuits; yet they do not adapt to the job situation as well as Eskimos, who value their traditional life and economy more highly. To some extent at least, the Eskimos' performance relates to their generally high level of skill, mechanical aptitude, and cooperativeness—qualities that are as valuable on the job as they are in hunting. The Indians seem to have a better understanding of how white men think and view the world, however, and this may help to explain their children's equal or (in some cases) superior performance in school.

Unearned Income

The Kutchin value money highly, are averse to the discomforts of hard work in the outdoors, live where jobs are hard to find, and have a long tradition of sharing. It is no surprise, then, that welfare has had a tremendous impact upon their lives. The people are eligible for a variety of governmental assistance programs that were set up to aid citizens with a life pattern drastically different from that of the Indian. But the law is the law, and so the Indians have been classified as poor, even though they live in the midst of relative plenty available to them by hunting and trapping.

Welfare has been perhaps the greatest influence in taking people away from the land, because it is destroying their initiative to pursue any kind of productive endeavor. The Indians who continue to work are frustrated when they see others being paid to do nothing:

I got a job here in the village, but it hardly gets me enough to feed my family good. Why should I work like hell on that job when the other guys get more every month for just sitting around doing nothing. That don't seem right to me. I'll be darned if I'm going to work when it's like that; so I might as well get that welfare, too, instead of working.

Although the Chalkyitsik people are quite willing to accept welfare, they are distressed by its effects. They see themselves becoming lazy, useless, and "spoiled." Their lives have become a meaningless routine of sitting around watching the seasons pass, waiting for a new welfare program that will "help" them more.

The Impact of Schooling

In some parts of Alaska schools became available to the Indians early in this century, whereas other areas such as the Black River had no schools until about thirty years ago. Around the turn of the century a famous Alaska missionary predicted the effects of education upon the Indian:

To keep a school in session when the population of a village is gone on its necessary occasions of hunting or trapping, and to have the annual recess when the population is returned again, is folly. . . . Moreover, it is folly to fail to recognize that the apprenticeship of an Indian boy to the arts by which he must make a living, the arts of hunting and trapping, is more important than schooling, however important the latter may be, and that any talk . . . of a compulsory education law which shall compel such boys to be in school at times when they should be off in the wilds with their parents, is worse than mere folly, and would, if carried out, be a fatal blunder. If such boys grow up incompetent to make a living out of the surrounding wilderness, whence shall their living come?

The next step would be the issuing of rations, and that would mean the ultimate degradation and extinction of the natives . . . is the writer perverse and barbarous and uncivilized if he avow his belief that a race of hardy, peaceful, independent, self-supporting illiterates is of more value and worthy of more respect than a race of literate paupers? [Stuck 1924, p. 356]

Obviously these words fell on deaf ears. The children have been taken completely away from the land, with no chance to acquire even the most basic knowledge of exploitative techniques. They spend their waking hours in the school, giving them no chance to travel with their parents. Some parents, anxious for their children to become educated, actively discourage them from hunting. And in school they are led away from all that is traditional, as their teachers stress the importance of jobs, moving to large towns and cities, and integrating into the white man's world.

Children who have any potential at all are taken "out" to high school once they finish eighth grade in the village. After four years away from home living in a city with youngsters from all over Alaska, the high-school graduates are released into the world. And what then? Both the grade school and the high-school graduates are completely alienated from their native way of life, but remain strongly attached to their own people. Many return to the village or to a neighboring large town, where there are few opportunities to make productive use of their education. Furthermore, those who have been to high school or had vocational training have acquired a peculiar ethic that places little value on settling down to a mundane job routine and entering the world of the native adults. Many have also developed serious alcohol problems.

Thus, even the ones who find jobs have difficulty holding them. The educated native youths fit into neither the culture of their parents nor that of the white man. They band together and carry on a subculture of their own, bound by an alliance of friendship and mutual understanding, profoundly alienated from all who do not share their peculiar background. They know and care little about the ways of their parents and ancestors. They are moving into a future that looks very uncertain indeed.

So the traditional lifeways of the Indians, their attachment to the land and their understanding of it, are largely dead today. The younger adults and children have never known the land, and they never will. The adults over forty continue to hunt and trap, especially in isolated villages like Chalkyitsik, but each year their interest and effort declines. They are looking more and more toward the new life, though they are not fully prepared to meet it. The outdoor life, hunting and trapping, still holds them, but only because it is at present the only way to make a living. Most of them are anxiously awaiting the day when they no longer must depend upon the land. At the same time, however, they are becoming aware that the "modern" life they are achieving is, at best, a mixed blessing.

20 Adaptive Skills: A Comparative Perspective

The Problem

Explorers and scientists who have come into contact with hunting and gathering peoples around the world have almost universally praised their remarkable fund of adaptive knowledge and their ingenious exploitative skills. Writers have been deeply impressed, and rightly so, by the ways these societies have adjusted to marginal and harsh surroundings. It is easy to understand, then, why anthropologists apparently make a tacit assumption that, given the limits of their material culture, hunter-gatherers will have a tendency to achieve something near perfection in the behavior and knowledge underlying their adaptation to the environment. In other words, within the limits imposed by technology they will approximate the most highly effective behavioral adaptation that is possible.

Certainly it is beyond question that these societies have developed an intimate acquaintance with their surroundings and considerable skill in exploiting them. This is essential to the survival of the group. But is it reasonable to assume that all hunting and gathering cultures are about equally well adapted to their environments? Or might some groups be relatively better adapted than others? There is a well-known propensity for cultures to become elaborated along certain lines while remaining less developed in

298

other respects. Given this tendency, it seems probable that once they had achieved adaptive adequacy some cultures would remain near that level, whereas others would go beyond it toward adaptive perfection.

This chapter examines certain aspects of environmental adaptation among the western Kutchin and North Alaskan Eskimos. It compares their degree of success in perfecting a cognitive, behavioral, and technological adjustment to their surroundings. I hasten to point out that it does not examine the total adaptive complex within these two cultures, but only those aspects related to exploitative skills and knowledge of the environment. Whenever the term "adaptation" is used, therefore, it should be interpreted with this limited scope in mind. Furthermore, *although the discussion concludes that one group has achieved a higher degree of adaptive perfection than the other, this implies only superiority on the part of that group and not inadequacy on the part of the other.*

Attempting to make an objective comparison along these lines is not a simple undertaking. First, it is based on certain personality features, attitudes, and bodies of knowledge which are difficult to compare cross-culturally. It is relatively easy to make an objective comparison of adaptive modes in terms of concrete elements such as technology or formalized cultural institutions. But the somewhat abstract and subjective qualities to be considered here are more difficult to assess and compare. Second, the two cultures in question occupy very different environments—the one Arctic tundra and sea ice, and the other subarctic forest. It is therefore essential to seek parallel or identical types of behavior which are in fact comparable despite environmental differences, and which constitute significant aspects of the overall adaptation.

During the course of this research I made an effort to compare the level of exploitative skills and knowledge among the Kutchin with that of the Eskimos (I am indebted to G. R. Bane for the initial suggestion that I make such a comparison). Although I quickly became certain that differences in the level of these skills existed, I had to find a means of translating impressions into a more concrete and objective form. I therefore noted specific personality features or attributes that might be considered adaptive, and what emerged was a catalog of characteristics which could be examined point by point to compare the exploitative skills of individual hunters.

These adaptive attributes, manifested in varying degrees, characterize hunters in both Kutchin and Eskimo culture. They are developed to the highest degree in the most skilled and successful individuals within these groups and to a lesser degree by those who are less proficient. It seems probable that these attributes should occur among members of other hunting and gathering societies regardless of environment or culture, therefore composing a universal basis for comparing adaptive skills.

If such a catalog of attributes exists, and if the same attributes characterize hunters in any culture, it should not be surprising to find that different peoples vary in the degree to which they have cultivated them among their members. A particular group may develop highly effective means of inculcating these qualities into the young men who will be its providers, whereas another group may be less successful along these lines. There will always be a range of individual variation, of course, but the overall level of adaptive qualities attained by the aggregate population of some cultures is perhaps higher than in others which emphasize them less. The net effect of a higher "average" development of these qualities within a culture is a more successful adaptation.

These adaptive characteristics include the following:

> knowledge
> practical resourcefulness
> foresight
> cooperation
> industry
> physical skills
> supportive values
> technical sophistication

This chapter attempts to show that although *both* cultures have inculcated their providers with these qualities to a fairly high level, the Eskimos have done so to a greater degree than the Kutchin. Eskimo culture appears to have a more institutionalized and explicit mechanism for developing these attributes, maximizing the extent to which they will occur in individual personalities. The degree of difference between these two groups is significant but not enormous, so that individual variations cause some overlap. Thus the better Kutchin hunters are as good as many Eskimos, but not equal to the best. When I hunted and trapped with the most expert Kutchin, I was continually struck by how Eskimolike they were in their approach and aptitudes. Indeed, they were Eskimolike, but only because they shared a high development of those adaptive qualities which probably characterize the most skilled individuals in hunting and gathering societies everywhere.

Supportive Data

This section considers in some detail each of the adaptive attributes listed above. It attempts to explain, illustrate, and appraise specific behavior patterns which are closely associated with the techniques and knowledge underlying environmental adaptation. And it compares the ways each of these patterns is manifested among the North Alaskan Eskimos and western Kutchin, with additional notes on a number of Athapaskan tribes.

Knowledge

The adaptive attribute of knowledge includes a number of essential contributory aspects. These include: (1) knowledge, (2) objectivity and empiricism, (3) curiosity, and (4) communication. Each of these aspects plays an important role in determining the amount and quality of knowledge which is amassed by the individual hunter and by the group as a whole.

Knowledge. The expert hunter's most important attribute is knowledge. The more a man knows about his environment and the multitude of exploitative techniques, the better equipped he is to deal with life effectively. This is true for normal day-to-day activities as well as those exceptional situations which are likely to confront him only occasionally. There are many traditional solutions to unusual or emergency conditions, but sometimes the hunter finds himself in a situation which demands a unique response. This is where his intelligence—his ability to work creatively with his fund of knowledge—is a crucial factor in success or survival.

Both Eskimo and Kutchin hunters are uncommonly knowledge-able about their environment and intelligent in their approach to exploiting it. But these qualities are developed to a significantly different level in most Eskimos than in most Kutchin. Eskimos are more concerned with knowledge of exploitative techniques than with anything else—it is the dominant interest in their lives. Each man has a tremendous fund of knowledge, and the more he knows the greater his prestige and the more he is respected.

The Kutchin are generally less concerned with amassing a large fund of knowledge regarding environmental exploitation, but there is a wide range of individual variation in this regard. Although knowledgeability is respected and desired, most of the men seem to feel that knowing enough to get by is sufficient. Less emphasis is placed upon learning exploitative skills and exchanging related information, and the general concern with these subjects is much lower than among the North Alaskan Eskimos.

The Kutchin (and Koyukon as well) often seek advice and information from Outsiders, lacking confidence that their own adaptive solutions are correct. Eskimos are so far beyond the knowledge and abilities of Outsiders within these realms that they would never think of requesting a white man's counsel. "I'm glad I'm not a white man," I was once told, "because they're always so stupid."

Caribou are an important resource among Eskimos and some of the Athapaskan groups and therefore afford an ideal opportunity for comparing exploitative knowledge. There is good evidence that the Eskimos are more knowledgeable regarding this species and more skilled in techniques for exploiting it. For example, a wildlife biologist who has traveled throughout Alaska collecting information on that animal from native hunters reported to me that Eskimos have a far more thoroughgoing knowledge of caribou behavior and ecology than any of the Athapaskan groups he has visited (James Hemming, personal communication). In general, Eskimos are natural historians par excellence, and the Indians are significantly less knowledgeable along these lines.

The Koyukon are by long tradition hunters of caribou; yet they are not as skilled as Eskimos at hunting this animal (G. R. Bane, personal communication). This is apparently true, as well, of the Slave and Dogrib Athapaskans,

who rush up to a band of caribou at top speed, hoping to get within shooting range before they begin to run, and hoping also that because of their peculiar antics the caribou will be convinced at once that they are not wolves, and will circle to get a better look or to get to leeward to prove it by the sense of smell. I have often seen this method used by Indians and never with great success. They may get one or two out of a band or they may get none. . . . But by more common-sense methods, one can usually get every animal of a band of six or eight. . . . I long ago discarded the haphazard methods of the Indian, which too often leave you hungry and empty-handed after several hours to begin the hunt all over again. [Stefansson 1921, pp. 229–30]

The "common sense" methods which Stefansson refers to are undoubtedly those he learned during his extensive travels with Eskimos, who prefer to stalk carefully on foot and shoot from concealment.

Similarly, the Eskimos use more effective methods for shooting any big game animal. When firearms replaced the bow and arrow, they gave up shooting animals in the heart in favor of bone-shattering neck, shoulder, or head shots. These shots knock the animal down, minimizing further movement. The Kutchin continue to use heart shots even though a wounded animal may travel considerable distance, causing them extra labor in retrieving the meat and, if the animal is a bear, threatening the hunter's safety.

Eskimos have gone far beyond the abilities of the Kutchin in understanding and predicting weather. Prediction is more difficult in the Kutchin environment, but they approach the problem in an unsystematic fashion. Indications are that the old white trappers surpass the Indians' skills as weather forecasters, because they are more careful to observe recurrent meteorological phenomena. Eskimos have developed a very accurate system of weather prediction, and it is doubtful that an Outsider would ever surpass their skill without using instruments unavailable to them.

Emergency responses are a critical area of adaptive knowledge, and here again there are differences between Eskimos and Athapaskans. The Eskimos almost invariably make the best response, often reacting so appropriately that the situation can hardly be termed an emergency. There are some very important instances in which their standard response to dangerous conditions is more effective than that of the Kutchin.

If they become lost in intense winter cold, the Kutchin and Koyukon believe that they will freeze to death if they fall asleep, and men have walked themselves to near-fatal exhaustion under these conditions. Eskimos react the opposite way, sleeping and resting as much as possible, exercising only to warm up. They have proved this method successful time and again when powerful storms caught them far from shelter. In this case the Indians' response is not only less effective but may be fatally incorrect. Similarly, the Kutchin and Koyukon treat frostbite or freezing by rubbing snow on the affected area or by immersing it in ice water. This is precisely the opposite of the Eskimos' (and medical scientists') long proved method of immediate warming. Again, the Indian method may be outright damaging.

During periods of extreme food shortage Eskimo groups fragment into small family units to wander in search of food, maximizing their chances that some will find food sources. By contrast, the Peel River Kutchin gathered together in large groups during times of starvation, feeling that they might as well die together (Slobodin 1962, p. 80). This tendency to congregate in one place and to give up rather than persevere under stressful conditions would severely limit their chances of finding food. Interestingly, Slobodin records accounts of Kutchin families who declined to face starvation with the majority and eventually found enough game to save the others.

These examples are sufficient, I think, to illustrate the differences in adaptive knowledge which characterize Eskimos and Kutchin. One is confronted with many more situations in daily life among the people which contribute to the impression that a significant disparity exists.

Objectivity and Empiricism. The Kutchin take an extremely individualistic approach to the realm of knowledge and belief. They are less likely than Eskimos to have standard, traditional, and highly accurate answers to the problems they face. There is, of course, a large body of knowledge related to everyday practical experience which is accepted by all or nearly all individuals within the group. But there is also a broad realm of idiosyncratic knowledge that is not universally known or accepted. Thus, some men "know" that otters prey on beavers, whereas others "know" they do not. One person reports that moose are attracted to salt licks near a certain lake; another says he knows the area and there are no salt licks. Yet both have lived for decades within a few miles of the place in question. Thus there is no deep concern for accuracy or universal acceptance, and speculations are often reported as truth.

Eskimos contrast sharply with this individualistic approach to belief and knowledge. They have few personal opinions on practical matters because most of their knowledge is traditional and standard-ized. For the Eskimo this makes good sense, because whenever a practical problem arises the traditional, given solution proves to be correct, and any effort to provide an original solution would almost certainly fall short of the traditional one. Small wonder, then, that he believes and acts in accordance with the answers he has learned. Eskimos are also highly scientific, expert at making accurate and objective observations of their surroundings and drawing correct conclusions. They are careful to report only what is accurate and unexaggerated, and to state things provisionally when they are uncertain.

Successful adaptation is dependent upon a body of knowledge and technique which is accurate and widely disseminated and which applies both to everyday practical solutions and to rare or unusual problems. The larger the fund of reliable information, the greater the potential for effective response. The Kutchin must operate with conflicting and often unproved information, whereas the Eskimos utilize a body of knowledge which is generally accepted and empiri-cally based. The Indians are *not* irrational or unlearned by *any* means, but their resource of factual data is not as large and reliable as that of the Eskimos. In the long run, this means a relatively lower productivity for individual hunters and therefore a lower level of adaptive success for the group.

Curiosity. The most expert hunters or trappers are men with an intense scientific curiosity about their environment and the ways of exploiting it. There are two aspects to their curiosity. First, they attempt to find out more about the "permanent" aspects of their environment by learning general patterns of ecology, animal behavior, and physical processes. And, second, they are attentive to temporary phenomena, such as snow or ice conditions, which have an important effect upon exploitative success.

Eskimos are highly inquisitive about all phenomena in their envi-ronment, and the Kutchin are somewhat less so. The Eskimos are passionately fond of watching animals and learning about them, whereas the Indians rarely devote much time to this. Similarly, Eskimos often study animal feeding habits by examining stomach contents, a method also used by biologists. Learning what an animal eats may lead to the discovery of better ways to locate and capture it. The Kutchin almost never look at stomach contents, and there-fore know less about the feeding habits of game species.

The Eskimos were fascinated by a bird-guide I carried in the field, often poring over it for hours on end. They always tried to identify each species, to show that they knew something about it, and to indicate whether they had seen or hunted it. Among the Kutchin the same book excited almost no interest. The Indians seem to limit their curiosity to natural phenomena which are of immediate, practical importance, whereas the Eskimos are con-cerned with information for its own sake, or what might be termed "basic research." They are very interested in "practical" or "ap-plied research," of course, but seem to be aware that nonpractical knowledge can also be converted to utilitarian gains.

Communication. It should be clear that communication of infor-mation is essential for developing an individual and group fund of knowledge, as well as for the exchange of information regarding present conditions or the immediate availability of game. Eskimos devote a major portion of their social life to the exchange of hunting information, but the Kutchin speak of these subjects rather infrequently.

The Indians tend to be secretive about their hunting-trapping activities and, in some cases, about the availability of game. Sometimes they may conceal knowledge of a resource because it is limited and the individual might lose out by telling others. But often a man will "save" a resource (such as a moose or bear den), then never get around to utilizing it. This has the maladaptive effect of decreasing overall village productivity, because if the information were made available such resources would be utilized by someone. Eskimos always attempt to inform others about the location of game, no matter how large or small the resource may be.

More important, Eskimo men devote practically all of their con-versation to subjects related to environmental exploitation. Every day there is a constant exchange of information and accounting of experiences, especially from the oldest and wisest men. This singular interest, to the virtual exclusion of all else, assures that each Eskimo acquires a very large body of exploitative knowledge during his lifetime. The modern Kutchin, on the other hand, spend only a small fraction of their time discussing these subjects, which seem to hold no great interest for them. General rules for exploitative procedures are sometimes spoken of, but accounts of experiences and observations are not often exchanged. Thus the Indians are largely deprived of an essential means for acquiring adaptive knowledge and skills.

Practical Resourcefulness

Both the Eskimos and the Kutchin live in difficult and challenging environments, where successful adaptation depends upon a high degree of imaginative and practical resourcefulness. For example, improvising equipment is often necessary where there are no repair shops, specialists, or large general stores. In some cases standard solutions are used when a recurrent situation arises, but often a unique problem occurs which demands a unique response.

Indians and Eskimos are both expert in this sort of improvisation, and it is reasonable to guess that all hunting and gathering peoples share this talent. But experience among the Athapaskans and Eskimos clearly indicates that the Eskimos have elaborated these skills to a comparatively higher level. Indeed, Eskimos are well known for their extraordinary resourcefulness, in dealing with everyday problems as well as unusual or emergency conditions.

The Outsider finds himself completely overshadowed by the creative ingenuity of the Eskimos—he is almost childlike in his inability to approximate their cleverness and imagination. A white man resigns himself to the hopelessness of a difficult situation whereas the Eskimo is just getting started on a workable solution. By contrast, the Indians often ask for an Outsider's help with a perplexing problem which they find it difficult to solve effectively. Certainly the Outsider finds himself much better able to equal the Indians when it comes to devising on-the-spot solutions to problems which arise in the course of outdoor activities.

Foresight

There is an obvious adaptive advantage in being able to anticipate long- and short-range variations in environmental conditions and resource availability, especially in surroundings like those of the Eskimo and Kutchin, where changes are an important facet of

everyday life. Long-range foresight means that the people will be
ready for each season's activities beforehand, will store food and
other supplies in anticipation of lean periods, and will always prepare themselves for the worst conditions rather than the best.

Of the two groups, Eskimos demonstrate considerably greater
foresight in coping with daily needs. They plan their activities
beforehand, carry all necessary equipment, anticipate and avoid
danger, and get work done on time. The Kutchin are not so adept
in these regards, and frequently suffer losses as a result. They are
strongly present-oriented, with minimal concern for long- and short-
range goals. This may cause delays in the start of activities or create
inconveniences when necessary items are unavailable out on the
trail.

Cooperation

Small groups of hunters can greatly increase their success by working smoothly together for a common gain. Among the Eskimos,
individuals and groups are able to cooperate very effectively; hunting crews function with practiced precision, and leadership is
asserted in ways that do not create disagreement or conflict. The
Kutchin and other Athapaskans are far more individualistic and
find it difficult to achieve smooth, effective small-group cooperation.
This may result from the relative infrequency with which they hunt
and travel in groups. When communal undertakings are attempted,
however, their success is often impaired by this pervasive individualism.

Industry

The importance of hard work and perseverance in adapting to a
harsh environment is obvious—the harder a man works at exploiting
his surroundings the better his chances of success. Acculturative
factors such as a waning interest in living off the land, "easy
money" from government assistance, and other changes have
caused a decline in ambition among Eskimos and Kutchin alike.
Despite these changes, members of both groups often work very
long and hard at making a living. Of the two, however, the Eskimos
take a significantly more industrious approach to their subsistence

life. In fact, I was often amazed by their ability to carry on intensive labor for sustained periods until an undertaking was thoroughly and successfully completed. This ambition and persistence certainly has its adaptive payoffs, and when these qualities are lacking group productivity can be seriously affected.

Physical Skills

Expert hunters must, of course, be physically adept, possessing such qualities as agility or athletic prowess, strength, quickness of reaction, toughness, conservation of energy, alertness, and sensory acuity. At first glance these skills might appear to be factors of individual inheritance and therefore variable within the same range from group to group. This is certainly true to a large extent, but cultures can select for these qualities and develop them to the highest level that inheritance will permit. The overall physical performance of providers may thus be improved by training and prestige factors.

Both the Kutchin and Eskimos seem to have developed the qualities listed above to a very high degree, and it is difficult indeed for Outsiders to equal either group in these attributes. A lifetime of training and practice makes them adept in these skills far beyond the level that most Outsiders can achieve in their relatively sheltered existence. If any difference exists between Eskimos and Kutchin, it is probably in quickness of reaction and physical agility, in both of which Eskimos may hold a slight edge.

One quality that has received considerable emphasis in both cultures is toughness—the ability to withstand prolonged exposure to cold, wetness, lack of sleep, or physical exertion. The traditional Kutchin trained their youngsters to withstand all types of physical privation by forcing them to endure daily periods of discomfort and strenuous exertion. It is surprising, in view of this traditional concern, that the Eskimos are more able to withstand physical privation and discomfort than the Indians.

The modern Kutchin (and Koyukon) readily admit to being cold or uncomfortable, though they are definitely not complainers. Eskimos are almost never willing to admit to any kind of discomfort lest they appear to be weaklings or children. They also seem to have such great resistence to discomfort that they hardly notice anything less than extreme chilling or exhaustion. Neither the Kutchin nor the Koyukon approach the Eskimos' fortitude under such conditions. For example, they are deterred from productive outdoor activities by temperatures that would elicit no adverse reaction from Eskimos. The Eskimos accept discomfort as a normal aspect of life, whereas the Indians avoid it as much as possible. "You talk about tough," an old Koyukon told me, "Eskimos, they're really tough people."

Supportive Values

"Supportive values" is something of a catchall category that includes a number of attitudes related to the hunting way of life. The attitudes, which are all in some way adaptive, include response to adversity, food preferences, ideas concerning luck and skill, conservation ethics, and valuation of the hunting life.

Eskimos are well known for their ability to accept with good humor the misfortunes which befall them in an environment where things frequently go wrong. Instead of becoming angry or frustrated they laugh at their errors, failures, and setbacks as if the world had played a great trick on them. Any other response, they feel, would leave them unprepared to face the essential realities of life in the far North. The Kutchin face adversity and misfortune more as the Outsider would, resigning themselves to these inevitable occurrences with complaints and feelings of frustration. "Sometimes I wonder how come God put us way up here instead of some warm, rich place," a Kutchin once told me. This attitude seems less adapted to adversity than that of the Eskimo, who faces an even harsher existence but accepts and enjoys it for what it is.

Eskimo and Indian food preferences are another kind of "attitude" that might be seen as adaptive. Both groups, for example, seem to prefer the most plentiful kinds of food, although the Kutchin apparently crave variety more than the Eskimos. A preference for common foods is adaptive in an environment where these are often the only foods available. Eskimos have achieved a measure of fame because they spurn almost no edible species of animal, in any state of freshness or decay, raw or cooked. They feel that a person should be able to eat everything because he may be required to do so during periods of scarcity.

The Athapaskans are more selective. Some species are tabooed or considered unfit for human consumption, and there is even a prohibition on bear meat for women among certain groups. Beyond this, the Indians have strong individual food preferences, such as a common distaste for beaver and porcupine. And they are also particular about how meat is prepared, generally preferring it fresh and well cooked. Taboos and dislikes are something that one might expect in a richer environment, for among people who often face great food scarcity a readiness to eat anything is certainly adaptive.

In view of the differences in adaptive skills among Eskimos and Kutchin, it is interesting to find that the two groups place a different emphasis on the role of luck and skill as determinants of exploitative success. The Eskimos, as one might expect, assign a paramount role to individual knowledge and skills, whereas the Kutchin say that luck is what really counts. "I heard lots about so-and-so is a good hunter or bad hunter, but I don't believe any of it myself. It's all luck. A man that gets lots of game, that's a lucky man. Doesn't mean he's better than anybody else." Such statements are heard repeatedly among the Indians, who, although they realize that skill and knowledge are important, most often ascribe their fortunes to luck.

The Kutchin have a well-developed conservation ethic, whereas the Eskimos do not share this adaptive characteristic. Indians rarely kill an animal without reason. Either they want the meat for food or the hide for sale, or they kill the animal to get rid of it (in the case of grizzly bears and ravens). The Eskimos, by contrast, sometimes engage in purposeless killing. Far more caribou may be shot than could be handled or used, for example, and seabirds are often shot without any attempt to retrieve them.

This also reflects a fundamental difference between the Indian and Eskimo personality, involving their attitudes toward hunting as a way of life. The Kutchin hunt as a means to an end. Hunting fulfills a role in life similar to that of the urban worker's job—it puts bread on the table. The Eskimo, on the other hand, hunts as an end in itself; he hunts in order to eat, of course, but above all he hunts to be an Eskimo. The ultimate compliment is to be told, "You're a hunter!" or "You're a man!" Being a hunter and being a man are inseparable. Part of the Eskimos' great adaptive success certainly relates to the fact that they live to hunt rather than merely hunt to live.

Technical Sophistication

An early naturalist wrote of the eastern Kutchin and Eskimos:

> I obtained a number of Eskimo implements, all of which exhibited much more skill in their manufacture than anything made by the Indians. [Kennicott 1869, p. 182]

Eskimos are famous for the ingenuity and sophistication of their technical culture, and are perhaps the most outstanding of the world's hunting and gathering peoples in the realm of technological elaboration. No one could argue that Athapaskans enjoy the technological genius of the Eskimos, though their material inventory (which includes devices like snowshoes and complex deadfalls) is impressive in its own right. At the individual level the Eskimos also appear to have a greater talent for dealing with technical problems. Certainly my own experience among Eskimos and Kutchin convinced me that the latter are significantly less adept in the effective manipulation of modern technology.

Honigmann (1949, p. 260) points out that the Kaska (like the Kutchin and Koyukon) seek no perfection in their manufactures beyond that required for adequate functioning. Thus, cabins may be rough and lacking in structural perfection, but they are serviceable. This kind of unembellished pragmatism contrasts with the Eskimo concern for technological perfection. Eskimos strive for practical functionalism, but go beyond this, both in overall design and in skill of manufacture. Products which are finished until they surpass mere adequacy, attaining polished refinement, pay a practical dividend in smooth and faultless operation.

There is no need to recite examples of the Eskimo technological genius, since many of them are common knowledge. In fact, several devices such as kayaks, parkas, skin boots, and dog teams have been adopted in one form or another by western cultures. Few elements of Athapaskan material culture survive among the Indians themselves, and snowshoes are their one notable contribution to the intrusive white society. In some cases Eskimo implements clearly excel their counterparts in Athapaskan cultures. For example, Stefansson (1921, p. 78) describes the great warmth of Eskimo clothing and shelters, then comments on the neighboring Indians:

> One winter I travelled about for several months with the Dog-rib and Yellow Knife Indians. I found they were so poorly clad that during the day when out of doors they had to be continually moving, for if they stopped for even half an hour at a time they became so chilled that their hands became numb. The Indians are really in continual fear for a large part of the winter of ever ceasing from active motion when out of doors. In the evenings their wigwams are cheerful with a roaring fire but by no means comfortable, for while your face is almost scorched with the heat of the flames, your back has hoar-frost forming upon it. At night the Indians go to sleep under their blankets, covering up their heads and shivering all night so the blankets shake.

The aboriginal Kutchin seem to have made better shelters than those described by Stefansson, but they were probably less effectively housed than the Alaskan Eskimos. And their clothing was less perfectly designed. Except for groups which had acquired them from Eskimos, the Kutchin did not use parkas (they had a hoodless coat), and they made no waterproof footgear.

Much remains to be said about the differences in technological sophistication that characterize Eskimos and Athapaskans. The strongest evidence for the superiority of Eskimos in this regard is seen in the direction of diffusion where the two cultures have come into contact. If the Eskimos are in fact more sophisticated, it should be reflected by a greater flow of material culture from Eskimos to Indians than in the opposite direction, and, as the following section will show, this is certainly the case.

Relationships between Eskimo and Athapaskan Culture

Eskimo culture seems to have had a uniformly great influence upon Athapaskan peoples wherever the two groups had frequent and intensive contact, whereas the Indians have not had much influence upon the Eskimos. As the distance increases from areas where the two cultures live in close proximity, the number of Eskimo elements decreases. Thus the Tranjik Kutchin have acquired only a small amount of Eskimo technology, whereas the Mackenzie River Kutchin and the Koyukon Indians of Alaska show a more pervasive effect (in material and nonmaterial culture), and groups such as the Ingalik are highly Eskimoized.

The Alaskan Kutchin formerly traveled all the way to the Arctic coast to trade with Eskimos, though groups like the Chandalar people could meet neighboring Nunamiut Eskimos without venturing far from home. During the postcontact era these meetings were mostly peaceful, but there is a history of warfare between the Indians and Eskimos. Osgood (1936*b*, p. 86) makes the interesting comment that the most important cause of warfare "is the desire to capture [Eskimo] possessions." He adds that many items had more trophy value than practical usefulness for their captors. But a survey of utilitarian items of Eskimo origin adopted by the Kutchin gives a somewhat different impression.

The Kutchin have used or do use the Eskimo semilunar knife or ulu (modified for use as a scraper), the parka, skin boots (and derivative canvas boots), dog traction, the two-pronged fish spear, the toggle-headed fish spear, snow goggles, and ice-fishing implements. The aboriginal footgear and the hand-drawn sled are probably of Eskimo origin (McKennan 1965, pp. 45, 46; Morice 1928, p. 77), and the traditional hunting canoe and skin boat may have undergone considerable Eskimo influence. There is little to indicate that the Kutchin had any significant effect on the Eskimos, except for the possible Indian origin of dome-shaped tents found among both groups (Oswalt 1967, p. 111). It is interesting to note that in trade relations the Kutchin and other Athapaskan peoples seem to have learned to speak Eskimo, whereas the Eskimos did not learn Indian languages (cf. Richardson 1852, p. 132; Oswalt 1967, p. 241).

The Eskimo influence on Kutchin culture is very moderate indeed compared with their influence on such Athapaskan groups as the Ingalik and Tanaina of western Alaska, who maintained close contact with the Eskimos. The traditional Ingalik culture is so completely pervaded by intrusive elements that it sometimes appears to be more Eskimo than Indian, and historic trends indicate that the Ingalik were being assimilated by Eskimos (Oswalt 1967, p. 190). This is particularly interesting because these Indians were living in an interior riverine environment where Eskimo culture was intrusive. One might have expected the Eskimos to do more borrowing, since they had moved away from their coastal element.

The Tanaina material culture was also heavily influenced by Eskimo elements, but in this case the Indians had moved into an environment (Cook Inlet area) formerly occupied by Eskimos. In their summary of traditional artifacts recovered from a Tanaina site in southwestern Alaska, VanStone and Townsend (1970, p. 132) note that:

all types can be duplicated in Eskimo archaeological collections from south-western Alaska. . . . The Eskimo-like, rather than Indian-like character of the traditional antler, bone, and stone objects reflects the proximity of the Eskimo-Tanaina boundary . . . and perhaps a general tendency for the Tanaina to be very receptive to the material culture of their Eskimo neighbors.

One case in which the influence went two ways is between the Kobuk River Eskimos and the neighboring Koyukon Athapaskans. These people have a long history of friendly contact and perhaps deep prehistoric interrelationships, which have influenced both significantly. The Kobuk people are living far from the coast in a forested interior environment, similar to that of nearly all Athapaskan peoples. Perhaps this, plus their long contact with the Koyukon, helps to explain their acceptance of elements from Athapaskan culture.

This may be an oversimplified view, however, since Eskimos have inhabited the middle Kobuk River for some two thousand years (Anderson 1968, p. 32), and some of their "Athapaskan" traits may in fact represent elements of an early "Arctic woodland culture" which underlies both Eskimo and Athapaskan cultures (Giddings 1952, p. 118). Or the Eskimos may have assimilated Athapaskan Indians who formerly occupied the upper Kobuk River, coming away with a strong Indian element in their culture.

Since the Eskimos occupied this interior environment for thousands of years and have obviously maintained close contact with Athapaskans (as well as neighboring coastal Eskimos), I find it most interesting that their culture has remained overwhelmingly Eskimo. Where the situation has been reversed, Athapaskans have tended to be assimilated into Eskimo culture, but this certainly has not occurred on the Kobuk. In fact a small group of Eskimos has lived within half a mile of a large Indian settlement on the Koyukuk since early in this century, and despite intensive daily contact it still retains important elements of its Eskimo identity.

Eskimo culture has proved itself sufficiently resilient and well adapted to remain clearly identifiable as "Eskimo" while it has been carried into a number of Arctic and subarctic environments. Eskimos have always adapted to new conditions within the framework of Eskimo technique and technology; variations have developed, but always around the same theme, retaining a strong Eskimo flavor. The Athapaskans, by contrast, have adjusted to varying habitats by incorporating into their culture the adaptive methods of neighboring peoples. They have adapted by hybridizing. In their contacts with Eskimos, the Indians found new elements of technology which filled needs previously answered inadequately by their own culture. Thus the pattern of one-way diffusion is strong evidence for the adaptive superiority of the Eskimos.

Conclusions

If there is a difference in the level of adaptive success attained by Eskimos and Athapaskans the immediate question is, Why does it exist? The following discussion considers three factors—acculturation, environment, and cultural orthogenesis—which may have some bearing upon this question. It is followed by a few summary remarks about the importance of differential adaptation.

Acculturation

Both the North Alaskan Eskimos and the western Kutchin have suffered important losses in adaptive skills and knowledge owing to acculturative influences, making today's hunters less perfectly adapted than their predecessors were. But the Indians have experienced more intensive acculturation and are generally more receptive to it than the Eskimos. There has been a greater loss of knowledge and skills on the part of the Indians, which has undoubtedly influenced the modern adaptive design. But there is evidence to indicate historical depth for these differences.

First, the transmission of adaptive technology from Eskimos to Athapaskans and our knowledge of the material inventories of both groups indicate greater technological sophistication in traditional Eskimo culture. Second, the differences in adaptive skills are so pervasive in nature that it is hard to accept the idea of recency.

In other words, it is highly unlikely that the whole range of adaptive behaviors, attitudes, and knowledge could be so thoroughly changed by 120 years of contact, particularly since the Indians remained heavily dependent upon hunting and trapping during most of this time. Third, there is evidence in the literature for historical depth in adaptive differences.

The explorer Stefansson was perhaps more familiar than anyone before or since with the exploitative knowledge and skills of Eskimos and Athapaskans. He lived among these people around the turn of the century in areas where very little acculturation had taken place, and so his comments are of particular interest:

> The marginal forest Indians, as, for instance, the Loucheaux [Kutchin] at the head of the Mackenzie Delta and on the Peel River, had winter tents and winter camps that were a sort of incomplete adaptation of Eskimo shelters. They were not as simple or comfortable as those Eskimo tents and houses of which they were imitations and are, therefore, not worth discussion in a practical manual, although of considerable interest for those who want a grasp of the cultural history of the two people. *That the Indians borrowed, or tried to borrow, from the Eskimos, and that the Eskimos did not borrow from Indians, seems logical for those who have lived among both peoples. For practically every forest Indian method or device is less well adapted to its purpose than the corresponding Eskimo feature.* [Stefansson 1944, p. 210; emphasis mine]

Regarding other Athapaskan groups, the same writer comments:

> when you go north from the Slavey and Dogrib to the Eskimo country, the conditions suddenly change. You now come into contact with a people who have . . . a system of living almost perfectly adapted to a cold climate, while the northern Indians have a system almost unbelievably ill-adapted to the conditions in which they live. [Stefansson 1921, pp. 78–79]

These early comments by a highly qualified observer, plus other evidence for historical depth, strongly indicate that a difference in adaptive skills and knowledge characterized traditional Eskimo and Kutchin cultures. Although acculturative influences might have increased the differences in modern times, they cannot be used to explain the differences during an earlier period.

Environment

The Arctic tundra and sea-ice environment inhabited by Eskimos presents significantly different adaptive challenges than does the

interior forest of the Kutchin. It is probable that more complex
and highly evolved adaptive skills and knowledge are required for
successful exploitation of the Eskimo environment. Eskimos might
be forced, therefore, to perfect a relatively better adaptation than
the Kutchin's to insure group survival. If both cultures were adapted
only to the level of adequacy within their own environments, then,
Eskimos would necessarily have a greater development of exploitative knowledge and technique and a more sophisticated technology.

It is almost certainly true that the greater adaptive challenges
which face the Eskimos are a factor in stimulating an elaboration
of skills and knowledge. But although environment is an initial factor, it is not the critical variable in explaining the nature and extent
of differences between the Eskimos and Kutchin, because the differences exist in both a relative and an absolute sense. The Kutchin
face a lesser adaptive challenge and have developed an adequate
or satisfactory adjustment to it; Eskimos face a greater adaptive
challenge and have achieved a superior adjustment to it, even moving toward adaptive perfection. The Eskimos might have "rested
on their laurels" once they attained adequacy, but they did not.
Environmental factors alone cannot explain this difference,
because there was just as much reason for the Kutchin to strive
toward adaptive perfection as there was for the Eskimos.

Many of the adaptive qualities discussed earlier in this chapter
are in fact comparable within both environments. Both the Kutchin
and the Eskimos faced extreme cold, for example, but the latter
developed better methods of dealing with it. Eskimos were more
effectively clothed and housed, and had devised more appropriate
responses to problems such as frostbite and emergency survival
situations. Similarly, both peoples utilized the caribou, but Eskimos
went further toward amassing a body of knowledge and hunting
technique related to this animal.

I do not believe that the presence of a somewhat greater environmental challenge can explain the differences outlined in this chapter.
The diffusion of many adaptive elements from Eskimos to Athapaskans proves that there was a use for them in the interior environment; but they were never developed there, and the general absence
of diffusion in the opposite direction is also of interest.

In summary, differences between the Eskimo and Indian environments can only be used to explain the amount of knowledge and

skill necessary to achieve adaptive adequacy. When developments beyond this level are considered, some other explanatory factor must be involved. Why have the Eskimos never been content with a static level of adaptive success, preferring to drive toward a level approaching perfection? I do not believe that any factor external to Eskimo culture itself will answer this question.

Cultural Orthogenesis

There is no difficulty in explaining the level of adaptive success achieved by the Kutchin, since they developed an adequate adjustment to their surroundings and then maintained it. The problem is to understand why the Eskimos went beyond this level and continued striving toward a higher elaboration of knowledge and skills. In my opinion Eskimo culture has generated its own internal drive beyond a mere survival level. In short, Eskimos have made adaptation a cultural "focus of interest," for reasons that defy explanation. They are more concerned with exploitative knowledge and skills than with anything else.

The phenomenon of cultural elaboration or focus of interest occurs among many of the world's peoples. One particular aspect of a culture is often developed far out of proportion to the rest. In some cases this development has its practical payoffs, as with the Eskimo concern for adaptation. Frequently, however, the greatest elaboration occurs within areas of culture less involved with the practicalities of living, such as kinship or ritual. In most cases it is impossible to explain why this phenomenon occurs, beyond stating that culture has a tendency to direct itself in ways that cannot be understood.

All we can do is call attention to the fact that there is a human tendency in the elaboration of culture to seize upon some aspect and go all out with it. "Cultural orthogenesis," it might be called, if we think of biological analogies; or, "the tendency to skewed elaboration of culture," if we prefer statistical images. [Hoebel 1968, p. 301]

Although culture responds creatively to its environmental surroundings, it is also powerfully directed by its own internal principles, which is why cultural adaptation and adaptive technology might be highly elaborated in one society and less developed in another, without environment's necessarily acting as the major creative force (Hatch 1971, p. 94). Both Eskimo and Kutchin cultures were highly responsive to pressures emanating from their surroundings, but once they had adapted successfully they reacted in different ways. Eskimo culture apparently generated its own energy to move in the direction of adaptive perfection, but the ultimate cause remains unknown. Cultural orthogenesis describes what took place, but does not explain why.

Whatever the reason for these differences, it should come as no surprise that they exist. Indeed, it would be surprising if two or more hunting and gathering cultures were found to have achieved an identical degree of adaptive and exploitative proficiency. There is little more reason to expect that all cultures will be equally well adjusted to their surroundings than that they will elaborate their kinship system, religion, or political organization to an identical degree. We are not reluctant to accept the idea that certain peoples are extraordinarily skilled with technology or uncommonly successful in farming or pastoralism. Differential skills in hunting and gathering societies are of the same order, and should be expected as a natural result of cultural elaboration beyond the level sufficient to insure survival.

Cultural ecologists have concerned themselves mostly with adaptive variables which are fairly concrete and therefore relatively easy to observe in the field. Ecological formulations generally concern themselves with the features of environment which most significantly influence culture, the level of technology or material culture which is utilized to exploit the environment, and the institutionalized aspects of culture known to be directly or indirectly influenced by exploitative or environmental factors (cf. Steward 1955, pp. 40–41). The elaborate systems of behavior and knowledge which give life to the exploitative technology are considered only in a most superficial way. Cultural ecologists tacitly assume that environment, technology, and exploitative institutions (cooperative hunts, group size) are the important variables, whereas all hunting and gathering cultures are presumed to be equally sophisticated in their exploitative knowledge.

But if the level of adaptive knowledge and skills is added to ecological formulations, the picture changes significantly. For example, if it were possible to put them in an equally productive and equally challenging environment, with an equally effective material culture, would the Eskimos and Kutchin exploit their surroundings and adapt to them with equal efficiency? I think not. The behavior and knowledge which give force to the technology would lend an adaptive advantage to the Eskimos. This facet of adaptation, which is rarely mentioned in discussions of cultural ecology, has a considerable effect upon the overall patterning and success of adjustment to the environment. It can influence population and demography, settlement patterns, and the development of sociocultural institutions.

Thus, material culture may not be the only indicator of a culture's exploitative efficiency, as has become traditional in ecological anthropology. The more subtle but vitally important factors of knowledge and skills, which may vary in elaboration from group to group, must be considered an essential aspect of adaptation.

This chapter is a beginning effort toward a method of objectifying the level of adaptive skills among hunting and gathering peoples anywhere in the world. If criteria such as those used for this comparison of Eskimos and Athapaskans are found to apply universally, then it will at least be possible to amass a body of comparable data upon many hunting and gathering cultures. Furthermore, if universal attributes of expert and successful hunters are discovered, it may be a step toward understanding factors which have influenced the entire course of human evolution. Since man lived as a hunter-gatherer for practically all of his evolutionary history, these attributes might be of key importance in understanding the human animal as he exists today.

Bibliography

Adney, Edwin T., and Chapelle, Howard I. 1964. *The bark canoes and skin boats of North America.* Washington, D.C.: Smithsonian Institution.

Alt, Kenneth T. 1969. *Taxonomy and ecology of the inconnu, Stenodus leucichthys nelma, in Alaska.* Biological papers of the University of Alaska, no. 12.

Anderson, Douglas D. 1968. A stone age campsite at the gateway to Americ *Scientific American,* vol. 218, no. 6.

Balikci, Asen. 1963a. *Vunta Kutchin social change.* Ottawa: Northern Co-ordination and Research Centre.

—————. 1963b. Family organization of the Vunta Kutchin. *Arctic Anthropology,* vol. 1, no. 2.

Bane, G. Ray. n.d. Environmental exploitation by the Eskimos of Wainwright, Alaska. Unpublished manuscript.

Barger, Walter K. 1969. Adaptation to town in Great Whale River. M.A. thesis, University of North Carolina, Chapel Hill.

Benedict, Ruth. 1934. *Patterns of culture.* Boston: Houghton Mifflin Company.

Birket-Smith, K. 1930. Contributions to Chipewyan ethnology. *Report of the Fifth Thule Expedition 1921–24,* vol. 5, no. 3.

Burt, H. D., and Grossenheider, P. H. 1952. *A field guide to the mammals.* Boston: Houghton Mifflin Company.

Cadzow, Donald. 1925*a*. Habitat of the Loucheux tribes. *Indian Notes,*
                        vol. 2, no. 3.
————————————. 1925*b*. Old Loucheux clothing. *Indian*
                        Notes, vol. 2, no. 4.
Campbell, John M. 1968. Territoriality among ancient hunters:
                        Interpretations from ethnography and nature.
                        In *Anthropological Archaeology in the*
                        Americas. Washington, D.C.: The
                        Anthropological Society of Washington.
Carroll, James A. 1957. *The first ten years in Alaska.* New York:
                        Exposition Press.
Cohen, R., and VanStone, J. W. 1963. Dependency and self-sufficiency
                        in Chipewyan stories. National Museum
                        of Canada, bulletin 194.
Cooper, John. 1938. *Snares, deadfalls and other traps of the northern*
                        Algonquin and northern Athapaskans.
                        Catholic University of America,
                        Anthropological Series, vol. 5.
Dall, W. H. 1870. *Alaska and its resources.* Boston.
Dawson, G. M. 1889. *Report on an exploration in the Yukon District.*
                        Annual Reports of the Canadian Geological
                        Survey, n.s., vol. 3, pt. 1.
Federal Field Committee for Development Planning in Alaska. 1968.
                        Alaska natives and the land. Washington,
                        D.C.: U.S. Government Printing Office.
Franklin, Sir John. 1828. *Narrative of a second expedition to the shores*
                        of the Polar Sea. London.
Giddings, J. L. 1952. *The Arctic woodland culture of the Kobuk River.*
                        University of Pennsylvania, Philadelphia,
                        Museum Monographs.
————————————. 1956. *Forest Eskimos.* University of
                        Alaska Museum bulletin, vol. 20, no. 2.
————————————. 1961. *Kobuk River people.* University of
                        Alaska, Studies of Northern Peoples, no. 1.
Goddard, P. E. 1906. Assimilation to environment as illustrated by
                        Athapaskan peoples. *Proceedings of the*
                        International Congress of Americanists,
                        vol. 15, no. 1.
Godsell, P H. 1938. *Red hunters of the snows.* Toronto.
Gubser, Nicholas J. 1965. *The Nunamiut Eskimos: Hunters of caribou.*
                        New Haven: Yale University Press.
Hallowell, A. Irving. 1949. The size of Algonkian hunting territories:
                        A function of ecological adjustment.
                        American Anthropologist, vol. 51.
Harding, A. R. 1935. *Deadfalls and snares.* Columbus, Ohio: A. R.
                        Harding Publishing Company.

—————————————. n.d. *Steel traps*. Columbus, Ohio: A. R. Harding Publishing Company.

Hardisty, W. L. 1866. The Loucheux Indians. *Annual Report of the Smithsonian Institution, 1866*.

Hatch, Elvin J. 1971. Benedict, Steward, and White. Unpublished manuscript.

Heller, Christine A. 1966. *Wild edible and poisonous plants of Alaska*. University of Alaska Extension, bulletin F-40.

Helm, June. 1961. *The Lynx Point people: The dynamics of a northern Athapaskan band*. National Museum of Canada, bulletin 176.

Helm, June, and Lurie, Nancy O. 1962. *The subsistence economy of the Dogrib Indians of Lac LaMartre in the Mackenzie District of the N.W.T*. Ottawa: Northern Co-ordination and Research Centre.

Hoebel, E. Adamson. 1968. *The law of primitive man*. New York: Antheneum.

Honigmann, John J. 1946. Ethnography and acculturation of the Fort Nelson Slave. *Yale University Publications in Anthropology*, no. 33.

—————————————. 1949. Culture and ethos of Kaska society. *Yale University Publications in Anthropology*, no. 40.

—————————————. 1965. *Eskimo townsmen*. Ottawa: Canadian Research Centre for Anthropology.

—————————————. 1968. Adaptation of Indians, Eskimos, and persons of partial indigenous background in a Canadian northern town. Paper presented to the 67th annual meeting of the American Anthropological Association.

Honigmann, John J., and Honigmann, Irma. 1959. Notes on Great Whale River ethos. *Anthropologica*, n.s., vol. 1, nos. 1, 2.

Irving, Lawrence. 1958. Naming of birds as part of the intellectual culture of Indians at Old Crow, Y.T. *Arctic*, vol. 11, no. 2.

Jones, Strachan. 1866. The Kutchin tribes. *Annual report of the Smithsonian Institution, 1866*.

Keith, Lloyd B. 1963. *Wildlife's ten year cycle*. Madison: University of Wisconsin Press.

Kennicott, Robert. 1869. Biography of Robert Kennicott and extracts from his journal. *Chicago Academy of Sciences Transactions*, vol. 1.

Kirby, W. W. A. 1864. A journey to the Youcan, Russian America. *Annual report of the Smithsonian Institution, 1864*.

Knight, Rolf. 1965. A re-examination of hunting, trapping, and territoriality among the northeastern Algonkian Indians. In *Man, culture, and animals,* ed. A. P. Vayda and T. Leeds. Washington, D.C.: American Association for the Advancement of Science.

Kreps, E. 1944. *The science of trapping.* Columbus, Ohio: A. R. Harding Publishing Company.

Laughlin, William S. 1968. Hunting: An integrating behavior system and its evolutionary importance. In *Man the hunter,* ed. R. B. Lee and I. De Vore. Chicago: Aldine Publishing Company.

Leacock, Eleanor B. 1954. *The Montagnais "hunting territory" and the fur trade.* American Anthropological Association memoir 78.

Lee, Richard B. 1969. !Kung Bushman subsistence: An input-output analysis. In *Environment and cultural behavior,* ed. A. P. Vayda. Garden City, N.Y.: Natural History Press.

Lee, Richard B., and DeVore, Irven. 1968. *Man the hunter.* Chicago: Aldine Publishing Company.

Leechman, Douglas. 1954. *The Vunta Kutchin.* National Museum of Canada, bulletin 130.

Leopold, A. Starker, and Darling, F. Fraser. 1953. *Wildlife in Alaska.* New York: Ronald Press Company.

McKennan, Robert A. 1935. Anent the Kutchin tribes. *American Anthropologist,* vol. 37, no. 2.

—————————. 1959. The Upper Tanana Indians. *Yale University Publications in Anthropology,* no. 55.

—————————. 1965. *The Chandalar Kutchin.* Arctic Institute of North America, technical paper no. 17.

Mason, J. A. 1946. Notes on the Indians of the Great Bear Lake area. *Yale University Publications in Anthropology,* no. 34.

Mason, Michael H. 1924. *The Arctic forests.* London: Potter and Stoughton.

Milan, Frederick A. 1964. The acculturation of the contemporary Eskimo of Wainwright, Alaska. *Anthropological Papers of the University of Alaska,* vol. 11, no. 2.

Morice, A. G. 1928. The fur trader in anthropology: And a few related questions. *American Anthropologist,* n.s., vol. 30.

—————————. n.d. *The great Déné race.* Vienna: Press of the Mechitharistes.

Mueller, Richard J. 1964. *Topical dictionary of Western Kutchin.*
          Fairbanks: Summer Institute of Linguistics.
Murie, Olaus. 1958. *A field guide to animal tracks.* Boston: Houghton
          Mifflin Company.
Murray, Alexander H. 1910. *Journal of the Yukon, 1847–48.* Publication
          of the Canadian Archives, no. 4.
Nelson, Richard K. 1966a. *Literature review of Eskimo knowledge of the
          sea ice environment.* Fort Wainwright,
          Alaska: Arctic Aeromedical Laboratory.
——————————. 1966b. *Alaskan Eskimo exploitation of the
          sea ice environment.* Fort Wainwright,
          Alaska: Arctic Aeromedical Laboratory.
——————————. 1969. *Hunters of the northern ice.* Chicago:
          University of Chicago Press.
Osgood, Cornelius. 1934. Kutchin tribal distribution and synonymy.
          American Anthropologist, vol. 36, no. 2
——————————. 1936a. The distribution of northern
          Athapaskan Indians. *Yale University
          Publications in Anthropology,* no. 7.
——————————. 1936b. Contributions to the ethnography of
          the Kutchin. *Yale University Publications in
          Anthropology,* no. 14.
——————————. 1937. Ethnography of the Tanaina. *Yale
          University Publications in Anthropology,* no.
          16.
——————————. 1940. Ingalik material culture. *Yale
          University Publications in Anthropology,*
          no. 22.
Oswalt, Wendell H. 1967. *Alaskan Eskimos.* San Francisco: Chandler
          Publishing Company.
Peterson, Roger T. 1961. *A field guide to the western birds.* Boston:
          Houghton Mifflin Company.
Pruitt, William O. 1967. *Animals of the North.* New York: Harper
          and Row.
Rausch, Robert A. n.d. *The moose in Alaska.* Alaska wildlife notebook
          series, no. 10. Juneau: Alaska Department
          of Fish and Game.
Rhode, Clarence J., and Barker, Will. 1953. *Alaska's fish and wildlife.*
          Washington, D.C.: U.S. Department of the
          Interior, Fish and Wildlife Service, circular
          17.
Richardson, Sir John. 1852. *Arctic searching expedition.* New York:
          Harper and Brothers.
Shimkin, Demitri B. 1955. The economy of a trapping center: The
          case of Fort Yukon, Alaska. *Economic
          Development and Culture Change,* vol. 3,
          no. 3.

Simpson, Thomas. 1843. *Narrative of discoveries on the north coast of
           America.* London.
Slobodin, Richard. 1962. *Band organization of the Peel River Kutchin.*
           National Museum of Canada, bulletin no. 179.
Spencer, Robert F. 1959. *The north Alaskan Eskimo.* Bureau of American
           Ethnology, bulletin 171.
Stefansson, Vilhjalmur. 1921. *The friendly arctic.* New York: Macmillan
           Company.
———————————. 1944. *Arctic manual.* New York: Macmillan
           Company.
———————————. 1962. *My life with the Eskimo.* New York:
           Collier Books.
Steward, Julian H. 1955. *Theory of culture change.* Urbana: University
           of Illinois Press.
Stuck, Hudson. 1924. *Ten thousand miles with a dog sled.* New York:
           C. Scribner's Sons.
Taylor, Robert F. 1950. *Pocket guide to Alaska trees.* Washington,
           D.C.: U.S. Department of Agriculture.
U.S. Department of Commerce, Weather Bureau. 1959. *Climates of
           the states: Alaska.* Washington, D.C.: U.S.
           Government Printing Office.
———————————. 1963. *Climatic summary of Alaska:
           Supplement for 1922 through 1952.*
           Washington, D.C.: U.S. Government
           Printing Office.
VanStone, James W. 1961. *The economy of a frontier community:
           A preliminary statement.* Ottawa: Northern
           Co-ordination and Research Centre.
———————————. 1963. Changing patterns of Indian trapping
           in the Canadian subarctic. *Arctic,* vol. 16.
———————————. 1965. *The changing culture of the Snowdrift
           Chipewyan.* National Museum of Canada,
           bulletin 14.
VanStone, James W., and Townsend, Joan B. 1970. *Kijik: An historic
           Tanaina Indian settlement.* Fieldiana,
           Anthropology, vol. 59.
Washburn, Bradford. 1963. Frostbite. *Polar Record,* vol. 2, no. 75.
West, Frederick Hadleigh. 1959. On the distribution and territories
           of the western Kutchin tribes.
           *Anthropological Papers of the University of
           Alaska,* vol. 7, no. 2.
Whymper, Frederick. 1868a. *Travel and adventure in Alaska.* London.
———————————. 1868b. A journey from Norton Sound, Bering
           Sea, to Fort Yukon. *Journal of the Royal
           Geographic Society,* vol. 38.

Index